TELLING
THE
STORY

This book is made possible by collaborative funding from the Office of Educational Activities of the Corporation for Public Broadcasting and the Station Services Department of National Public Radio. I particularly want to thank Clyde Robinson, NPR Senior Vice President, Representation, for his support and encouragement, as well as each of the authors listed below, who so generously gave their time and effort to the creation of this book.

Brian Brightly
Director
Education Services
National Public Radio

CONTRIBUTORS

Deborah Amos
Jonathan "Smokey" Baer
Edward Bliss, Jr.
Ted Clark
Dave Creagh
Janice F. Hill
Larry Josephson
Chris Koch
Robert Krulwich
Skip Pizzi
Scott Simon
Susan Stamberg
Flawn Williams

Telling the Story

The National Public Radio Guide to Radio Journalism

**Larry Josephson,
Editor**

Produced by the
Education Services and
Station Services Departments,
National Public Radio

**KENDALL/HUNT
PUBLISHING COMPANY**
Dubuque, Iowa

Copyright © 1983 by National Public Radio

Library of Congress Catalog Card Number: 82–83325

ISBN 0–8403–2861–3

Printed in the United States of America
10 9 8 7 6 5

CONTENTS

Preface

Radio is flourishing in the United States today. For National Public Radio member stations, there was an astonishing increase of two million listeners in 1981. Radio is not only alive, but is attracting a whole new generation of listeners, who find in its immediacy and intimacy a welcome companion in the workplace, on the highways, and at home.

We at National Public Radio (NPR) like to think we may have had something to do with the coming of this "second age" of radio. Since 1970, NPR has been serving as a national production and distribution center for a network of some 270 non–commercial, mostly FM, radio stations. Today, NPR produces and distributes more radio programming than any other network, and is the recognized standard-setter in the field. Our news and public affairs programs, such as "All Things Considered" and "Morning Edition," represent the best of radio journalism.

Whether you are already in radio, or simply curious about it as one of many mediums a journalist can work in, this book will expand your ideas about its possibilities. This book contains the combined advice and hard-won experience of men and women who've gone light-years beyond the old "rip–and–read" school of broadcast journalism. And there's a lot of knowledge here that will serve you well as a journalist, whether or not you ever pick up a microphone (though of course we hope you will).

Radio journalism requires a hardy breed. In contrast to the highly specialized role of a reporter in a large city newsroom or even a television station, most radio journalists must be able to assume many roles. At a local station, you may find yourself working simultaneously as a reporter, editor, producer, and audio engineer. This ability to create and control the final product is what attracts many to radio. Those who choose to embrace the medium will find that it rewards with a rare sense of accomplishment.

The modest means of radio—a tape recorder, a microphone—are one of the sources of its strength. It has always been an American premise that citizens should have access to a full range of information in an uncensored marketplace of ideas. As a technology that can be possessed by the many, rather than the few, radio insures that access.

One final note: radio journalism must be carried out by professionals prepared to accept and live with the responsibilities that accompany its unusual freedoms. In this book there is no chapter on journalistic ethics *per se,* but implicit in NPR's philosophy of news is the belief that our mission to inform must be conducted with fairness, impartiality, and without arrogance. Investigative journalism is a powerful instrument that has often worked in the public interest; its practitioners are advised to remember their own humanity and humility.

Frank Mankiewicz
President, National Public Radio

Introduction

by Larry Josephson

This book is about radio journalism: the art and craft, theory and practice, ethics and pragmatics, legal underpinnings and marketing of news and information radio.

Success in radio journalism rests on a pentagonal foundation of:

- *Personal Qualities,* such as talent, energy, imagination, intelligence, concentration and persistence.
- *Role Models,* persons whose style, skills and personal qualities we emulate in the process of creating our unique selves. These might include parents and other family members, teachers, peers, and one or two individuals at the top of their field from whom we can ethically take bits of technique or mannerism without risking the charge of imitation.
- *Professional Skills,* such as writing and speaking ability, tricks of the trade, thorough knowledge of and respect for equipment, and bureaucratic survival instincts.
- *Practice*—and then more practice.
- *Luck,* being at the right place at the right time or a serendipitous occurrence, a personal contact when and where you happen to need it.

Professional skills are what this book is all about. Some of the best people in public radio journalism and allied fields—mostly, but not exclusively, from National Public Radio—have distilled years of collective experience into these pages.

This book is divided into four parts. Part One, "Hard News," presents the fundamentals of news reporting. It includes a discussion of the editor's role and a chapter of the principles of writing news for broadcast.

Larry Josephson has spent more than 17 years in nearly every phase of public radio—on both sides of the microphone—as host, producer, reporter, fundraiser, engineer and station manager at Pacifica stations WBAI (New York) and KPFA (Berkeley); and now as President of the Radio Foundation, a public radio production and service organization based in New York City. He developed and produced the "Bob and Ray Public Radio Show," which brought the beloved comedy team back to radio. His documentary on a dwarf convention, "The Little People," won an Armstrong Award. Josephson has been a consultant to the Corporation of Public Broadcasting, National Public Radio, the National Telecommunications and Information Administration, the Carnegie Commission on the Future of Public Broadcasting, the City and State of New York and to a number of public radio stations and minority broadcasters. He has also taught radio production and management at New York University and at the New School for Social Research, and is the organizer of the "Airlie" Seminars on the Art of Radio, an annual conference of public radio producers, reporters, program executives and funders.

Part Two, "Features," contrasts soft news with hard news, examines further refinements in writing for *and with sound,* and takes the reader step-by-step through the development of a feature.

Part Three, "Recording, Editing and Production," is an excellent overview of the technical skills and equipment needed to practice radio journalism. Topics covered include field recording, tape editing and studio production.

Part Four, "The Law and the Market," reviews basic legal concepts every producer should know, and presents ways producers can fund, market and disribute their work.

The book concludes with an epilogue on the future of radio journalism in the face of changing technology.

The importance of basic journalistic and technical skills cannot be overemphasized. The old master painters were thoroughly acquainted with the preparation of paint, pigment, brush and canvas before the first line was drawn. A radio journalist's equipment should become an extension of his or her senses: a reporter should be able to operate in a riot or a rainstorm without thinking consciously about the tape recorder. An occasional glance at the machine and the monitoring of the recording through earphones should provide sufficient warning if the equipment is not working correctly. Similarly, a developed sixth sense should tell a journalist when a source may be trying to mislead—a warning that should be translated into one more phone call to check a fact or assertion.

With the exception of Edward Bliss, Jr., who had a long, distinguished career with CBS News, this book was written by professionals at the top of *public* radio journalism. For the most part, however, the skills, techniques and philosophies advanced herein will serve you well in *commercial* radio as well. There are, to be sure, important differences in style and convention between the two: public radio pieces tend to be longer and more "laid back," more concerned with the use of *sound* in telling a story. Nonetheless, many people have moved successfully from one to the other; former public radio reporters, editors and producers are well-represented in the ranks of the three commercial network news organizations, in both radio and television. (Much of this book applies to television journalism as well.)

As Chris Koch advises in Chapter 1, listen extensively to the work of the organization you want to work for. If after listening you still want to work for them, then you must to some degree adapt your style to theirs. You should adapt enough to gain entry and to survive, but not so much as to lose what you have most to offer—your individual character, intelligence, style and personality. *No one ever got to the top by being just like everyone else.*

No *book* can transform you into a successful radio journalist. But *Telling the Story* can give you an invaluable head start, by providing shortcuts, professional techniques, an exhaustive introduction to equipment and its proper use, and the unwritten rules and written regulations of the profession of radio journalism.

This book is the product of many talents—some credited on the title page, others not. I want to thank: my colleague and friend, Professor Daniel Mack of Fordham University, who designed the faculty manual which accompanies this text, for his valuable criticisms and suggestions; Karen Kearns of NPR Education Services, whose contributions as mediator and facilitator have been protean, and Mary Jane McKinven, the copy editor—both of whom readily acceded to difficult demands at the last minute in the service of excellence; Kathy Dobkin, my former assistant, who copy-edited early drafts of this book and in the process improved it greatly; and finally, my thanks to the chapter authors—busy people all—who applied themselves with exemplary dedication and skill to the task of setting down what they know and do so well for the benefit of new generations of radio journalists.

I
HARD NEWS

Fig. 1.1. News isn't news until it is observed and reported—news is the report of an event, not the event itself. National Public Radio was a major reporting presence at the 1980 political conventions, providing the most extensive election coverage of any radio network.

The Rules of the Game

by Chris Koch

What Is News?

Every journalist, whether working in broadcasting or print, must answer one very crucial question: What is news? There are probably as many definitions of news as there are journalists, but all definitions seem to have common threads. News generally involves an *event* which is *observed* either by the journalist or another individual, and this observation is *recreated* or *reported* to an *audience*. It is helpful to remember that news isn't news until someone decides that it is: news is the report of an event, not the event itself.

You can waste time trying to do news stories on vague ideas. Broadcast journalists, in particular, get into trouble when they try to do pieces about poverty, poor education, crime in the streets, corruption, inflation, freedom of speech and other abstractions. These are good topics for columnists and professors, but abstractions alone are not news stories. If journalists are interested in these things and want to do stories about them, then they will look for events.

A march by poor people or the formation of a welfare rights organization are legitimate stories about poverty. A patrol of a big city park by a local vigilante group or the police routine at precinct headquarters are ways of doing news stories about crime in the streets. Unemployment lines, pandemonium on Wall Street or the release of the latest economic indicators may be legitimate ways to cover inflation. *Look for the events.*

In general, the more powerful the event, the easier it will be to do a story, because strong stories tell themselves. If you are working on a story about prison conditions and a riot breaks out, your only problems are getting to the riot, recording the right sounds, asking the right questions of the right people and getting out in one piece. But if the prison is quiet, you will have to look for the events that evoke prison life—perhaps the slow movement of a new prisoner through a tough entry procedure, or the sounds of the night lock–up, or the sermon at Sunday chapel, or the conversations of guards and prisoners about past events.

There are different kinds of events and correspondingly different kinds of news stories about them. These stories are given different names, and even though the

Christopher Koch was the Executive Producer of National Public Radio's 90-minute evening news program, All Things Considered, *from July 1979 through October 1981, when he left to produce a television special based on* All Things Considered. *In February of 1981 the program was awarded its second Dupont Award for excellence in broadcasting. Before joining NPR, Koch was a producer/correspondent for a PBS documentary series, called F.Y.I., and an associate producer for the* ABC Close-up *documentary unit. He has spent over 20 years in radio and television broadcasting, taught literature and mass communications at Bennington College, and is a graduate of Reed College and Columbia University.*

names are by no means precise (the popular jargon changes from place to place), it is helpful to keep some distinctions in mind before you go to work.

Hard news generally refers to the breaking, daily stories that make up the front page of the newspapers, the bulk of the TV news shows and the leading articles in the newsweeklies. Hard news stories are about those political, military, economic and social events that appear to have a shaping influence on our lives.

The basic hard news story will convey the sense of such events—the taking of American hostages, the concession speech of an incumbent President, the agony of people's uncertainty in the wake of a violent eruption.

In most extended news programs—those that go beyond a capsule summary of the day's main events—these major stories will be accompanied by **sidebars,** reports that spin off from the main event and help explain it.

Types of Sidebars

If the major story is new or complicated, then it may be important to explain the events that led up to it. In these **backgrounders** reporters are interested in events that took place in the past. In radio, they will need archive tape and will need to talk to people who can describe earlier events.

Another typical sidebar is **vox pop.** The term comes from the Latin "vox populi" (voice of the people) and stands for the comments of ordinary people, collected at random, usually in public places. Sometimes the vox pop is strung together in a montage of different voices (one following the other) with no narration or linking comments by the reporter. Other times the reporter is heard asking questions.

Sound portraits are another typical sidebar. Here a reporter gathers sound from a series of small events and interweaves them with interviews, creating a sound impression of persons, places, or things.

Other types of sidebars may include stories on related topics, interviews with participants and observers, comments and analyses. These are usually part of extended news broadcasts, and may be used as a spin–off to the main story.

Know the Show

You can learn several different things by listening carefully to the news programs that you hope to work for—and to other news programs as well. For one thing, you can begin to develop critical standards that you can apply to your own work.

Listen carefully and consistently with a notebook in hand, asking yourself a series of questions. Which reporters appear most frequently? Does anything distinguish their work from the work of reporters who file less frequently? What pieces compel your attention and why?

Select several particularly interesting stories and record them for closer study. How long are they? What is the ratio between the narration (the things that reporters say) and **actualities** (the voices and sound that they record)? How many different interviews have been used? What other kinds of sounds have been incorporated into the report?

Transcribe the narration and analyze the writing of stories that seem particularly well-written. How long are the sentences? Are they full of vivid images, packed with information, or are they sparse links between actualities? No one way is necessarily any better than the other. Nor are you trying to imitate anyone. You are only figuring out what works or why. Everyone has a different style, and you shouldn't be afraid to develop your own. Good journalism can happen even when all the rules are broken.

Each news program has its own style, and that is another thing to listen for. Some programs give straight interviews to reporters and others insist that all one–on–one interviews be done by hosts. Some news shows are designed for a national audience and others are regional or local. If it's a national show, your stories will have to be interesting to a national audience. This does not necessarily mean that you should look for national personalities who are visiting your local area. Usually the national news staff will have access to these public figures and will prefer to do their own interviews.

Look, instead, for the local stories that speak to issues shared by people nationwide. And remember: If you listen carefully to the news programs, you'll get a much better idea about what might interest their editors and producers, the range of styles they will accept, the gaps in their coverage that you could fill, and other things that will help you file effectively and frequently.

Selecting a Story

An infinite number of things happen every day, but not many of them are news. What makes something news? Primarily, enough interest in the event. In order to make people interested, the story needs to have an **angle, the element that gets the audience to pay attention**. It's part of the reporter's job to find the angle and work it clearly into his story. Without it, you'll waste time pursuing ideas that never quite work out.

What follows are some truisms that should be chanted regularly or otherwise impressed on the mind of every beginning journalist.

- *Never do a story just because people ought to know about it for their own good or the good of the Republic.* Journalists are not professional moralists, and they have no special insight into what people ought to know. Leave moralizing to preachers and politicians.

- *People care about things that affect them.* The famine among 500,000 people in East Timor went almost unnoticed by most Americans. But the much smaller slaughter of combatants in the Iran–Iraq war was daily news, because that war affected our hostages and our oil supply.

5

- *Bad news, like gossip, travels more quickly and farther than good news.* Let's face it, you may hear about Uncle Harry's divorce faster than you hear about his marriage. Grandma calls when Junior breaks his leg, but you may never hear about Junior winning a school trophy. In news terms, the completion of a new wing at the local prison may get a brief mention on local programs, but a riot at the same prison could be national news.

- *Unusual events are more interesting to people than ordinary ones.* Thirty–five successful landings at the local airport are not newsworthy (unless the airport is under siege or the controllers are on strike), but the crash of the 36th plane is news.

There are general principles that will help you recognize good stories. They may also help you structure a questionable assignment by reminding you to look for an angle that will get people to listen to the story.

Where do the story ideas themselves come from?

- **Read the wires.** The national and local services of the Associated Press and United Press International carry the major stories on their wires services. If you have access to the wires, check them regularly. When you get an assignment, pull the wire copy. It will give you a head start on your research. But don't trust the wire services (or anyone else, for that matter) to be completely accurate or thorough. Do your own checking.

- **Keep in touch with the local press.** Read it carefully and don't ignore the small stories on page ten. Many news stories work their way to the front page over a period of time. Pay particular attention to the specialty newspapers and magazines. They will announce events and cover stories that could be interesting to a national audience before the major news organizations discover them.

- **Cultivate your sources.** The best ideas frequently come from sources. These are people who, for one reason or another, know about events before you do. They may work inside organizations and recognize good stories when they see them. They may be other reporters who can't use a particular good idea. They are frequently people whom you have reported on in the past, people who respect your journalism and trust you. Finally, keep your eyes and ears open for events that nobody else has noticed.

- **Keep your story ideas and your sources in a notebook.** Don't expect them all to be useful to you when you first hear about them. In many cases local stories can wait for a national news peg—a major news story to which you can tie a minor one. For example, if a national news program decided to do a piece on worker–ownership of failing companies, it could give you a peg for a local story on a specific experiment in your community. If Congress were to withdraw funding from the food stamp program, you could do a story on the impact of that legislation in your area if you talked to the local grocers, government officials, welfare rights leaders, and poor people who might be affected.

6

Understand the Assignment

Sometimes you will be assigned a story. Sometimes you will think up the idea yourself and get it accepted by the program for which you are filing. Occasionally, you will be working entirely on your own. In any case, someone is going to have to act as your **editor** and give you an outside, independent critique of your story idea. If this editing can be done by people involved with the show for which you are filing, so much the better. They can help you tailor your story to the show. If not, find a friend who can function as your editor.

Although editors are *sometimes* the final arbiters of what gets on the air, when they are working with reporters they should not be acting as judge, censor, or professor deciding on a grade. Editors do not usually know more about the story than the reporter. In their editing capacity they are essentially surrogates for the audience. They listen to the reporter's story idea with the ears of an intelligent listener, raising all the questions that any listener might raise. What do we need to know to understand this story? What story elements are redundant or obvious or too specialized? When does the story need more information to make sense?

If, in addition to being an intelligent, inquisitive listener, the editor knows something about the possibilities of broadcasting, he can be helpful in making the piece more effective radio, but that isn't essential. It *is* essential to have some outsider listen to your work *before* it goes on the air.

Before you begin to work, you and your editor should have a common understanding of the idea, the reason the story is of interest, the length you expect to file, the number of different components that you intend to include, the amount of research expected and the conditions and amount of your payment, if any. Decide on a deadline for filing and make sure that the time available is realistic for your story.

These early decisions should not lock you into any final conclusions. The story may change as a result of your research and field interviews. But your original conception will serve as a road map, and your subsequent conversations with your editor will help you discuss the story from common premises.

The key here is outside input. You need to talk your pieces through with other people, getting as much advice and input as you can. Of course, the advice will sometimes be conflicting, and in the end you will have to rely on your own news instincts. The quality of your judgment in these instances will measure your skill as a journalist.

Getting Started

If the story is dramatic enough, getting started is easy. If a ghetto is burning down or a plane has crashed or prisoners are rioting, grab your tape recorder and head for the action. But sooner or later you are probably going to have to do your homework and go back to the place where most stories begin: in research.

You can start your research with a press release, a wire story, a newspaper clipping or a tip from a source, but you will soon be on the phone. Because news is timely, there is rarely an extensive written record to look at. Because you are working under a deadline, there is seldom time to spend hours in the library or the county clerk's office.

Talk to the people who are involved in the story. What do they have to gain or lose? The losers are usually more interesting than the winners. Having already lost, they tend to be more reckless and more honest.

As people present their cases to you, they will buttress their arguments with information. Check the key facts with the **primary source** of the fact if you can. Remember, people frequently disagree on the facts. If it's a quote, the primary source is the person who said it. If it's a statistic, the primary source is the person who compiled it.

When you are talking to people in sensitive positions or about sensitive issues, make sure that you distinguish between information given **on the record** and that given **off the record.** If it's on the record, you can attribute the information to your source and you will probably want to record it on tape. If it's off the record, you must protect the confidentiality of your sources—despite pressure from some prosecutors and courts to reveal them—or your credibility as a journalist will be ruined.

The amount of research that you do will depend on the story and the time available. You could prepare a story on a prison riot from notes gathered during an afternoon at the scene, or you could research the causes of the riot for six months.

When you have finished your research, you should know the key people, the major issues and conflicts and the upcoming events. You should be in a position to rework your original idea, to structure your story and to make some preliminary decisions about what to record and what to look for in the field.

Before you set out, have a second conversation with your editor. Decide how you want to tell the story. You can simply write and read a script or you can produce a mini–documentary with all the sounds and devices of a full–scale documentary—interviews, recordings of events and different kind of **ambience** (the sound environment surrounding the story). You need to know what kind of story you plan to do so you can collect the right kind of tape in the field.

Keep in mind that you are telling a story. It should have a beginning, a middle, and an end. At the *beginning* the audience must be involved: something dramatic is going to happen; some goal important to us all is going to be contested; the situation of people that we care about is going to change. In the *middle* we may meet other characters and listen to pros and cons about the issues. We may get additional information and be exposed to other situations that bear on the main event. The *end* should tie the various threads together and take the listener to a stopping place. The expectations set out in the beginning should be fulfilled.

Objectivity and Fairness

Objectivity is always hotly debated in journalism. Today there is a school of journalists who argue that objectivity is impossible to achieve, so reporters might as well abandon the attempt and put all their own values and biases directly into their reporting where the audience can see them clearly and take them into account.

Some compelling journalism has been done this way, such as Hunter Thompson's account of his time with the Hell's Angels and Michael Herr's extraordinary look at the Vietnam War, *Dispatches*. But a lot of drivel has been written in the name of new journalism, too. Unless the reporter's perceptions are particularly revealing, unless his experiences are as powerful as the story that he's telling, the reporter's biases just get in the way of the main event—and they are usually boring to boot.

Of course, objectivity and fairness *are* impossible goals in an absolute sense. Any story is infinitely complex and any telling of it is a massive simplification. The reporter talks to some people but not others. He uses some of their remarks and not others. He records certain sounds and ignores others.

At every point in the reporting process, the journalist is making decisions about what to look for, what to ask, where to go, and what words to use to describe the things that he has heard and seen. All these decisions are made on the basis of each reporter's unique instincts, biases, and preconceptions. Different journalists tell the same story differently.

Despite the fact that objectivity is an unattainable goal, you strive for it by exercising journalistic discipline.

- **Be self-critical.** Bend over backwards to hear all sides and make a particular point of trying to understand the arguments of those with whom you disagree. Try to take everyone's point of view into account.

- **Be skeptical.** Pay most attention to people closest to the event—their biases will be most obvious, their recollections more vivid, and their explanation less filtered through value systems. Distrust secondary sources.

- **Be specific.** Stay with things that are actually happening and avoid speculating about motives, causes, feelings, meanings, and all such imponderables. Trust what you observed. Distrust the preconceived theories that people use to explain things.

If the people who appear in your piece feel comfortable with the way you have portrayed them—including those on opposite sides of some controversial issue—then you have probably been objective and fair. Honest journalism will inevitably anger some people. Be prepared for that and make sure that your facts support your portrayal.

Final Planning

Do one more thing before you go out to record. Sit down with your notebook and plan your field recordings and your production schedule. If you haven't already talked to the people you want to interview, do so before you arrive ready to record. Keep the conversation general. Find out what is on their minds. Be a good listener. You will find out more if you are sympathetic and genuinely want to get their story. Save your key questions for the taping. Most people say it best the first time. After that, they are more cautious and rehearsed. Make appointments and keep them.

If your story includes events, you will want to plan your interviews around them. For example, if you want to talk to people about why they are going to do something, it's best to interview them before they do it. If you want a vivid reaction to an event, talk to them as the event is going on or immediately afterwards. Obviously, if you want to know what impact the event has had on them, you will have to wait until it's over.

Make some preliminary decision about how you will record the event. What elements are important to your story? Where do you have to be and when should you be there? What other sounds do you need to enrich your report? These may be the background sounds that help place the story in a concrete location: the sounds of a receptionist answering a busy phone; the sounds of a car leaving a paved highway and turning onto a gravel road; the din of a factory in full production; or the hollow emptiness of a factory shut down during a strike.

Music can add realism and convey feeling, particularly if it's part of the location or the event, such as the Muzak of a hospital waiting room conveying the long and restless waiting in a public place, a radio or television clip that relates to the story, or the songs of demonstrators. According to FCC regulations, you must get written permission to rebroadcast another (American) TV or radio station. (See Chapter 12, "Basic Legal Concepts," for details.)

Make a list of the information that you need to collect to complete the story and ask people in the field for it. The more you get down as you go along, the less likely you are going to get stuck later trying to collect it over the phone.

Make some preliminary judgments about your **recording ratio**—the relationship between the raw tape you bring back and the length of the final story. Reporters tend to record too much. If you keep some ratio in mind—say twenty to one (that's one hour's tape for a three-minute piece) you will remind yourself to stay focused on the story and avoid an editing nightmare when you start to put the piece together later.

Finally, remember that when you are in the field the best laid plans may become irrelevant. Problems can occur that you didn't foresee or the story may go in a direction that you couldn't anticipate. Despite the pre–interview, the person to whom you are talking may have a whole new story to tell. Go with the story in the field even when it takes off in a different direction. Your advance planning may help you get back on course. At the very least, it will provide a yardstick against which you can measure your new story idea. But don't let yourself be locked into a weaker idea when a stronger one emerges.

Journalism is fascinating because the world is unpredictable and irreconcilable. Every situation has a crap–game quality that eludes the moralists and ideologues. People are far more complicated, and good and bad are distributed far more randomly, than the true believers and social planners want to accept. The moral and social ambiguity of real events is apparent to all good journalists. True believers frequently call that recognition cynicism, but it can just as easily be called compassion. If you infuse your reporting with a search for the truth and a respect for different points of view, you won't go far wrong.

2

Advancing the Story

by Ted Clark

There are two ways to approach journalism. **You can simply report the story, or you can advance it.** You can simply report the information at hand; or you can push beyond it. You can wait for developments to move the story forward, or you can be bored with that and move it forward yourself by reaching for new information and new insights.

The purpose of real journalism is to add to the body of information. That's why people listen. If your story adds nothing, it is simply a recounting of events— beautifully written perhaps, professionally delivered, but just a recounting.

It's especially important for broadcast journalists to bear this in mind. It's easy to think you have performed a service by taking a print story and rendering it for broadcast. Getting the mayor to say the same thing on tape that he said in the morning paper may seem like a useful endeavor, but it's not. Newspapers generally have more reporters than radio stations, and it's tempting to let newspapers do the real reporting while you transform it into radio. But don't yield to that temptation. **Advance the story.**

Try to find questions that haven't been answered yet. Eavesdrop on conversations in the bus, on the street. Find out what people are asking each other about the story. Chances are they're asking some questions that haven't occurred to the press corps. **Find answers.**

Some reporters keep a "call list" of community leaders, interest groups, or just plain thoughtful people—people to be telephoned on a regular basis. Their insights help to advance stories, and often they can provide tips about stories that are not yet in the news.

Reporters always call "the other side" in a story, but not just because it helps assure a fair story. It also helps advance the story, because the other side will have researched the issue in a unique way, to find new information in its own defense.

Think the story forward. Imagine it's a game of chess and it's up to you to think about what happens three or four moves ahead. The nation's air traffic controllers have threatened to strike. How will the current administration respond? Will it fire them all? What will be the controllers' next move? Will they ask controllers in other countries not to handle U.S. flights? How will the administration deal with that? If you think the story forward, you'll have interviews lined up before other reporters even think of them.

Ted Clark studied history in college. He began in journalism in 1975 as an apprentice in the Washington, D.C. bureau of Pacifica Radio and became bureau chief in 1977. He joined NPR in 1979 as Program Editor for All Things Considered *and was assigned to cover the White House in 1981.*

Think the story outward. Go outside the circles immediately affected. What will happen to the tourist industry and to small businesses that send perishable goods by plane? What does the President's action portend for his dealings with other public sector unions? With private unions? What effect will his action have on his popularity and his mandate to lead?

Think the story backward. What light can past events shed on the story today? Didn't the air traffic controllers support the President during the election campaign? Did that create false expectations on either side?

Another way to advance the story is to go from the theoretical to the real. If the Federal Aviation Administration says all planes are arriving on schedule, go to the airport and see if it's true. If not, that's news. The F.A.A.'s credibility becomes part of the story.

Profile the people making the news. What kind of man is the union president? Is he an experienced negotiator? Will he makes mistakes? How does the Transportation Secretary feel about unions in general? In profiling the newsmakers, you provide insights into the news. **The point is to make the listener think new thoughts.**

With that in mind, you should sometimes try to abandon the popular assumptions of a story. For example, the operative assumption in the Panama Canal story was that the United States had won friends in Latin America by agreeing to return the waterway. But the story is very different if you begin with the assumption, common in Central and South America, that the United States had no right to the Canal in the first place. Pursue that assumption and you'll gather very different information. *You'll advance the story.* Then try out the assumption that the United States should *never* have returned the canal, that it is vital to our national security. If you had done that in 1978, you might have met many of the people who later were swept into power with the Reagan Administration.

By trying out different assumptions, you'll be exploring the meaning of the story. Almost any story can be made more interesting this way. *So push beyond the obvious. Transcend boring assignments; advance the story.*

Some of the Perils

As a journalist, you deal in an elusive commodity: truth. Truth changes with every new piece of information. And perhaps the greatest peril of reporting is the notion that you know the truth about a story before you begin; you know the truth and all that remains is to gather the evidence. Reporters with that attitude are often blind to facts before their very eyes. They talk when they should be listening. They miss opportunities to advance the story.

In 1948, all the experts predicted that Thomas Dewey would defeat President Harry Truman. The election would serve only to provide the evidence. One newspaper went to press announcing boldly that Dewey had won before the evidence was in. But Harry Truman served another four years.

While journalists shouldn't be too sure about the truth, they can and should be sure about their values. Journalists must never lose the capacity to be angered, when the facts justify their anger.

Another peril is being lied to—not just outright lies, but lies from the best intentioned people—inadvertent lies, lies of omission, lies of dissimulation. There are many kinds.

There are artful denials. President Reagan promised in a speech that he would not cut the "social security benefits you've worked so hard to earn." He created the impression that all social security benefits were safe, but in fact he intended to cut the so-called minimum benefit. Minimum benefits are not exactly earned, however, they are given to anyone who needs them at a given age. The President chose his words carefully when he spoke of "benefits you've worked so hard *to earn.*"

There are diversionary techniques. Has the mayor put his relatives on the city payroll? "Charges like this come up every election year. I'm surprised that my opponent would resort to such gutter politicking. If I were you I'd ask him about the Mercedes he bought for his secretary."

There are attempts to belittle the truth. Watergate was a "third-rate burglary," according to White House Press Secretary Ron Ziegler in 1972. There is **disinformation,** stories planted in the press by governments eager to discredit their enemeies. There are flat-out lies when the stakes are high enough. And there are unwitting lies, told not out of malice, but out of simple ignorance. If reporters pass along any of these lies unchallenged in their stories, they become accomplices to some degree. Their reports give the lies greater validity.

There are other hazards to deal with besides the lie. *You will be flattered by people you are covering.* Press secretaries will tell you they admire your work, especially your sense of fair play. Watch out. It will be a little harder to be critical the next time. Richard Dudman, who wrote for the *St. Louis Post Dispatch,* tells the story. "Once [former Secretary of State] Kissinger asked my opinion on what he should say, in some great matter, and for a second I felt the headiness of being an important guy. But the truth is, Kissinger couldn't have cared less what I thought—it was a form of flattery. Reporters have to remember they are not sought out in Washington for their charm."

You will hear things out of context. A White House reporter had just heard President Reagan talk about the decline of Communism. Later, the reporter overheard a couple of the President's advisors. One was saying "The President told me 'It's the end of one era, but the beginning of another.' " The reporter thought Mr. Reagan had elaborated on his earlier remarks about Communism, and said so in the report he filed. But it later turned out the President had been talking to his aides about the sale of a major league baseball team in Chicago.

You will encounter the trappings of power, and be awed. Huge front offices, receptionists with frosty voices, countless reminders that you are about to talk to a very busy person. You will want to rush through your questions, and you will not think to follow up on them. Or perhaps you will find that the official is charming, witty—like the "good cop" after the "bad cop." And your defense, your skepticism, will fail. Just remember that VIPs are well schooled in these techniques.

And finally, you will occasionally cover people or causes you deeply admire. The perils here are obvious. It helps to bear in mind that honest and even harsh criticism is constructive and should be welcomed by people or causes that are honest.

General Assignment Reporting

The appeal of general assignment reporting is its variety. There are a million stories to choose from. While the diet of a general assignment reporter is varied, there are a few staples.

One of these is the **press conference.** It's not the place to go for scoops, but a press conference is often where news is happening. Press conferences are most useful to reporters who prepare before they go, who read the **clip file** who call "the other side," who have questions ready.

At press conferences, you'll be sharing the newsmaker with many other reporters, and it can be difficult to get your question in. You should learn to **seize the pauses.** The first pause comes after the initial introduction and presentation: a brief instant of awkwardness when no one knows who should talk first. Ask your question then, before the others do. Not only have you managed to get your first question in, you've made an impression on the person holding the news conference. You have become more visible, and it's easier to ask the next question.

Once the question and answer session (the "Q and A") is underway, if you're in a particularly competitive crowd of reporters, you may have to get the jump on them by asking your question before there's a pause, just as the speaker is concluding a sentence or a thought. This technique borders on the obnoxious, and if you don't want to risk being obnoxious you can often go up at the end of a press conference and pose a few questions quietly.

But while it's important to get your questions in, it's also very important to let the collective intelligence of the press conference work. Each reporter brings a different perspective and different information to the press conference, and the overall questioning can be much more incisive as a result. If a successful line of questioning is going on, join it if you will, but try not to interrupt it.

The press conference is an occasional event, but **press offices** are forever. Every general assignment reporter encounters them in corporations, in government, and in sports. Often they provide daily briefings. Sometimes reporters refer to people who work in press offices as "flacks," but this is not a complimentary term. They prefer to be called "public information or press officers." *Rule Number One: Press offices are there to make their bosses look as good as possible.*

Providing useful information is not the *primary* goal of press offices. But if you want on–the–record reactions, if you want someone to describe the mayor's position on rodenticides, if you want to get an interview with just the right official on some non–controversial subject, if you want information on schedules and itineraries—press offices can help.

Be prepared to go around them at times. A press officer may not want reporters to talk to a controversial figure, and may warn him not to talk if it's known you're trying to contact him. Similarly, if you're on to a story that's damaging to the institution in question, the press office will probably steer you away from the people who know what you need to know.

The Defense Department press office did not help Seymour Hersh break the Mylai Massacre story. He walked quietly into Lt. Calley's barracks one day, before anyone understood the enormity of what had happened at Mylai, and had a long talk with Calley about that day in March when U.S. troops opened fire on Vietnamese civilians.

The White House press office did not help Woodward and Bernstein with the Watergate story.

You may not always be able to talk to officials about controversial stories in their offices. Call them at home if necessary.

If you want to tape telephone interviews, remember that the people on the other end of the line have no way of knowing that they're being recorded unless you tell them. Make it clear that you want to tape and then make it clear when you've started to tape. A young reporter once lost his job because the congressman he interviewed on the phone didn't know his comments were being recorded. The reporter claimed he had abided by the letter, if not the spirit, of the rules. He began the interview by saying: "Hello, this is Jack taping for News Scope." (Names have been changed here to protect the innocent.) The congressman thought the "taping" was the reporter's last name.

As with press conferences, it's good to have a list of questions ready when you interview someone. The list can be liberating, allowing you to explore tangents or new directions without worrying that you'll forget to ask an important question.

Before the interview, many reporters think about *when* to ask the controversial questions. If they're likely to anger the interviewee, reporters will hold these questions until after they have the non–controversial answers they need. If reporters already have those answers and are looking for an unrehearsed reaction, they will often ask the provocative questions right away.

When you talk to people in their official capacity, as representatives of the local steel mill, for example, or the school board, you should operate on the assumption that you have every right to ask them questions. If their actions are going to affect the public, the public has the right to know about them.

For private individuals, or the private lives of public individuals, the ethics are very different, and so is the law. (See Chapter 12, "Basic Legal Concepts.") You don't automatically have the right to know what they are thinking or doing. If you want their stories, you may have to use gentle persuasion.

On a Beat

The time may come when general assignment reporting loses its allure. The excitement of covering a different story every day may give way to frustration. You can rarely do that follow-up story. You can't develop any real expertise.

That's the time to try a **beat.** It could be city hall, it could be crime, it could be Bangkok, it could be the arts. But whatever your beat, the first thing to do is read all about it; read everthing you can get your hands on, even things that are marginally related. Become voracious for information about your beat.

The next thing to do is develop **sources.** Official spokespersons are not usually sources. It's generally not the job of a source to deal with the press. Sources are people who do policy work within the organization you're covering. Many beat reporters try to meet mid–level sources to begin with: not the mayor, but the mayor's assistants; not the company president, but the vice–president in charge of operations. The big names make pronouncements, but the mid–level sources often originate policy changes, and can help a reporter to understand them. In addition, they can describe their bosses' motives, fears, regrets, and follow–up moves.

Some reporters meet sources by simply inviting them to lunch. They say: "I'm covering city hall, and believe that you can help me understand what goes on here. Your insights would make my reporting more fair. Let's have lunch. On me."

Some reporters simply walk into the office of a potential source and introduce themselves. And some reporters make a point of going up to the dais after a press conference and introducing themselves to the newsmaker there. In every case, the idea is to get acquainted, get familiar with each other, so the reporter doesn't have to call out of the blue on the day of the really big story.

Sources usually have pet products or projects and many reporters will sometimes admit to having filed newsworthy stories on these primarily to cultivate the sources. Another way to get acquainted is to do a series of portraits of people behind the scenes. Never pass up the opportunity to meet a source.

Sources won't always want to be quoted, but sometimes reporters can get off the record information placed on the record by asking another official to confirm it. This is not a good idea if the second official is likely to know who the primary source was. **The confidentiality of sources must be protected when they ask for it.**

What motivates sources? Often it's a sincere desire to enlighten the public. Sometimes sources may want to get air time for their point of view when a policy decision is pending. Sometimes they may want to sabotage an opponent. And sometimes the object is to lull a reporter into complacency, to lure a reporter into the family, or worse—to sandbag a reporter by giving false information at a critical moment.

Pack Journalism

There are hazards everywhere, even among your colleagues in the press corps. If you are covering a beat, you're likely to be in their company for long periods of time, and it's easy to start writing for *them* rather than for your real audience. *They* (not you) can end up deciding for what is or isn't news. That same collective intelligence that produces incisive questioning at a press conference can go astray and lead you into the practice of **pack journalism.** The *New Republic* once compared the Washington press corps to the pigeons in Lafayette Park, which take off all together sometimes, race madly around in a flock, and then settle together in another corner of the park, all without apparent reason.

But there are also benefits of being a part of the group. Reporters on a beat often "pool" resources. ("You stake out the back door, I'll stake out the front and we'll share whatever tape we get.") They can share insights and even sources on rare occasions.

To be or not to be a part of that group is a dilemma with no easy answer. I. F. Stone, an investigative reporter in Washington, opted out of the "family." He once said: "You pay something for everything you got. The establishment reporters, without a doubt, know a lot of things I don't know. But a lot of what they know isn't true. And a lot of what they know that is true, they can't print."

Putting the Story Together

Some reporters have daily deadlines, some weekly, some once a month, but you can't avoid them. Sooner or later you have to take all that information and extract the news. You have to write it down clearly and engagingly.

Paradoxically, the more you know about a story, the easier it is to write, once you have a basic outline in mind. If you know more than you need, you'll write with greater confidence. You'll know which word is exactly right. You won't have to be equivocal. Your syntax will not be tortured by your doubts.

Reporters who learn more than they need find the information valuable later. One week after American and Libyan war planes clashed over contested waters, an American plane had a close encounter with a missile from North Korea. Reporters who asked questions after the Libyan incident about other U.S. military operations in contested air space had a head start on the Korea story.

When you're gathering information, put out lots of calls. Really *work* the phone. Reporters can't afford to be idle while they're waiting for people to return their calls. There's almost always someone in another agency, in another office, or in a nearby town who has some useful information. Nearby colleges are often overlooked as sources of valuable information. Political science, history and fine-arts departments are full of experts and activists.

If there is just one person who knows what you need to know, be persistent. Don't be shy about calling back before that person has returned your call. Explain that you're on a tight deadline. Say you were out of the office for a moment and thought perhaps you had missed the return call.

Wire services can provide useful information, but they should be used judiciously. They are especially useful close to deadline when they can bring news of late–breaking developments across town. But the wires should be a supplement, not a substitute for your own reporting. To the degree that you use wire service information, your report will sound like dozens of others. And of course, it's important to confirm information taken from the wires whenever possible. This is the case with all secondhand information. If it's controversial, it *must* be confirmed before use.

After gathering this wealth of information, the best way to organize it into a story is to talk to someone else about it. Get back in touch with your editor. (You should already have talked to the editor at the beginning of the assignment. See the section on "Understanding the Assignment" in Chapter 1.) Most reporters find that once they've managed to explain the story to the editor, it's easier to explain it on the radio.

As you talk to the editor, or soon before, decide on your **lead.** A lead is the opening shot in a news story. In newspapers, the lead is one or two sentences long, contains the most important information, and conveys a sense of where the story is going.

In radio, there's another factor. You must think about ways to divide the lead with the person anchoring your newscast. If you don't give the anchor something provocative or newsworthy to say about your story, the anchor will simply sound dumb. Your report will not be an integral part of the newscast, but only attached to the newscast by the most tenuous of phrases: "And now for the latest on the economy we turn to. . . ."

Many reporters find it useful to write the **intros** to their own stories, in consultation with the program editor. That way, there's the smoothest possible flow from anchor to reporter.

If it's a hard news story, you might give the anchor the latest development to report, or perhaps the most important development. Your report should then begin in the most vivid way possible. It's a kind of partnership: the anchor gets listeners interested, and then you take them to the scene of the action.

So while a newspaper story could begin this way: "Today the Senate Ethics Committee recommended unanimously to expel Senator X, amid growing evidence that the full Senate will concur," a radio program would have the anchor saying something like: "The vote was unanimous. The Senate Ethics Committee has recommended expelling Senator X. If the full Senate goes along, and that seems more and more likely, it will be the first time since the Civil War that Senators have thrown out one of their own. More from reporter Y."

And the radio report would then begin: "It was a painful moment for Senator X and his colleagues. The committee chairman announced the decision in a subdued voice, as the committee members looked on silently. (Tape.)"

When you've settled on a lead, you have the heart of the story, and you should take a moment to sketch a rough outline. It will set your mind free. You can concentrate on writing, and not worry about forgetting an important element of the story.

As you write, remember that editors are there to be careful, reporters are there to be clear. Don't be reckless with the facts, but don't let caution paralyze you either. Write as simply as possible and as forcefully as possible. Your editor should keep you from painting with too broad a brush.

Write conversationally. Many broadcast reporters talk their stories as they write them. They try each sentence, each paragraph out loud. It's the best way to guarantee a comfortable, conversational style.

In radio, the active voice almost always sounds better than the passive voice. People usually talk in the active voice. They don't say "It was announced by the mayor today. . . ." They say "Today the mayor said. . . ." But sometimes the passive voice is unavoidable. Sometimes you won't know who did something and you'll have to write, "A young man was killed in his apartment last night. . . ." And sometimes reporters use the passive voice to help the pacing of their stories. (See Chapter 4, "Writing News for Radio.")

When the story is completely written, go back to your editor for one final edit.

Delivery

Before they go on the air, most reporters read their script out loud as many times as possible. Then, when they're on the air, or when they're recording, the words sound spontaneous and the script is almost secondary. Delivery is a very personal matter but there are some general guidelines, which add up to: **be natural.** Pause when you need to, breathe normally, swallow if you have to. Let your voice respond to what you're reading as it would to what you were saying in a normal conversation.

A frequent problem for beginning reporters is slowing down to a natural pace. Reading tends to make people talk faster, and you may have to make a deliberate effort to read more slowly than you think you should. Also, there's the danger of **singsong.** When you read out loud, your voice often rises and falls arbitrarily, and you may find your voice placing greater emphasis at the end of every sentence. You may find your pitch rising in the middle of every sentence, then falling at the end. In both cases, it's not natural: it's your voice doing arbitrary things. If you are really familiar with what you're reading, you can concentrate on the substance of it, and you'll find that your voice falls into more natural patterns. Sometimes, reporters will underline words that should be emphasized until it comes to them naturally. Sometimes, reporters write cues to themselves (or use symbols) in the margin of their scripts to denote "pause here," or "read deliberately here."

Use the voice you were born with, not the one you think a broadcaster should have. That one rarely "fits."

To enliven your delivery, if that's a problem, you might try smiling while you read. It's something you can get away with in radio because no one can see you.

The point is to feel what you are reading. If you do that, your voice will assume the proper tone. It's almost like acting. In fact, hosting a newsmagazine or delivering a news report unavoidably includes an element of performance—and acting is an element of any performance. But in radio journalism, acting skills are put to the service of the effective presentation of fact, not fantasy.

Being an Editor

At the end of a news day, a reporter should know everything about something, and an editor should know something about everything.

A good editor has the same sensibilities as a good reporter, and the ethics are pretty much the same. But an editor's concerns are "macro." An editor provides the context into which reporters place their pieces. So as you move from the role of reporter to that of editor and back to reporter again, you'll have to adjust your world view.

As an editor, you'll have to read more widely—even things that don't particularly interest you. They may interest your listeners. You are the listeners' advocate, and their first line of defense against boring or confusing stories.

As an editor, you have management responsibilities. At times you'll be a dispatcher (known as an **assignment editor**), sending reporters out across the news landscape. All assignments must emanate from a central point, or you'll have two reporters showing up at the same place and none at all at the really big story. And you have to make sure the reporters don't all file at the same time, which is otherwise likely to be a minute before the news program goes on the air.

Knowing what the good stories are *before* they happen is the art of being an editor, and there's no easy way to learn it. It comes with experience. But experience teaches the following: **Be well informed.** Project the trend of a story. Where is it likely to go next? The day after the mayor announces a new anti–crime initiative, send a reporter to the police precinct station to see if it will work. If it looks as though the federal deficit is going to be larger than expected, have a reporter standing by at the Office of Management and Budget for the inevitable announcement of further cuts in spending. **Use your own sources.** Contact the people on your own call list to find out what's brewing.

In many parts of the country, the wire services print "daybooks" every morning, sometimes the night before. These are listings of events that may interest the press: speeches, ribbon cuttings, ceremonies, hearings and the like. Not all the events are good stories, of course. Some are public relations stunts. Here, as always, the guiding principle should be: Do my listeners care about it? Look for reasons why they might be interested. "Bronx Man Leads Russian Revolution" was the headline in the *Bronx Home News* in November 1917. The editor had discovered that Leon Trotsky once lived in the Bronx.

Get your name on mailing lists. Ask press officers to write you or call whenever something is happening. They'll be happy to do it, seekers of publicity that they are.

As editors make assignments they try to create a good "mix" of stories: not just hard news; not just features. This mix helps to assure a lively and well–placed news program.

And, of course, the assignment process is a consultative one. Reporters will tell editors about good stories, and editors will try to match reporters with stories that are right for them. It's not productive to be arbitrary or dictatorial in assigning reporters. But there are times when editors have to overrule reluctant reporters if that's the only way to get the story covered.

You should have reporters call you as soon as they have a substantial amount of information. Use this occasion to help them formulate the stories in their minds, to think of follow–up questions, and to decide upon leads. This is an important opportunity to pass on other information you have learned from the wires or from other reporters in the field. Editors should be clearinghouses for information, should be (in journalistic parlance) **the desk.** This prevents contradictions within your news program, and it makes all your reporters sound better–informed. It's a kind of cross-pollination that leads to new insights. And as you receive all this information, be looking for patterns.

Barry Sussman was the District of Columbia Editor of the *Washington Post* in the summer of '72 when the Watergate story began. In his book *The Powers That Be,* David Halberstam describes him this way: "Sussman was not simply encouraging, he brainstormed the story, trying to put the pieces together, fitting them and refitting them until finally, slowly, there was the beginning of a pattern. Where other editors on a story so difficult might have cast doubt upon the fragments the young reporters were bringing in, Sussman offered only constant encouragement. Sussman always believed there was more."

Two or more hours before air time, you should know which stories are going to be ready for your news program, and which are not. You should have a pretty good idea of which stories are most important, and you should begin to design your newscast or news program.

Traditionally, the hard news stories go first, but a better standard might be: **put the stories that most interest your listeners first.** Intersperse long stories with short ones, hard ones with soft, analyses with produced, on–the–scene reports. Use commentaries, even satire. News programs should not be predictable except in this respect: listeners should know that they will hear the most important story first. You may want to end your program with the most thought–provoking story and leave your listeners with something to muse about.

There will be days, of course, when one story dominates all others. When President Reagan was shot, for example, most Washington news bureaus assigned all their reporters to different aspects of the same story. One went to the hospital for reports on the President's condition. One went to the White House to see how it was functioning. One went to the scene of the shooting, etc. On days like that it is especially important that all information be cleared through one point before being aired, or contradictions and mistakes will abound. And on days like that, features and satires may seem inappropriate.

About an hour before "air," it's time for final edits. You should try to take one last look at the wires, in case there have been late–breaking developments that your reporters should know about.

Listen to reporters with total concentration. Block out the chaos around you for those few moments. Make notes to yourself as comments or suggestions occur to you. Hear the reporter out before you suggest changes. You should have a sense of the story as a whole before you try to fix it. If the story is too boring to be fixed, or if you are unsure about the information in it, drop it. Try again the next day. There's no law that says you *have to* put something on the air. Have a stockpile of pretaped "evergreen" material nearby, to fill the hole when a story drops out.

You won't have much time to make changes during the final edit. That's why it's essential to stay in touch with reporters throughout the news day.

Reporters and editors will have arguments, but their conflict should be constructive. From that inevitable tension, a better story will often emerge. Good editors respect reporters who are prepared to fight to keep a point of information or style in their reports. It's a sign of intellectual rigor. And good reporters welcome tough editors who pay close attention. When an editor cares about a story, an editor is really caring about the reporter, and in the end, about the listener.

3

Interviewing

by Susan Stamberg and Larry Josephson

This chapter is devoted to one of the most important tools of journalism, the interview. Interview stories come in all sizes and shapes, but generally fall into two categories: 1) the **news interview,** one shedding light on a current topic; and 2) the **personality interview,** where a person reveals him or herself in conversation.

Successful journalists continually work on their interview style and strategies. As Susan Stamberg, co-host of National Public Radio's evening news program, *All Things Considered,* explains: "Somewhere there is the perfect interview. Maybe someday I'll end up doing it. Meanwhile, I continue to work toward it."

This chapter begins with an interview with Stamberg, one of the most popular and respected interviewers in the nation. The second half of the chapter sets out some guidelines to be remembered in the interviewing process. You will learn that interview styles are as personal as thumbprints; no formula exists that works for all reporters in all situations. But careful attention to the basics presented here will increase the chances that your interviews produce results—and excellent radio.

In Search of the Perfect Interview

Susan Stamberg, interviewed
by Larry Josephson

Larry: Susan, do you have a set of rules—do's and don'ts—about interviewing? Are there things that you never do or things that you always do?

Susan: Not really. I suppose I carry rules around as a part of my subconscious professional baggage, but if I ever had to stop and think, "Today I'll do a–b–c–d, but I'll never do x–y– and z," I'd never find surprises. I would

Susan Stamberg, the first woman to anchor a national nightly news program in the United States, has been co-host of NPR's All Things Considered (ATC) *since 1971. Prior to joining NPR, she was producer and host of a nightly newsmagazine aired on WAMU-FM, Washington, D.C. She also served as program director and general manager for WAMU from 1963 to 1966. A native of New York City, Stamberg graduated from Barnard College. Her book,* Every Night at Five: Susan Stamberg's All Things Considered Book *(New York: Pantheon, 1982) offers excellent examples of interviews.*

Photo by Barbara Bordnick

Fig. 3.1. Susan Stamberg is co-host of *All Things Considered*, NPR's nightly newsmagazine.

anatomize myself to death, become so rule–ridden that all the spontaneity and magic would be lost. In fact, what worries me about this book is that people might read through it as if it were a set of rules. Then they might begin interviewing and think, "Susan Stamberg says never do this, and always do that." The truth is: Sometimes do this and sometimes do that, and sometimes never do this and sometimes always do that. Mostly, I think you should play your hunches and be open to the infinite range of possibilities that exist in any interview.

Larry: How much do you prepare for an interview with someone who's written a book? Do you do a lot of research?

Susan: The most research was for two major literary interviews—one with Joan Didion, the other with Tillie Olson—each of which ran for a full half-hour on *All Things Considered.* In both cases I not only read everything they had written, but everything that other people had written about them. With non–fiction books, it varies. Sometimes the book itself is enough, sometimes you'll need to do supplementary research to find other angles that might make the interview livelier. That kind of research is done mostly by phone calls. If you have a book with a very clear point of view on adoption, for example, you can call two or three family service organizations and say, "I'm reading a book; the author says this, this, this, and this—do you agree?" The calls may broaden your base of information.

Some years ago I interviewed Dick Cavett and asked him whether he always read the books before he interviewed the authors. Cavett said he made a point of *never* reading the books, because he didn't want to lose his edge of curiosity. If he read the book he would already know too much and come to the interview so well armed that he might forget to ask the most simple, basic questions. I found that shocking and irresponsible at the time. Then, some years later, I had to interview an author whose book I simply hadn't had the time to read. Well, it turned out to be one of my better interviews. Maybe it was for Cavett's reason, or maybe it was that I was so edgy from not having done all my usual homework ahead of time, that it just gave me a little bit more adrenalin.

Larry: So you dipped into your store of common sense. . . .

Susan: I think that's what you do even with research. You bring everything that you have ever done to bear on the interview you are doing at the moment. The research is an ongoing process, really. It's being in love with ideas in some way, or keeping in touch with ideas and being alive to them.

Larry: Why do research? Does it put you in a position to challenge someone you're interviewing?

Susan: Sure, but I'm not very enthusiastic about challenging. I don't like to do confrontational interviews—it's not my style. I *can* do them, and when I must, the research is preparation for battle. But for me, the research is a chance to think about the subject and decide what to do in the interview. I want always to go in with some idea about the person's work so that I can engage them in a dialogue, an exchange of views. I try to avoid the tell–me–everything–you–know–about–navy–blue–sweaters kind of interview. If I come to the interview with research information that navy blue is a power color, and you've written a definitive book on navy blue sweaters, I've got something interesting to talk with you about. That's the real reason for research. Not to gird for the challenge, but to provide a background of ideas. The challenge will happen, because I come in armed with those ideas, that perspective on the subject.

Also, research is a courtesy. If someone's taken the time to write a 400 page book, I think it's a courtesy to take the time, myself, to read the book, so I'm familiar with what's occupied my guest for so long. If I interview Laurence Olivier and my first question is, "Tell me, Sir Laurence, how did you get into theater?" I'm asking an extremely rude question. I should already know all that about him, through research. Then I don't waste his time by asking him something he's already told 5,000 interviewers. Not only would that be rude, I'd also risk boring him to death. But if I have spent a little bit of time first reading and thinking about his career, I will come up with some interesting questions. He will get interested in answering them. Then I'll get something lively on tape. Basically, you do research so you don't waste time—your time or the time of your guest.

Larry: What about questions? Any taboos there?

Susan: I avoid the question, "How do you feel?" I won't ask it directly because it's an obvious question, and the answer either may be none of my business or quite predictable. I'm thinking of the "What's–it–like–to–be–a–widow,–Mrs.–Kennedy?" kind of hideous TV news questions. I try never to ask exploitative questions. I remember the writer Joan Didion saying in our interview that one of the biggest problems she has as a journalist is asking people how much money they make. She said, "The most basic questions that journalists need to ask, I can't ask." I feel exactly that way. "How hard was it for you after your wife left you?" I can't ask questions like that. So I always find ways around it, other things to ask.

I have difficulty, sometimes, finding the proper angle with creative people. I feel it's insulting to ask a poet, "What does your poem mean?" In asking that, I'm either saying I am ignorant, or that the poet has failed. I asked folk singer Pete Seeger for advice at a time when I wasn't satisfied with the way I was interviewing artists. He said what you can always do is ask them what was in their mind at the moment of creation. That was a great help. The artists can explain *themselves* to you, rather than their work and give you insights about the creative process.

It is important to develop a line of questioning, to avoid the "vacuum–cleaner" kind of interview. The vacuum–cleaner approach is much more common in print journalism, but I've been on the other end of enough broadcast interviews to despair at how frequently it's done by my colleagues. Here's what I mean by vacuum cleaner: Ask any question, as it occurs to you, in any order. Just get it all. Draw it in like a vacuum cleaner. Print journalists do this all the time, because they can always go back, sort and juggle their notes. But in radio, you must create a structure that gives the interview a beginning, middle, and end, with some line of investigation. I think it's crucial to build that into the interview as it's taped. You can do a lot of saving through editing and re-arranging, but you can't always rescue a disjointed interview.

Larry: Do you have a rough idea, at least in your mind, of how the interview is going to be structured—how the final cut will sound—before you even start?

Susan: Yes. Again, it's a way of not wasting time. And, at the same time, I'm prepared to completely abandon the structure, if, in the course of the conversation, something comes up that I hadn't expected or predicted. But I always try to go in with *something*—a framework for myself.

Novice interviewers often come in with a list of seven questions, and never listen to the answers. They're so busy looking at the next question that they miss three or four points being made in the answer that would be interesting to follow up. I do take notes in with me most of the time, for a very simple reason. On a day with several interviews, one on the Consumer Price Index, another with a writer, and something else on science, I'm going to lose my concentration if I don't make myself at least a bare outline of the points for each subject. In preparation, I'll sit down ahead and just think, or make notes to myself before I go into the interview, so I've got something to look at. But I try not to let myself get tied down to one set of questions.

Larry: So, in other words, when you go in, you kind of have the beginning, middle, and end—at least conditionally—traced out so you don't have to just do a lot of things and hope that whoever edits your interview can make something out of it?

Susan: Yes. I think it's wrong to hand over a jumbled tape. I think that's irresponsible. It leaves the burden on the editor. The burden should be on me, as the interviewer.

Larry: You don't generally edit your own interviews, do you?

Susan: I did for years. But in the last two or three years, we've gotten more editors. When *All Things Considered* began, I edited almost all of my own work, simply because there were so few tape editors. In those days I was doing five or six interviews a day *and* editing them. That was really too much. Now we have content editors who sit in the control room making notes on the news interviews. When I'm finished taping, I can go in and look over the notes. If I have strong feelings about how the piece should be cut, I'll express them. Then we both will confer with the actual tape cutter about the major points, and how the cuts should be made.

Larry: Do you feel that the experience with the razor blade in the early days helped you be a better interviewer?

Susan: Of course. It can't help but help! When you make a sloppy tape that goes in 43 different directions and the burden is on you to cut and shape it into something coherent, you're hearing all your own clutter. You're hearing the places where you're going off the track. You're hearing the places where you're losing control of the interview and letting the guest run away with it. Each time that happens, you learn not to do it the next time.

Larry: What about location—where would you prefer to talk to the subject? In the studio, in their habitat, or on the phone?

Susan: It's an interesting question. Location is partly about power, and it depends on the kind of power I want to have in an interview. If I bring a John Ehrlichmann into my studio, then he's on my turf, and it's going to affect his behavior in some way. But if I have to go to him, in that impressive White House, with all its flags and symbols of office, I'm at a disadvantage. So for somebody like that, I'd rather bring him into my studio if I can, where the power symbols of broadcasting are on display. That evens out the relationship a bit. On the other hand, I would never bring someone who's not a professional speaker into our studio. It's so stressful and unnatural to sit at that table under our pizzazzy television lights, surrounded all the equipment, and try to talk in a human fashion. *I* find that hard, and I'm paid to do it. Imagine how a truck driver or a sculptor or a teenager—anyone who's not used to public speaking— would feel! So I try to be sensitive to who the guest is, and if I feel they would be intimidated by the hardware and show-biz stuff, I go to them if at all possible.

Location is not just about power. It's also about comfort. You go to the place where your person will be most relaxed and most at ease. In the first years of *All Things Considered,* most interviews were done by telephone because our staff was so small. There was no travel budget and few reporters we could send out, so we had to bring the world in to us. The way to do it was by phone. It worked wonderfully, even though the engineers hated it because it's such terrible quality. (I've never cared about the quality of line. All I care about is what's being said.) If I couldn't go to the guy's truck to talk to him while he was driving, he could talk to me on the telephone at his house, or from a diner, or wherever he was, and that again was his natural turf.

Also, the microphone inside that telephone is the microphone that most people are used to dealing with every day of their lives. They're extremely comfortable with it, and they will talk to me through it the way that they would to a good friend or neighbor. They will be instantly relaxed and there'll be a rapport that is very lovely to hear.

Larry: Have you ever said, "This isn't working?"

Susan: Yes. I've said, "This is really what I wanted to talk about," or, "Why don't we start again?" Or, I'll just say—explicitly, because I know it can be edited later—"Wait, we're really getting off the subject. Let's get back on track." But sometimes what I'm getting is just boring. The chemistry is not good, or the guest is an uninteresting speaker. If it's a factual subject that you must get on the air that day, you complete the interview, thank the guest, say goodbye, and go back and find someone who's a livelier speaker, or more articulate. You do have to be prepared to write some things off. I've got a stack of tapes now, back at the office, that I think I'll throw out; they are interviews that just didn't work.

Larry: How do you conceive of your role as interviewer?

Susan: What you can never forget is that you're not just there talking to that person across the table. You're there in behalf of the listener. You're always the listener's advocate. Your job is to extract information that the listener needs. Then there's the performance part of the job. Your questions have to be expressed in a way that makes *you* interesting to listen to, as well as your guest. You are participating in the dynamics of the interchange, not just sitting on the side, observing.

Larry: Do you try to ask questions that the listener would ask, or that the listener would not have thought to ask?

Susan: I really do both. My research should provide me with more sophisticated questions than the listener would ask, but I also try to keep confident in my own curiosity. One of the best lessons I ever learned about interviewing came from a *Mister Rogers' Neighborhood* program on which Neil Armstrong appeared after the moon walk. Fred Rogers asked him questions that children had sent in. One of the questions was, "How do you urinate in space?" I thought that was sensational! That's just the kind of question your mother told you never to ask. Your mother was wrong. It's something people are really curious about. Go ahead and ask those questions. Ask the symphony conductor, "Do your arms ever get tired?" Ask it simply because it's something you're dying to know. And then, and this is really the most important point about interviewing, listen very carefully to the answer, and see whether it raises other questions or sparks new curiosities. The questions you ask, whether simple or sophisticated, are never as important as listening to the answers. The answers should suggest new questions. Then the task becomes choosing the one follow-up question that will advance the conversation, out of the many questions that occur to you as you listen to the answer.

Larry: How do you avoid conversational conflict—talking over someone? Besides, of course, listening? How do you structure your questions so that they don't start answering while you're still asking?

Susan: I don't mind that. In fact, I rather like it. It means that we've gotten very busy and there's a lot going on in the studio. That's how people talk in real life: they don't wait for sentences to be finished, they hear where you're going, anticipate the end of a sentence, and just jump in and continue it. I don't mind that kind of scrambling up at all. Sometimes I fall into a pattern of asking questions that are overly long and complicated. I end up giving a little speech. That's when the editing block helps—you can cut a question in half, or cut internally so that you have the beginning and end of it, without the entire epic.

31

Larry: But the point here, again, is that you constantly think about how you're going to sound in the finished product—the edited interview.

Susan: Yes. You can never forget that there is a final product, a product at the end of the line, that must be polished and smooth. You try to hear the edits as you tape the interview. Again, it's all part of the performance.

Larry: Let me lean on the word "performance," because I think that's important. I think there's a tradition in journalism of holding that word to be an anathema. Are you comfortable with the fact that you are a performer as well as a journalist in your role as an interviewer?

Susan: I'm definitely a performer and I'm not in the least embarrassed about it. I was uneasy with the idea of performance in the early years, when I was a little less confident about my journalistic ability. In the beginning you tend to stress that what you're doing is journalism, it's professional, it has nothing to do with show business. I've come to realize over the years that it's foolish to be embarrassed. If you can get people to listen by making it sound as interesting as possible, as dazzling as possible, as engaging as possible, then you're doing your job. You can't inform people, you can't educate them, unless they're listening to you. Anybody can be competent—those kinds of questioners are a dime a dozen. Interviews become magical when they're done by somebody like Studs Terkel or Bill Moyers. Someone with a thinking mind, who's dealing with ideas and presenting the guest in the liveliest fashion.

Larry: What is your background? What had you done? Who are you as a person? I don't think many people know. What do you bring to this, in terms of life experience and in terms of professional experience?

Susan: I bring no journalism, no broadcasting classes. My background was in the liberal arts and the humanities. I was an English major at Barnard College, and my interest has always been in the human drama of situations. So if I can approach news as a novel—as events that involve people, their lives, and their interactions, then I get extremely interested. If I just have to approach news as facts, or statistics, or chronologies, that doesn't engage me. I think it was the training as an English major that has stood me in good stead all of these years. I had a broad liberal arts background, my interest always was in the arts, in creativity, in ideas. If you can take that interest and bring it to bear on news and daily reporting, then you won't lose the heart of the story.

Larry: So, could we extract out of this that the best preparation for interviewing is to be a well–rounded human being, rather than a student of the Seven Rules of Interviewing. . . ?

Susan: Get a broad liberal arts education, learn as many different kinds of things as you can, and keep your level of curiosity and energy up. It will always pay off. Everything you have ever done will serve you well in this kind of work. Every life experience you've ever had will be useful, some day, sitting behind a microphone across the table from somebody.

Larry: Read a lot, talk a lot, talk to people. . . .

Susan: Keep in touch. Find out what's going on. Find out what's on people's minds. But also, have confidence in yourself and your own instincts and curiosity. You have to have done a lot of different things in your life, and to have been alert all the while. That could mean a range of different kinds of jobs and encounters with a wide variety of people—not getting stuck in one rut, not only talking with fellow students, not only talking with people your own age, not only talking with people 20 years older than you are, but seeking out variety. And having a broad range of interests. If you only care about politics, then you may be perceived as one–dimensional. But if you also care about music, and sculpture, and you have also taken a course at some time in your life in Sanskirt, then you are enriched. And very well–prepared.

Some of the most interesting interviews I've ever heard were done by people who'd never done a broadcast interview in their lives, but who brought to the situation layers of experience from the lives they'd already led. A psychologist came into the studios of WHA in Madison, Wisconsin and did a series of interviews with people about their work, and their attitudes toward their work. It was some of the most wonderful conversation I've heard. We ran it on *All Things Considered.* Now, granted, as a psychologist he was a professional asker–of–questions. He knew how to listen, how to reinforce. But those interviews were marvelous because of the environment he created for the people he was talking to, and the sense he gave them that they were safe, that they could feel free to talk to him. What you do in an interview situation will have to be strongly related to who you are and what you bring to the encounter. If you are naturally shy, or naturally hostile, aggressive, you can't hide that; you can't lie to a microphone. What you are is going to come out. If you are naturally enthusiastic and curious, that will come out too. So, you bring yourself.

Larry: Do you have any parting words for those who would aspire to be interviewers?

Susan: Yes, Larry, I do. I have one parting word: plastics.* No. Maybe the most important thing to remember is that you're not going to get it right the first time. The story of my life in broadcasting (which has lasted about 16 years) is that I keep doing it and doing it and doing it, and someday I'm going to get it right. We all have these radio programs in our minds, and they're all so much more perfect than anything that gets out into the air. Somewhere there is the perfect interview. Maybe some day I'll end up doing it. Meanwhile, I continue to work toward it.

*If you don't get this joke, go see the Dustin Hoffman film, *The Graduate.* [Ed.]

Surviving the Interview

As a reporter, you are not there to dominate the interview, but to control and channel it for maximum results. Stamberg has described how she approaches an interview; here is a brief sampler of additional advice:

Make your questions as specific as possible: "What has been the impact of the new development on Ninth Street?" may yield more than "What do you think of urban renewal?" Ask for examples. Avoid yes/no questions. Know that people have answered these questions before; understand why they are giving you a certain piece of the puzzle. Learn to pause and wait: what comes out of a subject's mouth after a moment's hesitation might be the most interesting part of the interview. Don't be afraid to ask the same question twice if you didn't understand the answer the first time. Be tough but cheerful. Don't confine the interview to straight question-and-answer: get the person to read to you, demonstrate something, *perform*.

Making the Initial Contact

Your first hurdle will be getting your subject to grant an interview. Ideally, an appointment should be made by writing or phoning several days in advance. If there's a big rush for a story, such advance notice may be impossible. But remember that dropping abruptly into someone's life and asking for a half–hour or more of their time can be interpreted as rude or presumptuous. Be gracious.

If you're making contact by phone, identify yourself and your organization, what you are working on and where the interviewee fits in, and approximately how long the interview will take. Introductions should be precise and phrased to engage the subject's interest. You can even write out what you're going to say over the phone, if you think you're going to forget it. One tip: some people may shy away from the notion of a formal "interview," which may conjure up visions of merciless cross–examination. Instead, ask for some time to elicit their views, advice, or criticism on a given topic. An interview by any other name can be just as successful.

In determining a site for the interview, keep in mind potential problems of background noise or interruption. A restaurant can be a relaxing setting, but the clink of glassware will show up on your tape. There are stories that may be enhanced by actualities, but a serious discussion of foreign policy calls for a quiet setting. Try to anticipate potential distractions. You want the interviewee's undivided attention.

Immediately Prior to the Interview

NPR correspondent Robert Krulwich recommends that you consult the following checklist immediately prior to the interview, if you are taping away from the studio:

1. **Check batteries.** If they run down during the interview, you will want to kill yourself later.
2. **Bring twice as much tape as you think you will need.**
3. **Label at least one cassette before you begin,** so that later you don't inadvertently record over the interview.
4. **Before—just before—you meet your subject, talk into your tape recorder** and play back what you have recorded to make sure it's working.
5. **Make sure the tape cassette is properly loaded and rewound** to the beginning of the tape, not to the leader (the plastic non-magnetic tape at the very beginning of the cassette.) That way, you won't miss the first few words and you'll be less likely to have to flip your cassette over during the interview.

During the Interview: Equipment Etiquette

The presence of a tape recorder can have a "chilling" effect on the most willing of interview subjects. Krulwich suggests that whether or not your subject appears to be nervous about the tape recorder, refer to it (that is, talk about it, look at it, fuss with it) *as little as possible.*

According to Krulwich, the best approach is to walk into the room and set the tape recorder down where *you* want it. If the room has couch and a coffee table, place it on the coffee table and ask the subject to join you. He or she may prefer to stay at a desk, or in chair that is far away. Take command. Explain that the two of you have to be within arm's reach. *You are the recording expert.* If you gently insist, you will win.

Once you and your subject are conveniently seated, begin informally. Don't suck in your breath and say, "OK, here we go"—that's too scary. The better approach is to review familiar territory. ("We're going to have a 10–to–15–minute discussion, I'm going to take it back to the station, edit it down. . . .") While you are talking, start the tape recorder. Don't bring the microphone to your mouth right away, just go on explaining ("This is for our show, *All Things Considered* . . . have you heard it. . . . etc.") and gradually, bring the microphone into play.

If you show that *you* don't particularly care where the microphone is at any given moment, your subject may adopt the same attitude. If the interviewee interrupts you and asks, "Have we started?", answer, "Yes," and jump right on to your next question. Mentally you should be focusing on what the subject is saying: watch the person's face or eyes. Look as little as possible at the machine.

Do's

1. **Do put your microphone just below the subject's mouth,** angled like an ice cream cone, just below the lower lip.
2. **Do follow the subject.** If the subject leans back in the chair or steps back, gently close in. You can give the interviewee (and your sore arm) a breather by dropping the mike down when he or she's on a tangent you don't care about. But when the answer is important, the closer you are to that lower lip, the happier you will be later on in the editing stage.

Don'ts

1. **Don't ever let your subject take control of the microphone.** Sometimes, after you have asked your first question, the subject will curl a hand around the mike handle and pull the mike away. Ask for it back. Explain that it is your job to hold the equipment. The subject might grab it back again a minute later. Take it back again. Without the microphone, you can't control your own questions, and you can't interrupt when you please. You have lost control of the interview.
2. **Don't lose an important remark because the subject turned away from the mike at a crucial moment.** Example: "I'll tell you who killed the mayor. I've got his name right here. It's . . . (and then the subject steps back to read from a notebook and the name comes in soft and distant). Jump right in and ask the question again. "I missed that. Who killed the mayor?" You want your crucial tape to be recorded at a consistent sound level.
3. **Don't leave an interview without checking to make sure the tape did, in fact, record.** Spot check your tapes. Play back random portions through the built–in speaker or (preferably) using headphones so your subject won't be tempted to revise his or her remarks as they are played back. If the tape is blank, it is too embarrassing to try to redo the whole thing at a later date. Better to discover the problem before you leave, try to conceal your horror and pain, fiddle with the dials for a second and then say, "Look, just to make sure I have this right," and go ahead and re–ask a crucial question, turning the machine back on. The subject will wonder a little about you, but at least you will have *some* recorded material. And some is a lot, lot better than none.

Some Legal Considerations in Interviews: Consent

Janice Hill of NPR's legal division advises all reporters to remember certain legal aspects of interviewing. Chief among these is the concept of "consent."

If you are doing interviews in person, and have clearly identified yourself and have told the participant that you are taping for broadcast, then legally the participant has consented to the broadcast of his or her remarks by talking to you, and no written agreement from the participant is needed.

If you are doing a phone interview, the Federal Communications Commission requires that you tell the person on the line that they are being recorded or are on the air. (The exception to this rule is the case of a radio "call–in" program, where it is assumed callers know they are on the air.) Again, consent need not be in writing: if you have informed your interviewee, the person consents by talking to you. You should tape your announcement and keep it with your outtakes of the interview.

It's important to keep the concept of "consent" clearly in mind. If someone asks to review or edit their remarks, and you agree, then as a matter of contract you can't use the material without getting their consent. You are bound by any conditions you agree to, so be careful. You need not agree to let anyone audition or edit what you put together before broadcast. If someone insists on it, and you desperately need the interview, then you should make it clear that you will not let them change or edit the material in any way.

The whole topic of "off–the–record" remarks is a complicated one, and you and your editor or station management should establish some ground rules. If your station does have policies in this area, you should inform the subject of them at the start of the interview.

If an interviewee suddenly announces that what they are about to say is "off–the–record," you must decide whether it's worth it and tell them immediately if you agree or disagree. This is a difficult judgment call, one that depends ultimately on what is in the listener's best interests. If you want to use the subject's full remarks on the air, then don't just remain mute, but say, "No, this is on–the–record," or "I'm still recording for broadcast." If you go off–the–record, then indicate when you have begun taping for on–the–record again. Once consent is denied for part of the interview, it must be re–established for any subsequent portion, if that portion is to be broadcast.

4

Writing News for Radio

by Edward Bliss, Jr.

The writer of news for radio must write the purest, most readily–understood prose of any medium. The reason is no secret. The writer for radio, unlike the writer for a magazine or newspaper, must write so as to be understood the first time. The words are spoken and, once spoken, are irretrievable. There is no calling them back for review.

The challenge is all the greater because listeners are not listening, intently, hanging onto every word. Most are doing something else: dressing, fixing a meal, brushing their teeth, or driving a car. Their attention is divided. Your message— the information you have for them—must be delivered cleanly, with utmost clarity. It has to be understandable to the highest degree.

You will be reporting all kinds of stories, and the most difficult will be stories in the realm of ideas. The late Frank McGee of NBC News said, "The most hazardous undertaking in the world is the transmitting of an idea." Democracy, our whole way of life, depends on how well that is done.

And every day it becomes more difficult. Every day the world becomes more complex. I think of Three Mile Island and its double hazard: radioactivity and the inability of scientist and reporter to communicate with one another. I think of what reporters have to know today and how well they must know how to write.

Two Basic Rules

There are two basic rules in writing news for radio. The first rule is to **adopt a style that is conversational.** Write as you, in the company of people you respect, would speak. The second rule is to **write simply.**

This does not mean writing down to the listener. It means writing clearly, in an uncomplicated, unpretentious way. The late Ben Gross, dean of radio–TV critics, expressed for himself what you should strive to do. He said, "I try to make

Educated at Yale, Edward Bliss, Jr. reported for Ohio newspapers before joining CBS News, where he worked 25 years as a writer, editor and producer. His last CBS assignment was as news editor for "The CBS Evening News with Walter Cronkite." Later he founded the broadcast journalism program at American University and was a visiting professor of broadcast journalism at the University of North Carolina at Chapel Hill. He is currently a news consultant to major television stations and is at work on a comprehensive history of broadcast news. Mr. Bliss has edited Edward R. Murrow's broadcasts for publication by Alfred E. Knopf and is co-author of a textbook, Writing News for Broadcast *(Columbia University Press, 2d ed., 1978). This chapter was adapted by Mr. Bliss from that text with the permission of Columbia University Press.*

my criticism short and simple, in literate, interesting language that will appeal to a truck driver or college professor." That means writing without condescension and being, at the same time, broadly understood.

How do you do this? **You write in plain English.** You don't use words like *effectuate, ancillary, prioritize,* and *interface.* You don't say in a news story:

The city plans to *utilize* those funds for housing for the elderly.

Instead, you say:

The city plans to *use* those funds for housing for the elderly.

You write short sentences. This does not mean you never write a long sentence. There are long sentences which, with built–in pauses and a natural flow of thought, are readily comprehended. But these are exceptions. If a compound sentence seems a bit long, there is a way to make it appear less formidable. The trick is to place a period after the first clause and start the second clause as a new sentence. Thus:

Such sales have been banned for more than a year now, but much of the traffic still goes on in ways reminiscent of the Prohibition era, when bootleg beer was big business.

becomes:

Such sales have been banned for more than a year now. But much of the traffic still goes on in ways reminiscent of the Prohibition era, when bootleg beer was big business.

Now the one has the *appearance* of two sentences. The period gives the person speaking a clear opportunity for catching his or her breath. And note the obvious pause after the word *era.* Pauses are important. They not only help the reader but allow the listener to absorb the pieces of information that make up your story. In this particular example, without the pauses, the sentence would not be fit for broadcast.

Write simply. Edward R. Murrow said there were no words to describe the Battle of Britain, but with simple words he told how it was. Here is a detail of that picture he painted with words. Notice how simple they are and how well, together, they sound:

Once I saw The Damnation of Faust *presented in the open air at Salzburg. London reminds me of that tonight, only the stage is so much larger. Once tonight an anti–aircraft battery opened fire just as I drove past it. It lifted me from the seat, and a hot wind swept over the car. It was impossible to see. When I drove on, the streets of London reminded me of a ghost town in Nevada; not a soul to be seen.*

Here is a picture—a mood—that few scenes on television could create. That is the advantage you have, writing for radio. You paint pictures, not for the eye, but for the mind. And the mind touches up the picture, adding its own color, giving it strength.

Murrow's broadcast on the liberation of Buchenwald, the German concentration camp, is another good example:

> As we walked out into the courtyard, a man fell dead. Two others—they must have been over sixty—were crawling toward the latrine. I saw it but will not describe it.

There was no need to. Remember the power of simplicity, the power of restraint.

Here is how an unsimple subject—death—was treated by Harry Reasoner. It is part of a commentary carried by CBS Radio on the day Ernie Kovacs, the comedian, died in an automobile accident. Reasoner said:

> Somebody dies in an unprepared hurry and you are touched with a dozen quick and recent memories: the sweetness of last evening, the uselessness of a mean word or an undone promise. It could be you, with all those untidy memories of recent days never to be straightened out. There's a shiver in the sunlight, touching the warmth of life that you've been reminded you hold only for a moment.

The style is conversational. Reasoner is speaking. He says *there's* and *you've*. He uses ordinary, everyday words—none more than three syllables. Commonplace words. But he combines them, as do good writers, uncommonly well.

There are good reasons for writing conversationally. A clean, easy–flowing, unpretentious sentence is readable. The broadcaster is less apt to stumble. But, more important, such sentences, because of their naturalness, are easier for listeners to understand. Continually, as long as they have lived, your listeners have received information through conversation. They are accustomed to learning about what has happened in their home, in the place where they work and in their community by word of mouth. They comprehend more readily what is written this way for the ear, rather than what is written for the eye. **Radio is an aural medium.** Everything you write, as well as every piece of tape you select, should be done with this basic fact in mind.

Up to now, we have been talking about radio news writing in a fairly general way. We need to get into more of the specifics, some of which are pretty workaday but all, I hope, of a kind to help you in your career.

The Wire Services

Let's start with the wire services, which supplement the reports of your correspondents.

Although these services are reputable and have distinguished histories, don't hesitate to question anything in the wire copy that strikes you as wrong. Although copy now moves at a speed which seems magical—up to 1,200 words a minute—it still is subject to human error.

Devise a system for sorting and labeling the wire copy you plan to use in your newscast. Save only those stories you are likely to use. Otherwise, you will be swamped.

Remember that stories on the "A" wire are written in the style used for newspapers. You must rewrite them—*translate* them—into the language of radio. Stories on the broadcast wire, which *are* written for radio, usually can be improved. There is no copy that cannot be helped by putting it through the typewriter, and a trained mind, one more time.

Work Rules

When you sit down to write, there are certain basic procedures to follow:

- Type your stories. Make at least one carbon copy.
- Double space. Leave margins of more than an inch.
- End lines with complete words. Don't hyphenate at the end of a line.
- If possible, write each story on a separate page. This makes revisions easier as the news changes.
- Write the word MORE in capital letters at the bottom of the page if the story is continued. In any case, pages should end with complete sentences.
- When you cross out words, cross them out completely. Leave no doubt that they have been eliminated.
- If you make a correction in spelling, rewrite the entire word.
- Mark tape inserts clearly (with outcue).
- Produce a clean script. Retype if there are many revisions and if time permits.
- Number your pages.
- Put your name (or initials) in the upper left-hand corner of each page, along with identification of the program.
- Mark the end of each script with # # # or some other symbol so you will know that there's no more to read, without having to think about it.

Numbers

Write out numbers *one* through *nine*. Use figures for 10 through 999.

When you encounter thousands, millions and billions, don't use a string of zeros. Write:

- *12-thousand, not 12,000*
- *32-million, not 32,000,000*
- *5-billion (or five billion), not 5,000,000,000*

Round off large numbers. Instead of saying, "The mayor estimated the cost at 32–million, 13–thousand dollars," say "The mayor estimated the cost at a little more than 32–million dollars."

At times, it is good to translate. "Nine and a half million dollars" is the same as "9–million, 500–thousand dollars" and easier for the listener to absorb. Simplify, without distorting, wherever you can. The fewer numbers, the less confusion.

Symbols

You may have noticed that in the preceding section the dollar sign does not appear. This is because symbols should *not* be used in a broadcast script. Instead of $, #, and %, write *dollar, number, percent.* With the word written out, there is less opportunity for error.

Abbreviations

Few abbreviations are used in broadcast writing. Names of states are written in full—*Illinois,* not IL, as the Postal Service prescribes, or Ill., as some people still abbreviate it. Military titles are also written out in full—*Captain* John Smith, not Capt. John Smith; *General* George Washington, not Gen. George Washington. In the same way, write *Colonel,* not Col., *Major,* not Maj.

The Alphabet Soup

During President Roosevelt's New Deal, scores of government agencies sprang up with strange alphabetical names, such as *WPA* (Works Progress Administration), *PWA* (Public Works Administration) and *NRA* (National Recovery Administration). A few of these, like the *FBI,* have survived.

In a radio script, *FBI* should be written *F-B-I*. Similarly, it should be *G-O-P* and *U-N*. Although periods are permissible, and certainly grammatical, in setting off these initials, hyphens are favored in order that the period may be reserved for the end of the sentence. This, again, is a device for avoiding confusion.

The initials of many organizations should be used *only* after the full names of the organizations have appeared in the story. It would be wrong, for example, to use the initials *UMW* without referring first to the *United Mine Workers*. However, terms like *FBI* and *YMCA* are so common that they may be used by themselves. If you are uncertain how recognizable the initials are, better give the organization's full name. That way, you will be sure.

Dates

You write what you, or the person for whom you are writing, actually will say. For example, for August 26, write *August 26th*. You add the "th" because that is how the date will be read on the air. In the same way, you write *January 2nd*, not January 2, and *May 23rd*, not May 23.

Names

Get them right.

Don't use names unnecessarily. "A spokesman for the airline made the announcement." No need to name the spokesman. "Police say more than 200–thousand dollars was taken." No need to name the policeman or woman.

Don't clutter sentences with unneeded first names. Skip the first name if the person is well known and you give the title. Thus: *President Reagan, Senator Kennedy of Massachusetts, Governor Brown of California.*

As a general rule, omit initials in names. For example, write *Henry Kissinger,* instead of Henry A. Kissinger, and *Howard Baker,* instead of Howard H. Baker, Jr. The exception is if the initial has become a kind of trademark, as in *George M. Cohan* and *Edward R. Murrow.*

Some nicknames are acceptable, but decide between the given name and the nickname. Don't use both. It is overkill when you write Henry ("Scoop") Jackson and Thomas ("Tip") O'Neill. Make it one or the other.

Avoid starting a story with an unfamiliar name. Instead of:

Paul Bortz, a department store executive, has been elected president of the Chamber of Commerce,

write

A department store executive, Paul Bortz, has been elected president of the Chamber of Commerce.

Pronunciation

Mispronunciation not only hampers communication but damages credibility. So make sure you know how to pronounce the words you use—*all* the words—not just proper names. Don't take any pronunciation for granted. *Moscow,* for example, should be pronounced MOSS'-co, not Moss-COW'. *Prevent* should be pronounced pre-VENT', not per-vent.

A biographical dictionary or gazetteer can be a big help. If it's the troublesome name of a foreign official, try the appropriate consulate or embassy. Perhaps someone in the appropriate foreign language department at a college or university can help. When you get the correct pronunciation, write it in. You may want to write a phonetic transcription of the correct pronunciation. Then rehearse it, so you or the person you are writing for will not stumble on the air. If you have *any* doubt, check.

The Lead

The lead—how you start your story—is the most important sentence. Often it is the most difficult. This is because ideally it should arouse interest, be uncomplicated—simple, almost to the point of being simplistic—and yet informative and completely accurate. You should not be discouraged if the right words don't come to you at once. Experienced reporters, composing a lead, often make several drafts.

The leads you write for radio, unlike the old–fashioned newspaper lead, do not attempt to tell who, what, when, where, why and how. All those facts, crammed into a lead, are too much to throw at a listener all at once. Take this newspaper lead:

> *Since the start of the United Fund drive on Friday, volunteer workers have raised $603,853 toward the 1981 goal of $3,000,000 it was announced yesterday at a campaign meeting in the Southern Hotel.*

Rewritten for radio, it might read:

> *Volunteer workers for the United Fund already have raised more than 600–thousand dollars toward this year's goal of three million dollars. The campaign started Friday.*

The story could then go on and report further details, including perhaps a direct quote from one of the campaign directors at the hotel. The lead, rewritten for radio, is less complicated, so more easily understood. The first sentence, which ran 33 words in the newspaper version, now runs 21 words. The figure, $603,853, has been streamlined to read "more than 600-thousand dollars." The year, 1981, becomes simply "this year." The fact that the campaign began on Friday is reported in a separate four-word sentence.

This is not the only way the newspaper lead could have been rewritten. It could have been simplified still further—and made more interesting—with a lead sentence that said simply, "This year's United Fund drive has gotten off to a good start." A lead can be verbless, like this one used by John Chancellor: "A considerable surprise from the government of Cuba today." And there is the so–called umbrella lead: "Congress had a busy day." In all these leads, the style is conversational. The sentences are clean. And they are natural.

As a general rule, do not use a quotation as a lead. The listener may confuse you with the person you are quoting.

Lead-Ins

Lead–ins are the introductions to a correspondent's report or taped actuality. They should set up the report, or actuality, in such a way that the listener will appreciate the significance. The lead–in should *not* skim the cream off the reporter's story. It should, however, include any essential fact the reporter does not have or that is not on the tape. For example, the reporter on the scene of a fatal plane crash may not have the official death toll, while the newsroom has the figure because of a phone call made to the airline's public relations office. If you use tape of a newsmaker speaking, add at least one sentence for the anchor to read coming out of the tape. That's called a wrap-around. It gives a sense of completeness to your report. It rounds it out.

Quotations

Try to limit direct quotations to one sentence—the shorter, the better. If you use a quotation consisting of several sentences, the listener will not know until after he has done some guessing where the quotation ended. In short, a long quotation should be avoided because it is confusing.

It is not necessary every time to start and end a quotation with the words *quote* and *unquote*. Often a quotation can be identified simply by voice inflection or by such attributing phrases as: "The Soviet leader denounced what he *called* "American imperialism;" or "A spokesman *described* Congress' action as "a callous refusal to meet the public need."

If you are quoting someone and omit language within the quotation, do not indicate the omitted matter with the three periods (. . .) used by newspapers. Your listener can't see them. Besides, in broadcast writing, the three periods often are used to denote a pause. And a final word of warning. *When you edit a quotation, do no distort what was said.*

A Late Night Problem

If your program goes on the air at midnight, or within an hour or two after midnight, avoid saying *yesterday, today,* or *tomorrow.* If you do, although it is technically a new day, listeners will be confused. The problem can be solved by naming the day of the week—Monday, Tuesday, Wednesday, etc.—or if the story is about something that happened the previous day, simply by using the perfect tense. That is, instead of *"There was a bad train wreck late Wednesday near Cleveland"* say *"There has been a bad train wreck near Cleveland."*

To avoid confusion, wire services often name the day in their leads. There is a awkwardness in this practice; it is not something we generally do in conversation. It also can result in unintentional humor, as when a correspondent began a sentence by saying, "Reagan's press secretary Friday said. . . ." *Remember: your enemy is confusion.*

Choosing Words

Words are your building blocks. Choose them carefully, remembering that the verb is most important. Active verbs are more dynamic than passive verbs. As Professor John Bremner of the University of Kansas says, active voice is a vigorous voice, "the voice of a Zola, a John the Baptist." For example, think of "Reagan Beats Carter" and "Carter is Beaten by Reagan" and ask yourself which headline carries more force.

Choose the right word. For many years, the editor who rode herd on words appearing in the *New York Times* was Ted Bernstein. When he saw a headline that read: "Elm Beetle Infestation Ravishing Thousands in Greenwich," he wrote a note to the guilty party on the copy desk. The note said, "Keep your mind on your work, buster. The word you want is *ravaging.*" Discussing the difference between *lend* and *loan,* he said you are free to use *loan* as a verb "if you are not offended by 'Friends, Romans, countrymen, loan me your ears.' "

Discriminate between *rob* and *steal. To rob* is to take from someone personally by violence or threat of violence. Say, at pistol point. If someone takes your bicycle while you are in a store, that's stealing. You weren't robbed. If someone slips into your house at night, undetected, and takes your TV set, that's burglary, not robbery.

Further is not the same as *farther.* One is degree, the other, distance. For example, "He did not pursue the subject further." "She jogged farther."

Save the word *prison* for penitentiaries, where people are incarcerated for fairly long periods of time. *Jails* are for persons convicted of minor offenses or awaiting trial.

Feel should not be used as a synonym for *believe. To feel* is to be convinced emotionally rather than intellectually. "His parents feel certain he is safe." They want desperately to believe it. "Scientists believe Saturn has other moons." They reached this conclusion—this belief—through hard evidence.

Be wary of *pointed out.* You can point out only what exists. If you say that someone pointed out something, you are accepting the statement as fact. Ask yourself, *is* it a fact?

Be careful with the verb *to claim.* Generally, it implies skepticism. You do not quite trust what was said. During World War II, on American radio, Berlin *claimed,* but Washington *said.* We believed the news from Washington; we were skeptical of reports from Berlin.

Also beware of fad words like *supportive.* Instead of "The mayor is supportive of her project," why not write, "The mayor supports her project?" The sentence is stronger, written this simpler way.

Avoid phrases like *ad hoc* and *sine qua non.* Not all your listeners know Latin. Say *by way of* Milwaukee, not *via* Milwaukee, and *before* leaving, not *prior to* leaving.

A little word that wears well is *said.* It usually serves better than stated, which carries an air of formality, and always better than *asserted* and *averred.* Don't be afraid to use the same word twice—or three or four times—if it's the right word.

47

A word often wrongly used is *meanwhile.* "Negotiations about the release of the hostages continue. *Meanwhile,* The Senate completed action on an omnibus tax bill." The adverb *meanwhile* should be used only when a close relationship exists in subject matter, and intervening time is actually meant. In the above example there is obviously no relationship in subject between the two events. Precision in language should be preserved.

Whenever possible, use short words. *Home* is better than *residence, buy* than *purchase, start* than *commence, end* than *terminate* or *conclude.*

Writing Tight

Don't waste words. In everything you write, look for and eliminate what serves no purpose. Watch for redundancies. *"Three were killed and nine others injured."* You don't need others. *"The reason for this is because of its scarcity."* You don't need *because of.*

Watch for inflated phrases. Such a phrase is *due to the fact that,* which means *because. In an effort to* simply means *to.* One word, *many,* does the work of four words, *a great number of.* That notorious phrase *at this point in time,* is, of course, a long way of saying *now.*

Ration your adjectives. The strength of your sentence lies in its nouns and verbs, the right nouns and right verbs. Consider that there are only three adjectives in the entire 23rd Psalm. Excess words not only perform no service, they clutter sentences, making them less easily understood.

All About THAT

A question often asked is: "When do you use *that* and when do you leave it out?" The question applies to *that* as a conjunction. The answer is that you leave it out in a sentence like "The President said he will attend." There's no reason to say, "The President said *that* he will attend." The *that* is superfluous here, a waste.

But take this sentence: "He adds the numbers are increasing." Here you do need the *that.* You need it because listeners don't hear a sentence all at once. They hear it piecemeal. In this instance, they hear "He adds the numbers" and get one idea—the wrong one—and don't get the right idea until after hearing the whole sentence. So you should say, "He adds *that* the numbers are increasing." The *that* shows where the sentence is headed. You have telegraphed your punch, as it were. You have made a signal that you are paraphrasing. Nobody is adding numbers. And notice that, just now, I said, "You have made a signal *that* you are paraphrasing." Otherwise, the sentence would read "You have made a signal you are paraphrasing." Are you paraphrasing a signal? So the test whether to use *that* is: Does the sentence without it momentarily mislead? Is there any ambiguity?

There is another problem. It concerns *that* as a relative pronoun—when to say *that* and when to say *which*. According to grammarians, *that* is correct when it defines. Example: "They debated the tax cut *that* the President wants." The *that* defines—identifies—the tax measure being debated. *Which* is correct when it doesn't define. Example: "Paley's memoirs, *which* I found interesting, were published by Doubleday." The *which* doesn't define. You already know whose memoirs. So, *which* is correct.

You use *that* more often than *which* in broadcast writing because *which* clauses occur less frequently in conversation than in print, and you are—or should be—writing conversationally. So much for *that!*

Double Meanings

Your sentence may look right on the page but sound wrong on the air. This example from a Boston radio station: *Police waited for hours outside the hospital, and their patience paid off.* Read that sentence aloud, and you will know what I mean. Always test what you write by reading it aloud—*sotto voce,* if you want, but test it for readability, and sound, all the same. Another example: *Agents said he had been working for several years as an imported car salesman.* Which reminds me of the time I heard a journalist refer to "the black doctor's bag." Be sure, in writing, that you say what you mean to say.

There are words you should use with care because they sound so much like other words with different meanings. These include:

threw/through
flout/flaunt
accept/except
one/won
two/too
won't/want

Cliches

Avoid them. A cliche is a word or phrase, once useful because of its originality and aptness, now badly overworked. A few dreary examples:

gild the lily
it all began
slept like a log
green with envy
clear as crystal
busy as a beaver
cool as a cucumber
sober as a judge

tired as a dog
back to the drawing board
raise your consciousness
remains to be seen
hit the hay
sack out

How often have you heard, "The plane (or planes) roared overhead?" On D–Day Ed Murrow heard Allied bombers overhead, and he said, "It was the sound of a giant factory in the sky." When you catch yourself using a cliche, think how you can say it in an original way.

Sound

In the Old Testament, Job asks, "Doth not the ear try words?" Try your words. Listen to the sound of your sentences. Read them aloud. Is there anything in them that causes you to stumble? If so, smooth them out. Does the sentence seem to trail off at the end? Fix it with a good terminal noun or verb, preferably of one syllable.

Beware of three or more short declarative sentences in succession. They have a weary, leaden sound. So do two or more sentences in succession ending with the same word.

If you are a writer, you are also an artist. I think of what John Dos Passos said of his English composition professor at Harvard: "He had an old-fashioned schoolmaster's concern for the neatness of the langauge, a Yankee zest for the shipshape phrase, and a sharp nose for sham." I like what Dos Passos says in that statement. But listen to the sound!

II
FEATURES

Fig. 5.1. While covering a major expedition in Antarctica, NPR Science Correspondent Ira Flatow took time out to do a feature on the only natives of this vast and frozen continent. Many features are by-product of "hard news," but anything that rouses your curiosity can be the starting point for a feature story.

|| 5 ||
Conceiving Features
by Robert Krulwich

Every feature begins with an idea, and developing that idea for the radio is much more than a writing job. For me, the writing part—sitting at the typewriter and knocking out a script—comes second to last. My features go through five stages:

1. Finding the Idea
2. Creating an Outline
3. Isolating the Tape
4. Writing
5. Refining

The rest of this chapter describes how I do all five along with some do's and don't's.

Finding an Idea for a Feature Story

There are basically two ways to do feature stories: find them yourself, or follow up someone else's story.

When editors assign features, they usually take the second approach. Very often they ask reporters to get the "local angle" on a major news story, so if the United States has just landed a man on the moon, editors across the country will want to know if anyone in their town, or any relative of someone in town, was part of the effort. These stories are called **sidebars, soft pieces,** or **color stories.** Seasonal stories, "Area Jews Celebrate Passover," are in the same category. Follow–up features are generally more fun if you think them up yourself; that is why it's best to read the morning paper *before* you get to work and hold on to any story that makes you so curious you want to know more.

So, if you read in the paper that 17 of the 18 lawyers the Governor nominated to be judges were not approved by the state legislature, you might wonder how the 18th lawyer got through. Or, if you see a story announcing that Paul Smith has been appointed President of the Hills School, replacing John Jones, who held the job for the last four months, you might wonder what happened to Mr. Jones

Robert Krulwich is NPR's Business and Economics Correspondent. Prior to joining NPR (first as National Editor), he served as Washington bureau chief of Pacifica Radio and of Rolling Stone *magazine. A graduate of Columbia University Law School, Krulwich has won numerous awards for excellence in economic broadcasting.*

and why they have such high turnover. If this doesn't come naturally, pick out a few stories and force yourself to think of some aspect that the paper overlooked.

Another tip: if you read the morning paper and you discover that you know a central figure, or better, someone who is friends with, related to, works or bowls with that figure, you've got yourself a **source.** Give that person a call, if possible, before you see your editor or tell your editor that you want to make the call. Then ask your source "Your son was at the Hills School when John Jones got there. Was Jones a good principal? Why did he leave?"

The other way to get feature story ideas is hard to explain. Some people can get up in the morning and by the time they get to work, they have seen something odd in a store window, overheard a suspicious conversation, or met a man whose wife is about to be named Ambassador to Trinidad. Good reporters are always making mental notes. They never stop reporting. The littlest thing can get them going:

- A tube of toothpaste can start a reporter wondering: why does toothpaste always come in a tube? Tubes break. They don't fit on the sink. Why hasn't anyone put toothpaste in a jar, with a pump? There must be a reason. . . .

- A friend mentions that a friend of hers is training a) to become a pilot; b) to become a shoe salesman; c) to stop smoking; and the reporter thinks maybe there are features here. . . .

- The local movie theater has been showing the same film for nine weeks; there are only 30,000 people in town. Everyone who wants to see that movie has seen it. A reporter may wonder: why is it still there? There must be an explanation. . . .

The key is: *anything that makes you curious could turn into a feature. Anything.* Then, when the editor calls you in to suggest a feature, before he drags out his idea, hit him with yours. Editors will normally yield to a reporter excited about a story, if they think he or she is any good.

Do's

Do follow up a lead. A friend of yours says in passing, "Strange, but that's the third boy to get leukemia in the same neighborhood. In fact, they live on the same street." If you think there may be more than coincidence involved, ask for the boys' names, the name of the street, the hospital they went to, and write the information down. *Don't trust your memory.*

Do check out stories promptly. Don't sit on a lead. Call right away. Someone else could get the story.

Don't's

Don't quit a story because the first interview goes badly. If the person you talked to was abrupt, insulting, confusing, or gave you too much information, that is not a reason to stop. Don't let yourself be intimidated. Try one more call. The second call is almost always easier.

Don't be embarrassed to ask a friend, relative or acquaintance for an interview, even if asking is awkward. Being a little pushy is part of being a reporter. You will be constantly amazed at how many doors can be opened just by asking, forcefully (but politely). Reporters are forever imagining privacy difficulties that don't materialize. If you have ever been interviewed, then you know the experience: at the start, you are nervous and careful, but as the conversation warms up, you find yourself saying all kinds of things you never expected to say, and only afterwards do you wonder, "what came over me?" Whatever it is, it comes over almost everyone. This does not mean you should betray confidences. Some exchanges, even if they would make good stories, are really *off the record.*

Don't trust newspaper accounts. They are not always accurate. Before assuming a statement to be true, check it out yourself. "Mrs. Lesko, the *Chronicle* says your collie dug up $48 in the front yard. Is that right?"

Creating an Outline: How to Organize a Feature Story

A straight news story offers facts in order of importance: the classic who, what, when, where, why, with appropriate supporting paragraphs in the appropriate order. But features flow any way they have to to hold an audience. So I cannot tell you how to structure a feature, only that you must have a structure.

Features require a peculiar way of thinking, common to reporters and story tellers: experience has to be turned instantly into narrative outline. For example, suppose my editor tells me he has heard that a famous music magazine has decided to change its name from *Crawdaddy* to *Feature.* He wants to know why. "Check it out," he says.

The beginning reporter is likely to rush over to the magazine without further thought. He or she will arrive on the scene, find the person in charge, and say something like, "Excuse me, I hear you are switching names. Tell me about it." This doesn't work very well. Asked a general question, a source will usually give a general answer like, "Yes, we're changing names. The new one comes out next month." This leaves your source with the burden of shaping your story, and it may not be until you are back in the office that you will notice a small remark that could have been the focus of your story, if only you had followed up on it. A better approach is to try to imagine a possible shape for your story *before* you start interviewing.

Scene I: Publisher notices two newsstands downtown where *Crawdaddy* has been put next to the sports magazines. It sits between *Trout and Stream* and *Reel 'n Rod.* He wonders why.

Scene II: Publisher gets a marketing report that says two out of every five newsstand dealers think *Crawdaddy* is about Southern fish.

Scene III: Publishers sends colorful mailing to 10,000 newsdealers saying that *Crawdaddy* is about music, and belongs next to *Rolling Stone* and *High Times.*

Scene IV: Nothing changes. Publisher decides to get a new name.

Scene V: Newsdealers react. . . .

Not one word of this has been verified. It is probably entirely untrue. But, with an outline, however imaginary, I have something that gets me going and guides my way. I now have a better sense of what to do next.

First, the story line (as I imagine it, anyway) seems a little nutty, so I am excited. This is important. If the editor's suggestion had triggered a dull scenario, I would have argued that it was a dumb idea and I should be assigned something else. But I like it. So I am motivated. Second, my five scenes suggest a definite line of questioning: What was wrong with the name *Crawdaddy?* Who discovered the problem? Why change to *Feature?* Were there competing alternatives? How will they explain the change to customers? Third, I can guess at a short list of people to talk to: a) whoever discovered the problem; 2) the person(s) who decided to change the name; c) readers; d) maybe newsdealers, if my hunch is correct.

Now I am on my way. I make calls, ask questions, and let's suppose that my first interview, with the publisher, goes terribly. Let us assume that he is dull, frightened and monotonal. Unfortunately, *he* was the one who discovered that *Crawdaddy* was, indeed, placed with the wrong magazines on the newsstands: not the fishing magazines, as it happens—it was stacked alongside *TeenScene* and *Teen Age* and the comic books. *Crawdaddy* is intended for the 16 through 35 year old reader, not the 8 to 14 set, so the wrong people were seeing it. I also learned (again from my dull, monotonal publisher) that he ordered an investigation and found that when newsdealers looked at the cover design and the funky name *Crawdaddy,* the magazine so resembled the other teen/fan magazines that the dealers just assumed they belonged together.

Yes, there was a meeting (but the publisher says everyone who was there is too busy to talk with me). Yes, they decided to make the magazine look more adult. Yes, that is why they dropped *Crawdaddy* and chose *Feature. Feature,* he says, has definite adult appeal. End of interview.

What to do? My original scenario assumed a colorful, bright narrator who would tell the magazine's story. Then I would talk to readers and newsdealers. But my narrator is a drag, and no one else on the staff has permission to talk on tape.

I know my original outline won't work. If I let the publisher tell his story for three or four minutes and throw in the newsdealers at the end, the audience will never stay with the piece—too dull—and if the dealers are any good, all my strong tape will come in a jumble at the very end. So I decide on a new outline that will introduce the dealers earlier in the story. I imagine:

Scene I: Publisher sees magazines in the wrong place.
Scene II: Dealers say they thought it was a teeny-bopper magazine.
Scene III: Publisher redesigns cover; changes name.
Scene IV: Dealers react.

That feels more lively. It depends less on the publisher, and it switches back and forth from the executive to the newsstand. It won't be dull. So with this substitute outline in my head, I go to interview the newsdealers. I tell them what the publisher has said, and ask them to react, step–by–step, to his narrative.

They are marvelous. One tells me yes, he put *Crawdaddy* with the comics, but he knows they are changing the cover, and from now on *Feature* will be where it belongs: with the literary magazines—that is what he remembers being told. The other dealer says *Crawdaddy's* problem is not its name. "It stinks. It wouldn't sell if they called it *Newsweek*," he says.

As we are talking, I can feel the story falling into place.

  Scene I: Publisher sees his magazine in the wrong place.
  Scene II: Dealers say they thought it was a teeny-bopper magazine.
  Scene III: Publisher redesigns cover; changes name.
  Scene IV: Dealer #2 says it won't work. The magazine stinks.
  Scene V: Publisher talks of plans to "educate" dealers.
  Scene VI: Dealer #1 tells me from now on it goes with the poetry journals.

Because I have a working outline in my head, I walk away from those dealers with a story that is almost finished. I don't have to dub off the full interviews, only the parts I need. Walking back to the office, I can start composing the introduction in my head. When I am up against a short deadline, having that outline constantly on tap is a terrific help.

However, I must be careful. Because I begin most interviews with a preconceived outline, it is easy to miss a better story, if one should come along. Should one of the dealers mention that *Feature* is going to cut its price in half, and so is *Rolling Stone,* bells should go off, if I am alert, and I must immediately switch scenarios:

  Scene I: *Feature* starts a price war among music magazines.
  Scene II: *Rolling Stone* reacts and drops its price.
  Scene III: So does *Record World.* . . .

Now I've got a business story. I don't completely ditch my earlier *Crawdaddy* scenario; I can go back to it if the business story proves uninteresting, or incorrect, but I decide to switch gears. Also, I have to be willing to let my outline become more complicated. My initial scenarios are often fairy-tale simple. The characters always tell the truth.

Suppose, however, that some of the dealers tell me that they hear *Feature* may never be delivered. The magazine, they understand, is too deeply in debt and is about to go under. If they are right, I am going to look very foolish talking for four minutes on the radio about a name change when the product itself is about to disappear. So, I have to check their story, and if the publisher denies it, I might include the rumor and the denial in my script, and if the publisher *won't* deny it, then I would call my editor and ask whether we want to run the story at all. We would have to restructure the outline to include the magazine's financial problems—which could get unwieldy.

But, if I had gone from person to person with no structure in my head, I could never have controlled my interviews as effectively. I would have been less certain what to ask, what to emphasize, who to talk to, and most of all, when to stop. And once I stopped, with no structure in my head, I would have to relisten to all my interviews and superimpose an outline. That takes too much time. To make deadlines, reporters have to be efficient and mental outlines are wonderfully efficient.

Isolating the Tape

This part is easy. When I am interviewing somebody, I always know when I have just had a good moment. Sometimes it is a concise answer that fits perfectly into my outline (or creates a perfectly good alternate outline). Sometimes it is a funny exchange that will be easy to listen to. Sometimes (and these are best), it is a remark that is perfect as a cap to my story and will fit wonderfully at the very end (I can hear myself signing off immediately afterward). As soon as I have such a moment, I think, "I can use that," and in it goes into the outline that is building in my mind. When I am walking back to the office, I play that moment back on my cassette recorder to hear if it was as good as I thought.

Beginning reporters too often feel compelled to use tape segments that contain official or "important" statements. For example, the mayor intoning in his official voice, "This was the worst earthquake we've had in eastern Michigan in 50 years." In fact, you can say that just as well yourself, in your script ("Mayor Jones called it the worst earthquake. . .").

You will find you can usually convey *information* more succinctly than the person you interview. The *tape* that is best is the tape that conveys mood, emotion, involvement, or context—things you can't convey as well yourself.

A word of warning, however. Since vivid tape (or good pictures) is so helpful to broadcast reporters, we often structure our stories around those moments, even if we have to stretch or take a weird detour to fit them. This is dangerous. I have a weakness for nice tape that is as strong as the next fellow's and I don't like to let a good moment go, but I know I must not distort a point or break a narrative flow just to accommodate a few seconds of flashy tape. Sometimes, tape must go. I have found that if I postpone the surgery to a later stage (the "writing" stage that follows) it is much less painful.

Therefore, after I have finished my interviews, I select all the "best moments"—even the ones that don't quite fit my outline. I arrange them in order of probable appearance as suggested by my outline on single reel. Each moment is separated by **leader tape** (colored tape that cannot be recorded on, used for visual identification of parts of a reel; see Chapter 10, "Tape Editing") so when I play the reel through I can hear my story in rough outline, minus the connecting, scripted parts. I listen through at least once, mentally "writing in" the connecting material. Then I sit down to write.

Writing

As I said earlier, for hard news, the form is all important: hard news always begins with the hard lead, followed by supporting material, spoken in the neutral "broadcast" voice. *Features,* on the other hand, can have personality. The reporter can speak in his or her own voice, or give a minor player a major voice, or let the scene play itself exactly as it was recorded. The choices are so varied that I cannot lay down hard rules for feature writing, but I *can* offer some tips.

You are allowed to use "I." When I write a story about an experience I had, I choose the first person form. I try to write my script as though I was talking to a friend across a table.

I compose out loud. I sit at the typewriter, write a paragraph, and then I speak it. If it sounds like myself talking, I move on. If it sounds like my written self, I try again.

I am not offended by laughs, grunts, snorts, giggles and sighs—my own or anyone else's. It is OK to make human noises on the radio. When appropriate, I will give myself a stage direction in the script, "Sigh here."

When is that appropriate? I find that when I am writing out of a tape cut that finishes with lots of people laughing it is sometimes correct *not* to break the mood. If they were laughing at a joke, I may keep the laugh going for an instant more, or at least speak my next lines smiling.

A mood or tone established on tape does not have to end just because the tape runs out. That is true *before* a tape cut too. If I have a bad scene on tape that begins with a woman crying, I anticipate the mood. My words may look neutral on paper ("I met Janet Jones in her apartment. The door was open and I just walked in. . . ."), but *I* know what's coming. This is going to be sad, so I put a little sadness in my voice ahead of time. A mood is established that makes the transition smoother. That way, the audience is not distracted when I move from script to tape, and the story flows more easily. I do change moods, but only when it fits the narrative.

There is a tendency, especially among beginning reporters, to draw too clear a line between tape and script. Tape and script are not separate entities, standing side by side; they must sound like two interdependent parts of a whole.

Suppose I go out and do a feature on acute depression. It is my first feature and I get an interview with a famous psychiatrist, who has just written a book on the subject. He says there are four types. He describes Type A beautifully; he is brief, clear and to the point. On Type B, he has a stuttering attack, which makes him nervous and hard to follow. On Type C, he is so–so and Type D takes too long.

I come back to the office. My outline is obvious. I will report on all four categories of depression. Since the tape on Type A is good, I will use it. To avoid the stuttering episode, I throw away the tape on Type B and script that section. I have to have more of the doctor in the story, so I go back to the tape for Category C and I write up Type D.

I end up with a story that moves like a fox trot; four steps, tape–script–tape–script, each separate, each equal. Boring. When a story moves in so predictable and regular a rhythm, the audience knows what is coming and if they aren't that interested in the subject, they will nod out. Each segment is self-contained, like unfriendly neighbors in an apartment house. Each makes its point, then ends. Novice reporters often fall into this pattern.

There are other options. You could start with tape segment A, where the doctor does well, then roll into segment B, still on tape, until the doctor begins his stuttering fit, and then just pick up in script after his second or third stammer. That way, the reporter appears to be rescuing the doctor. That adds a dimension to the story (it *is* interesting when a psychiatrist stutters), but more important, it is a more lively transition from tape to script.

When you finish describing Type B depression, you don't have to go back to the doctor for Type C. Begin describing the third category yourself, and pass off to the doctor only when he was at his best in that segment, even if you give him just two or three sentences. A short tape cut is OK. There is no such thing as too long or too short for tape or script segments. I have inserted a one word cut of tape that lasted one second. I do whatever suits me, as long as it moves the story along, keeps the audience listening and is faithful to the material. Remember, there are all kinds of ways to alter the rhythm of a story. Here are a few more ideas:

1. *Start a sentence in the script and have someone on tape finish it.*

Script:	"Yes, doctors say they are working on a cure. . . ."
Tape:	"But we won't have one for another ten years. . . ."
Script:	"says Dr. T. B. Gross."

2. *Don't return to script between each cut of tape. Go from script to several, consecutive tape cuts.*

Script:	"Doctors say they are working on a cure. . . ."
Tape of Dr. Jones:	"Yes, but that's a long way off. . . ."
Tape of Dr. Smith:	"I'd say 10, 11, years. . . ."
Tape of Dr. Gray:	"At least that or maybe more. . . ."

   (Notice that each tape cut is quite short. This works best if the three voices are very distinctive. So it would be nice if Dr. Smith were a man, and Drs. Jones and Gray women, so the voice changes would be obvious.)

3. *Start the story in a specific location (a hospital laboratory) and then leave the scene. The change in/or absence of atmosphere will alter the rhythm.*

Tape Ambience:	hospital/hospital/hospital/hospital/studio/studio/studio/studio
Script:	"The doctors are still looking for a vaccine. But they are out of money."

4. *Use tape to punctuate a script. Take a single word, (an enthusiastic "yes!"), or a short sequence ("yes! yes!" or "Oh no!") and drop it in to break up your script.*

Script:	"He drew the line in . . . slowly . . . and then he saw the fish. . . ."
Tape:	"YES!"
Script:	"It was a beauty!"
Script:	"She says she looked up, and that is when she saw him. . . ."
Tape:	"Oh no!"
Script:	"He was hanging off the balcony. . . ."

Refining

It is time to make my final cuts. Now that I have completed first or rough cut, my story will get much shorter. In this last review, precious moments on tape hit the floor. Beautiful lines drop away. I am editing for a consistent, even pace.

I not only cut, I sometimes add. I might mix in some new sound recorded at one of the places I visited—background sound of people playing or street traffic—because I find that a "bed" of non-studio sound can pull a section together.

This can be a dangerous time, too. I sometimes get so carried away tightening and cutting that I will chop out a minor, but important detail so that a complicated idea becomes too simple, and the story is no longer as precise, or as clear or honest as it should be. So I have devised a test. It is the last thing I do before I go into the studio to record.

I ask myself: can I bring all the people I interviewed for this story into this studio and read this script and play this tape right in front of them without shame, and when I finish, can I look them in the eye (all of them) and defend everything I have just said?

If I can, I go in and record.

6

Writing for the Ear

by Scott Simon

Several years ago I was part of a documentary team that was taken by a well–regarded and civilized producer to a spot in the western part of this country (the exact circumstances of this venture will be by necessity disguised). We were to produce a one–hour program that would leave a listener with an accurate and compassionate sense of the community that we'd inhabited for one week, and an appreciation for a way of living which would be odd and unknown to most of our audience. We taped everything, soaking up sound with shot–gun microphones, hand–held microphones, wireless microphones strapped into improvident places, microphones strung out of trees and over tanned, hard and mostly soundless prairies. "What I'd like to do," said our producer, "is create a whole hour of sound that will communicate this story, with no script at all. I guess that's something we always shoot for."

After several months of difficult stereophonic production, the documentary was ready. I listened to it while kneeling on the rug, my ears purposefully trained at the identical height of the woofers (or was it tweeters?). A great deal of it I liked quite a bit. But sound spattered unexpectedly at parts: squeals, jangles, chimes, and commotion would bustle across the speakers and tramp over my mental interior, without much sense. I listened with an unpleasant edge of internal tension, like someone overhearing a house intruder, and trying to determine exactly where he is in the house and what he's stealing. After a while, it was only tedious.

That documentary comes to mind now because after a time it occurred to me that what had been missing from the mix of a successful product was good writing: a voice which could have poked about, implored, queried, become friendly or abrasive, empathetic or instructive. The *voice* of a piece—which is what your writing becomes—is what provides the vision to a story. It is literally the eyes of our audience, the nose, the fingers, the mind. Good writing can give unexpected worth (even if it's just the shine of style) to a piece that is otherwise unremarkable. Bad writing can injure your ability to communicate a good story.

Furthermore, nothing else can offer identifiable *character* to your work like good, sensitive, imaginative writing. It can heighten good reporting into something memorable. It is the first skill most of us are told we have to master in this craft, yet the one that is often first left to settle after we have begun to gain our

Scott Simon is National Public Radio's Chicago bureau chief, where he produces news reports and human affairs features for NPR's two daily news and informaton programs, Morning Edition *and* All Things Considered. *He has produced stories out of 32 states, Canada, and Central America. Simon is a graduate of the University of Chicago and put in brief stints as a reporter with Chicago television station WTTW and* Newsweek *magazine before coming to NPR.*

way. I will raise many questions here to which I've been able to offer (cannily enough) no really explicit answers. But we might approach our inquiry (good, non–specific, academic word, gets you out of the sentence without forcing you to a conclusion) into writing by posing a series of *expostulations* (bad word for a script, too obscure, difficult to pronounce, sounds too much like the captions in a marriage manual).

Contractions are preferred, wherever possible. A radio script, when read, needs to be understood as *spoken* language. This is not an excuse for ill–considered, sloppy language, but a conversational tone often helps to communicate. Therefore, "don't" as opposed to "do not," etc., except where the latter is needed for emphasis.

Use a thesaurus, and don't feel you need to keep it hidden. It should be no more a cause for embarrassment than a physician who refers to *Gray's Anatomy* on an occasional point. The English language, as we have noticed, is rich and subtle and varied; you cannot be expected to remember all of it. But having all of it available for your discriminating selection can make your writing stronger.

Read as you write. Try reading aloud a sequence of words as you write to test the rhythm, sense and the ease with which you can read it in a studio. I once worked at a desk just fifteen feet behind a local sports reporter who bellowed as he did this, chanting and barking out scores and predictions. Unfortunately, he had three sportscasts scheduled each day, and it was a bit like trying to write while seated beneath the amplifier–speaker at a commuter railroad station. A soft, just scarcely audible reading to yourself should be sufficient.

While I believe in reviewing scripts from end to end, and making appropriate alterations after review, I do *not* believe in pulling up short at some particularly perplexing word or phrase, stopping, then returning when the script is otherwise complete. In my mind, that's too much like leaving certain struts and braces out of a building until it's topped off, then trying to return and install them in a complete structure. Too often, something will collapse. Writing needs cohesion and rhythm, needs to build and move from one exact word into the next. This was the opening of a piece we did on the fiftieth anniversary of Twinkies snack cakes:

Simon (script): *(sounds of unwrapping, munching and chewing, down for voice-over-sound)* "There may not be a more familiar . . . friendlier–looking insignia of American life than these tiny, twin, almost–orange confections sealed into cellophane wrap. . . ."

Voice: *(chewing)* "I dunno . . . Twinkies. . . ."

Simon: They're sold over the counter in snack-shops, supermarkets, gas stations . . . in the vending machines of carwashes, at cigar stands along Park Avenue . . . where they teeter over copies of the *Wall Street Journal* and *Paris-Match.* . . . They're with us always, Twinkies . . . like elevator music . . . sold, we're told, in the PX of Army camps in Thule, Greenland . . . plastic-wrapped ambassadors . . . in their way . . . from the abundance of American life. . . .

The words are meant to strike off one another in a certain order. It is necessary to have "familiar" set up before the phrase "friendlier–looking insignia of American life" for the balance of that sentence to work. "Tiny, twin, almost–orange confections sealed into cellophane wrap" builds from the alliteration of the two "t" sounds, into the alliteration of "almost-orange" into the play of "s" sounds in "sealed into cellophane wrap." It would have been perfectly accurate, of course, to write something like "small, paired, reddish–brown baked goods wrapped in cellophane" but not, I think, as interesting. Which brings us to this very general, inexplicable point.

Strive for rhythm in your words. There may not be a more difficult concept to convey about writing than this one. It has to do with bringing a balance, harmony, even a certain melody to your scripts. It is *not* "moon, June, spoon" writing. What is it then? That's hard to answer. I hope that a number of the segments here will suggest the principle and use of rhythm in good writing.

Write script-ease. In this instance, I am exercising a fantasy by urging you to look past, if not exactly ignore, some of the norms of grammatical construction *when necessary.* The "necessary" grows from the fact that *radio is a spoken medium.* A word like "ain't" will grate, when enunciated aloud, as much as it does when read. But there are other constructions that, while not strictly correct English sentences, can be vivid and effective. I endorse the method of script writing that separates words into more or less the same phrases you can read in a single breath. That separation is often best indicated by a sequence of dots (. . .). Even a prolonged sentence, rendered in this manner, can be comfortably read and made comprehensible:

I remember riding the south–side subway down to interview Frank Collin once . . . Nazi headquarters here . . . Rockwell Hall . . . is located in a literal ground–floor bunker of a converted shoe-shop . . . windows battened–down with plywood . . . a red-iron door, with an eye-sized slit for identifying visitors the only source of occasional light. . . . Frank Collin lived and worked in a single room above the headquarters . . . an enormous portrait of Adolph Hitler hung above the fireplace . . . the picture bleary and washed-out looking . . . the Führer as seen through funhouse glass. . . .

Outline. And take notes. An academically correct, categorized and subcategorized outline is not necessary, but some black–and–white scribbling of the themes and points you want to make, the scenes and detail you wish to describe, will help you plot the proper approach. It's been a source of displeasure to me to come across a number of radio reporters who care for nothing much more than those parts of a story which can be acquired through the business end of a microphone. If you rely solely on that information which can be recorded or remembered, you may be cheating the audience from the benefit of a reporter's practiced, firsthand observations. Which brings us to the intrinsic point:

Describe. Probably the most surprising, best-obscured virtue of radio is what it provides to the eye. The mind's eye can be stimulated by vigorous writing, directed and filled with selected detail which might not be noticed in film or video. It can offer the powerful sensation of *being there,* by offering, in close–up phrasing, the small glints of detail that can affect the feel and texture of an event. *Describe.* If profiling an individual, it's often good to begin by scrutinizing the distinct traits of physical appearance, especially as they seem to bear on character or career. Here's the opening of an election–year profile of Timothy Hagen, the "boss" of the Cuyahoga County (Cleveland) Ohio Democratic organization:

> **Music:** ("Happy Days Are Here Again")
>
> **Hagen:** *(into phone)* Hello, is Ethel Kennedy in? Tim Hagen from Ohio.
>
> **Simon:** Something used-up and unpleasant can come into the face of someone at the close of a long political campaign. It's a skin-bleaching really . . . a bloating of the cheeks, neck and eye sockets . . . A swelling collar of pastry, glazed doughnuts, acid-sour coffee, room service hamburgers, and dulling, late-night drinking all swallowed in full stride between engagements. Tim Hagen has been campaigning, more or less full time, for twelve years.
>
> **Hagen:** Ethel? . . . How are you? . . . I don't know, did the Senator call you last night or yesterday at all? You're scheduled to come into Toledo on Sunday. . . . Do you know that yet? . . .

The odd point about that passage is that you would still find it difficult, after the metaphors and similes have stilled, to recognize Tim Hagen on the street; the description nowhere mentions the color of his hair, his eyes, his height. Yet the mind's eye, I hope, colors in the mottled complexion I was trying to convey. As another example, though, I think that you might almost be able to recreate sections of an artist's drawing from this opening description of the offices of the City News Bureau of Chicago, an inner–city wire service:

> **Newsroom noises in . . .**
>
> **Simon:** The City News Bureau occupies the corner office on a floor fifteen stories up from the street. It hangs like an opera box over the tracks of the West Loop elevated train . . . and in this confusing period of Chicago spring, as the afternoon warms, windows are wrenched open to the clatter of trains,

sprinting past. There are no video displays in this news-room; the desks are glazed in grime. And reporters type, sometimes, listing to the side, so as not to sit on the bared inner coil of a desk chair.

Sound of teletype . . . .

Simon: There are actual iron teletype machines in here that slug, swipe, and slam out words, not squirt them quietly in inky whispers as on more contemporary units. The sound, the swelter, the crunch of soot, cigar ash, and coffee grounds aren't intended to make the employees of this organization entertain even the idea of spending a comfortable career here.

Interviewee: Most people who worked at the City News Bureau at least in the years I was there, recall it the way Marines recall boot camp.

Simon: Pulitzer Prize winning columnist Mike Royko, who began as an editor at City News.

In other stories, however, where the nature of the tape is such that a subject can best present and describe themselves, it is necessary to:

Play to tape. I would encourage a certain amount of this just in the general course of constructing a piece. I, at least, prefer the method of carefully auditing and logging each second of tape recorded for a given story, taking care to star (*) those moments which stand up best, then deciding which tape to use, determining what order, rather than scripting as the first step, then locating tape to fit. That method may indeed be more responsible in the case of a hard news piece, where the most attractive tape may not reflect the most important elements of a story. But I don't believe that the same rule obtains for features, even sober–minded news features.

I prefer tape which is active and expressive, something which contains the sound of thinking, musing, recollection, thoughts or events actually unfolding. In some rare instances you may interview people whose sense of self and narrative is so complete and entertaining that any log you might make of the tape would be lined with stars. In such cases it is best-advised to let the tape play through and apply script only sparingly, as a highlight rather than a base. Here's a seg-ment of a piece we did on a telephone answering service in New York City, fea-turing its founder, Clifford Harris:

Harris: *(into phone)* . . . Can I help you? . . . Yes, I can, who is this? . . . What do you want, Lena? . . . Well, you can't have messages. No one calls you. You're not pop–u–lahr. *(ringing phone)* Well, look, I gotta run, I'm being made famous. OK, bye–bye. *(to Simon)* Anyway, what was the question?

67

Simon: One thing I can't help but think about, and it does hearken back to that old Judy Holliday movie about an answering service. She becomes infatuated with one of the clients . . . does that happen?

Harris: Yes, it does. The problem is you build up these crazy fantasies in your mind about them, over the phone. And they never quite live up to what you expect them to be so it's not really fair to them because I meet them and after a half an hour I'm very disappointed with them and I think that they can tell it. And no one wants their answering service to, like, be disappointed in them.

Simon: As you may have gathered, this small office off of Broadway, with a window that fronts on an alleyway, is actually an interesting place from which to watch New York, or a part of it . . . and Clifford Harris likes that about it, that from a telephone on a scarred desk he can clue together an idea of the kinds of people that he services. But still, he speaks of leaving the business.

Harris: It's just the fact that I'm tired of taking other people's messages. I want to go out and make my own. The first thing I'll do is go and get my own answering service, and I will drive them insane. You kind of, like, find out what other people are doing in the city while you're sitting here doing nothing. You realize that there are a lot of things that go on in this city, a lot of people who are just, like, out on the fringe.

Simon: And everywhere around the room, cellophane–taped from the ceiling to baseboard, there are thousands of pictures of his clients, 8-by-10 posed publicity glossies that are sent to agents and directors by those looking for work, their names and telephone numbers run beneath their set smiles. And Clifford Harris can find this sad.

Harris: Because this is just like a small part of it. There are many, many more actors and actresses than this. And very, very few of these people will be even able to make a living at it, much less obtain any kind of status. *(ringing phone)* It is kind of, well, it's real sad. I'm depressed already, excuse me . . . *(to phone)* Can I help you?

Simon: For National Public Radio, this is Scott Simon in New York City.

Harris: *(continuing into phone)* Oh, we are always sharp this early in the morning. You sound like you're better than you were . . . *(fading out).*

This piece rendered into script underscores a point that's too easily forgotten: the tape of a piece and your script are equal partners in the ultimate product. Dull, witless actuality will debase, rather than enhance, good writing; and dull, witless, thoughtless or uninspired writing can only frustrate good tape.

The benefits of careful and imaginative writing are most apparent, I think, in those stories where good tape is illuminated and made whole by good writing; words, sounds, phrases which, if left just to themselves might be puzzling and incomplete, can be lifted up by good writing. One summer NPR's Ceil Muller and I spent an evening in the emergency room of an animal hospital in New York City:

(traffic sounds)

Simon: The New York City Animal Medical Center sits just below the bridge at 59th Street looking over the East River into the borough of Queens. And at night you cannot see the traffic really, but you hear it. . . . Iron sounds rattling out from under the girders . . . *(sounds heard)* An Emergency Room facility at a veterinary hospital is unusual . . . and here, the waiting room winding off of the second floor ramp looks like something between a *New Yorker* cartoon and a more ordinary trauma center, with some dogs sitting primly in plaster splints or gauze muzzles . . . families struggling to leash in their St. Bernard from lunging at a cocker spaniel . . . and a pair of women grinding tears from their eyes, the lid of an empty cat carrier thumping onto their chairs. The Chief of Staff in the Emergency room is Dr. John Caves.

Doctor: So what's up?

Woman: She is growing weak, and for about the past three days, she hasn't hardly eaten a thing.

Doctor: She's about 15 now.

Woman: Yeah, well she's in her sixteenth year.

Doctor: OK, what about vomiting?

Woman: Well, no, not that I know of . . . *(fading under)*

Simon: The cat is named Cassandra. Her fur is ticked brown, black, and white, and she seems quite slender, peering around the Doctor's fingers as he presses the palms of his hands in carefully below her ribs.

Woman: She's very weak. She couldn't jump up on the table today by herself.

Simon:	Dr. Caves seems quietly, clearly concerned over the condition of his patient, who slumps without complaint as he takes her temperature, but squirms her face away from the cradle of his elbow as he tries to feed her beef liver baby food from the tip of his finger. Most alarmingly of all, Cassandra has not groomed herself in several days, whether from weakness, the summer heat, or advancing disinterest. The human equivalent of that might be a man so dispirited he refuses to rub the sleep from his eyes each morning.
Doctor:	*(fading in mid-sentence)* I can't foreclose anything. I'm reluctant to give her a clean bill of health. That's not really legitimate in a cat her age . . . *(fading under)*
Simon:	And as Dr. Caves leaves the room for the paperwork to admit Cassandra, the woman who's lived with her for sixteen years holds the cat's ear against her cheek.
Woman:	*(consoling Cassandra)* I love ya . . . even if you do smell bad.

Isolate and characterize. Some large, endlessly–unfolding stories (wars, economic crises, political campaigns) can be made fresh and worth hearing by consciously isolating a smaller element from them and using that to suggest the contours of the whole event. During the presidential election of 1980, I was assigned to cover the John Anderson campaign on a daily basis for several weeks. Just before election day we took the scraps of several interviews and various sounds to present a portrait of the "Advance Children," as the young political advance workers of the Anderson campaign were called. It was a story meant to convey a sense of what nearly *all* political campaigns feel like, a sense of what it is to be young and committed and about to be overwhelmed.

Simon:	Recently the Children's Advance issued a new travelling credential for the Anderson campaign. It's more of a cartoon sketch really . . . the stubby, prop-run airplane with "Stardust," the candidate's Secret Service moniker, whittled on the side . . . A small, crayon-orange sun winking from above, a fluffy, feathered cherub of an American eagle holding like a teddy bear to the tail of the aircraft. . . . The speeches, the rallies, swirl up and depart from the center of this fusillage, which carries the campaign from stop to stop. . . . The aisle of the airplane by now is strung up with rubber snakes and lizards, pennants from various places are taped onto the overhead racks. . . . There's a gallery of Polaroid pictures . . . with the candidate in Mickey Mouse ears and the Chief of the Secret Service detail sitting on the candidate's wife's lap . . . Lee Brillhart, a recent graduate of Pomona College, is an Advance Child.

70

Brillhart: It's the only place we keep going back to . . . you know, travelling on a 747 is sort of flying in a little cocoon, insulated from the rest of the world and you're in your own little world. And it gets very easy to get wrapped up in it and sort of to lose track of what else is going on out there.

Simon: The ordinary rules do seem suspended inside here. On take–off and landing there are no amplified injunctions on fastening seatbelts or storing luggage; instead, the attendants pour out drinks and peanuts, often stumbling like passengers on a cruise ship tumbling through foul weather. In a tradition begun and now mostly observed by the television crews, whirring rotary whistles are blown full force at the take-offs and landings. It's been discovered that if you hold one of these small sirens flush against one of the overhead air jets they can shriek on without interruption for the length of the flight.

(sounds of these whistles throughout the above)

Peterson: Almost have to be debriefed after you get off of this thing. It's like coming out of space or something. You almost have to go through withdrawal in order to get back into the mainstream.

Simon: Maybe the most helpful lesson to be taken from this is the way in which reality can become refracted . . . or the often illusionary experience of American political campaigning. . . . Even as the polls have charted the decline of this particular campaign, the trappings of success remain. We arrive in darkened airports which quickly sprout light from the sun guns of television cameras. The reporters wait with courtesy for a word with the candidate; there are crowds to cheer him. . . . And always the sensation of being at the center of something great, even if that's not always the case. . . . And even in successful political campaigns frequently an exaggerated truth. . . . Again, Advance Child Lee Brillhart.

Brillhart: I look at some of the recent polls that have come out, and then we go to rallies where we have three or four thousand people, and we come to airports where we have people waiting and cheering wildly. It's really hard to reconcile those two things.

Simon:	As this campaign has come into its final days, an enormous wistfulness has been settling on it. Some of the Advance Children place down the telephone, and then twist away from sight to cry in one moment, then compose themselves in the next. . . . The Advance People have been tendering "good-byes" to local campaign people . . . exchanging hugs, kisses, scraps of phone numbers and addresses.

At the other end of this is the idea of enlarging a single, irreducible event so that it contains more. In a piece observing the tenth anniversary of the first manned landing on the moon, we tried to measure the impact of that event by examining its resonance in the life of Neil Armstrong:

Simon:	*(over music)* Ten years after the event it may not be ludicrous to introduce Neil Armstrong as the principal partner in the three-man team of Armstrong, Edwin Aldren, and Michael Collins . . . American astronauts whose television presentation of the first steps of human beings onto the surface of the moon remains the most widely-watched show in the world. No Superbowl game, Movie–of–the–Week has supplanted that. *(Actuality of moon landing drops in here.)* And if his face remains unfamiliar to millions of human beings, remember that at the moment of his unmatched eminence, Neil Armstrong was a swaddled white image on a late–night TV screen . . . diffused, indistinct, and unreal.
Armstrong: *(from moon)*	That's one small step for man . . . one giant leap for mankind.
Reporter:	How has the experience changed you as a person in the last ten years? How are you different?
Armstrong:	I don't think I'm different. I think I have the same kind of perspectives that I had in those days.
Reporter:	A cloudless night in Ohio where I was, I looked up and I saw a full moon. When you stand on the Earth and look up and see a full moon, what do you think? You know, you were there.
Armstrong:	Well, I still probably look at it more now than I did when I was younger, but it's probably because I see a different thing than I saw earlier. I used to see a flat disk in the sky, and now I see places . . . places that I've been and can relate to. *(Back to actuality of being cleared for take-off, held under.)*

Simon:	But were we expecting something else from Neil Armstrong? Asking that this man launched atop our tax dollars, in a racing ship pointed to the light in our sky, at least report that he had seen the face of God . . . Or like the cosmonaut Gherman Titov, say that he had tried the door to heaven and found no one to be at home? Were we hoping that when he turned his head to see us, our Earth, hanging as an ornament over the ocean of storms, small and distinct enough to be lost in the sky, he could tell us what held the world in place?

It is possible, I think, to mix the elements of basic reportage with a style and treatment more commonly applied to features. In part, this is enabled by the conversational nature of radio—its ability to tell a story. It permits freer movement from one approach to another. It surprises me sometimes to meet a colleague who has returned from a reporting trip, hear them relate all sorts of telling anecdotes about what they saw or heard or experienced, and then find so little of that on the air. The injunction, I think, should be "tell it to me" [on the air].

Particularize. If something is large, *how* large? If small, is it small as a Pekinese dog? Small as a child's tricycle? Small as a baby elephant, which, in turn, is much larger than a baby ferret? The point is to detail descriptions and action not only for their narrative worth, but in the interest of precision and accuracy in telling a story. It is possible to be excessive about this. Here are two segments from descriptions I wrote in a piece on Quebec's Premier Levesque:

. . . amiable, animated, Napoleon–small, and incessant smoker, the ash from a cigarette sprinkling onto his shoulders often, as he pulls back twines of his concrete–gray hair horizontally across the half–crescent of his head before public appearances. . . . Reneve Levesque's last major rally of the referendum campaign was held this weekend in the hockey stadium in Verdun west on Montreal Island. He was introduced thunderously, looking fuzzy and indistinct through the veil of flame-blue cigarette smoke, like an ill–tuned television picture. The Premier seemed exhausted, wan, his skin a mottled nicotine orange under stage light.

"By the time you were done with him," said my editor, "I didn't know if he was blue or orange or *what* the hell color he was." He preferred a phrase I had describing a rancher from western Canada who'd come to visit Premier Levesque and urge him to stay within the confederation: "his newly-learnt French pinching like a pair of tight boots." "It's the difference," he said, "between the rich tapestry of an Elizabethan work, and the isolated beauty of an uncluttered Japanese flower arrangement."

A final caution: if you begin to develop a distinctive style—a separate and identifiable *voice* in your work, which is your own—you may also begin to invite imitation, or, somewhat less welcome, parody. Or, worse, *self*–parody, a set of verbal gimmicks you can thoughtlessly bring into play on days you are exhausted of imagination or ideas. Occasionally, as something of a signal that we're aware of this jeopardy, I enjoy producing satires, parodies of ourselves. This is the opening passage of a piece we did purporting to report on the success of a scientific program researching communication between *homo sapiens* and coho salmon:

Simon: As the spring drifts to Warnock, Wisconsin, the winter's overlay of ice, like a great white goosedown quilt spread out like the robe of a thoroughbred horse over the shoulders of Lake Michigan, begins to recede . . . and deep beneath the moss-colored cover of the lake, coho salmon begin to swirl, as the lake, slapping sloop and shore, begins again to take on life.

That is, of course, pure crap. But to those not listening with great attention, it sounded quite plausible—quite like *me*—and that can be distressing. It is, however, a risk, I think, that is worth taking. It is the easiest price to suffer of trying to be original.

[A word of warning: One must be a very good and disciplined writer indeed to work in Scott Simon's narrative style, which is bit like high-wire act: the danger of falling into an abyss of excess is an ever-present part of the enjoyment of it. In lesser hands Scott's style, if not applied with restraint and taste, could produce unintended laughter.—Ed.]

7

Producing Features

by Deborah Amos

Defining Elements of the Story

A radio story is a shared experience between you and the listener. Preliminary research is as important as taking notes in the field, but your tape and your script tell the story, give this shared experience a beginning, a middle, and an end. The tape and the script not only allow the listener to share *your* experience but also the experience of the people involved in the story.

How do you turn hours and hours of tape into a finished radio story? This essay will explore some of the ways to do that. There are plenty of approaches to produce a radio piece, almost as many ways as there are producers, but some techniques are common to all productions. Take what you can use and invent new techniques as you go along.

It all begins with the tape, what you record in the field or the studio. You can involve the listener in the story only if he or she can identify with the people who are involved. Even if the story is about some*thing,* rather than a person, you must find a way to put a person in the story. It is that simple. Every something affects someone; and people must be heard talking about your subject. The more complicated the story is, the more this holds true. The writer John McPhee, in his book, *The Curve of Binding Energy,* made nuclear engineering quite understandable and interesting, simply by telling the story of *one* nuclear engineer. In one scene McPhee had his subject explain atom splitting as he and McPhee were playing billiards. It was a concrete metaphor that worked wonderfully, and of course, the same scene would work in a radio story.

A Thanksgiving Goose Story

There are general approaches to preparing a story. To illustrate those approaches, we will focus on one assignment, a story about goose hunting at Thanksgiving.

Deborah Amos is Special Projects Producer at NPR. Prior to joining NPR in 1977 as director of the weekend All Things Considered, *she worked in cable, commercial and public television for five years. A broadcast major from the University of Florida, Deborah is an enthusiastic convert to radio: "Before coming to NPR, I thought radio was just rock 'n roll—but I was wrong!"*

Let's go back to the beginning of the assignment. It was an assignment for a Thanksgiving Day show for *All Things Considered,* a report on goose hunting on the Eastern Shore of Maryland. Every winter nearly a million geese fly south to nest in the corn fields and ponds of Maryland. Thousands of hunters come to the area during hunting season; many take home a bird for Thanksgiving dinner. The story was to be about hunting.

Story preparation begins on the phone. We called the local newspapers to find out when the season opened. One newspaper had run articles about goose hunting in Maryland with the names of hunters so most of the research was already done for us—including leads to sources (hunters, guides, dogs). Some books about hunting pointed out that: 1) hunting dogs were important; 2) hunting guides were a skilled part of the hunt; and 3) a duck/goose blind would probably be a pretty noisy place.

Before You Leave

Before leaving on an assignment, have a few interviews set up. Work the phone hard before you leave, and even harder after you get there. Ask everyone you interview who else you should talk to. If the story is controversial, ask them who their most worthy opponents are and then go do those interviews. Talk to officials and professionals and shop clerks and parking lot attendants. Know what you must cover and cover those subjects with a number of interviews. It is better to have too many than too few choices back at your editing station, better to be in a position to use only your very best interviews in the finished piece. But remember, if you just go out to fill in the blanks of a story you have already done in your mind, you won't have the story—*not the real story.*

When you are in the field and sense the story starting to evolve, that's the time to trust your judgment and follow the new flow of the story. When we asked a couple of hunters to name their opponent, they directed us to the "meanest" and most strict federal game warden in all of Maryland. We called him for an interview, and he talked about the personality quirks of the hunters. We had expected a dry discussion about the law and law enforcement. Instead, we were surprised by his stories of agents hiding in a corn field all night to document hunters breaking the law. *His* stories were as passionate as the hunters' stories. We knew we would use this interview in the final production.

After interviewing many hunters for our goose hunting story, we found a man who seemed quite different from most of the others. He had spent most of his life training hunting dogs. He would talk about his animals with a warmth and sincerity that could be heard in his voice. When he called to his dog during the interview, the dog walked over to the microphone and whimpered just loud enough to be recorded. It was a lovely moment and it captured the contradictions of the hunter—a person who loves the outdoors, nature and animals, but who loves hunting and shoots beautiful birds out of the sky.

We had recorded many hunters but used only this interview in the final story. It was a great find. The other interviews didn't go to waste, however, because each interview gave us a few more details about hunting, which we used as research. You can never do too many interviews, but don't be afraid to leave the bad ones on the editing room floor.

Location Recording

Sound recording on location is simple: *get it all, get everything,* keeping in mind that you only use ten, or even five percent in your completed production. Keep in mind that each interview has a distinct environment and the listener should be able to hear that place. The sound you record on location will set the stage. When you are in a quiet room interviewing the mayor, record the sound of the room. Use that sound under your narration. When interviewing the local elementary school principal near a playground, record some extra sound in that playground. Record the playground without the principal speaking. These pieces of sound are called **ambience beds** or **ambience tracks.** Because no foreground voices are recorded, these pieces of sound are like pictures, and they can be used as a source of sound mixed under your script. It places you and the interview in a place, the school yard, a quiet office, and it gives the listener a picture of where you are.

Record long ambience tracks. If you are impatient, consult your watch as you record an ambience track: whether thirty seconds or five minutes, record as much as you may need for a long script passage, and then record some more. It is often the sound you didn't bother to record that turns out to be the sound you really need.

The opening of the story about goose hunting required an opening sound of geese. We needed to use a lot of descriptive copy to begin the piece to set up the premise of the story, and we wanted to bring the Eastern Shore of Maryland, the hunters and the geese to the listener. How *do* you get a picture of the geese with the hunters on the Eastern Shore of Maryland?

The day before hunting season opened, we set up our microphones in a cemetery. This cemetery serves as a bird sanctuary and ten thousand geese were spending a quiet Sunday feeding, chattering and flying about. We recorded over two hours of "ambience." During those two hours of taping the wind blew, a car drove by, an airplane flew overhead, and the geese decided to all fly up in the air in an enormous swell of sound.

In the editing room we located about two minutes of usable goose squawking without wind noise, or cars or airplanes. We also had a lovely piece with the sounds of birds flying up in the air: two distinct, different sound pictures. We used both kinds of sound for ambience in the opening of the piece. We mixed the birds with sounds of shotguns being loaded and of shotguns being fired. Two pictures, the hunters and the birds, made a third picture when mixed together— a picture of the Eastern Shore of Maryland during goose hunting season. We had the opening of our story.

During our trip to the Eastern Shore, we discovered a goose calling contest at the local high school. We recorded hours of tape at the contest. We recorded from the stage, with the microphones close to the contestants and the announcer on stage. We recorded the audience clapping for a winner. We recorded the auditorium from the back of the hall and the hubbub of a crowd of people waiting for the event to begin. When we got the tape back home, there were plenty of possibilities. After the production was finished, there was also plenty of tape on the editing room floor. *The more angles you try in the field, the more choices you will have when it's time to edit the tape.*

Listening in the Field

Listening sessions in the field are also essential. It's the only way to really be sure you've got what you came for. Listen to all of the material on good earphones while you're on site. If something isn't working, don't hesitate to record it again. Most of the people you interview want to be as helpful as they can and want to sound as good as they can—they'll do it again for you if they have to. Better yet, to cut down on technical mistakes in the field, always wear headphones when you are recording. Most interviewees won't feel uncomfortable when you slip on the headphones if you explain they are necessary to make everything sound right.

Finally, if you have time to listen, log the tape while you're in the field. Mark the good parts and then build on them for your next interview. A gap in the story may occur to you as you're listening to an interview done early one morning. You can fill in the gap in the afternoon. Better to find that gap while you're still on site.

Early one morning in a duck blind with two hunters, a dog and a hunting guide, we recorded a flock of geese coming toward the blind. The guide was calling the geese closer to the hunters, and the hunters stood and shot at the birds. They missed and the birds flew away. Tension subsided in the blind. Much later, in the afternoon, we were to interview the hunting guide, so we had time to listen to the sequence recorded that morning in the duck blind. We decided it was probably going to go into the final piece, and fashioned our afternoon interview to link with our morning sound recordings.

Then, it was home with the tape. Some words of caution here. At this point, a lot of time, effort, money, and emotional strain is on those tape reels or cassettes. There can be *no* excuse for not getting the tape back safely. Label the tapes clearly, number them in the order they were recorded, and put all of them into one bag and *never* let go of that bag, except to have it *hand* inspected at airport security.

Cataloging Your Material

Some producers like to start right in working on the story they've just recorded in the field. Others want time for the experience to settle. This should be a personal choice, but deadlines usually dictate the decision. You should try for at least enough time away from the tape so that the material is fresh again.

All this material should be logged. Use a stopwatch, or the tape counter in your recorder, to keep running times. Make detailed notes on the content and quality of each segment of tape. Put some kind of mark next to the counter number of the tape you may want to use. Some producers transcribe verbatim everything that was recorded. Some producers hardly make any notes. Do what you want or can, but you will need to know what you have and where it is. When it comes time to listen, you'll find you have three distinct types of tape: 1) hot tape; 2) explaining tape; and 3) sound tape.

Hot Tape

Remember our hunter? All of his interview was **hot tape.** He told hunting stories, old hunter stories, and good dog stories, and it was hard choosing the best of the best tape for the finished story. But the best tape came by accident: our hunter, sitting in his chair, called his dog. We had a nice moment between the two of them. Most listeners can share that experience because they can hear how it feels.

Hot tape makes the story interesting. Hot tape grabs your ear. It can be emotional, a strong statement spoken with energy and feeling. Hot tape sounds like people are involved with the story.

When looking for hot tape, forget editorial aspects for a moment. What you're listening for are statements made *interestingly:* with humor, with passion, with pathos. This is not to say that every good radio piece has to contain tape of people crying. Emotion is easy to use and therefore, some feel, a quick and cheap way to tell a story. Hot tape answers the question, "how did it feel?" That question itself is demeaning and it should not be asked, or if asked, should not be included in the finished production. But there are many ways to get the answer. You will hear it *after* the premise, especially if you have asked people to tell you stories that *explain* the premise, if you have asked them to tell you the best story they've ever heard that explains why such and such is so. Always keep in mind that the premise can usually be *written* better and more concisely than someone will do it on tape.

Explaining Tape

Explaining tape is a close cousin of, but not the same as, hot tape. It is tape in which a person explains the premise of the story, what the situation is, what the situation means, or gives his or her opinion about the issue. Explaining tape is needed to present the premise in someone else's voice. For explaining tape to work, the premises must be stated in complete thoughts—sentences that are complete and do not need lots of script to explain or string together. Often entire features can be put together with just the people involved in the story, and without use of a reporter/narrator. (It's much easier to do this with features than with news reports.)

The explaining tape in the goose hunting piece came from the federal game warden. He told us the laws a hunter must obey, the number of geese that hunters can legally kill, and the kind of work a warden does.

Sound Tape

Sound tape is the ambience bed. When listening to this kind of tape, it's important to have a stopwatch, and to make careful notes about what sort of sound you have. You must know what ambience beds you need and how long they must run. If they are too short, you'll have to budget production time to double, triple, or infinitely loop the sound.

Listen for the quality of the ambient material. Sometimes authentic ambience will not work behind your interview because it is accoustically too dense or too thin. For example, you wouldn't use an alarm bell under a narrator. Some sounds are just too heavy to use as voice–over ambience. A woman's voice will not sound right if placed over ambience of other women talking in the background; the frequencies will compete, and the ear will become confused.

We recorded many hours of ambience tape for our goose hunting production: geese at a sanctuary; the street ambience of downtown Easton, Maryland, during the annual Water Fowl Festival; a goose calling contest; a hotel lobby with hunters milling around at 4 a.m.; a small ferry carrying cars full of hunters; a restaurant kitchen where wild goose was being prepared; the CB radio in the game warden's office. We gathered a lot and used very little, choosing only the very best sound tape and matching it with the best interviews.

Accoustical Distance

It may help to think in cinematic terms. Take notes of your *full-up* (or foreground) sounds: a train whistle, a loud dog bark, a car door slam, a gun shot are like close-ups in film. They convey single images, and the listener must be able to recognize them without being able to see the image and without narration to describe it. You can use these sounds to make transitions or to end scenes. You should also note full–up sounds that can possibly be used as ambience beds.

Don't forget that once you have recorded something in a "long–shot," from a distance, you can't expect to be able to use it up front in the mix. It just won't be strong enough. But if you record as close as you can, it's then quite easy to place the sound in front. Occasionally, close–up sound can be mixed up in the background, using echo, equalization and level reduction to simulate a background.

Our full–up sound in the goose piece included: a goose calling contestant practicing in a hallway; a telephone conversation between a hunter and a guide; a clock in a hotel lobby striking 4 a.m.; a hotel clerk making wake-up calls to sleepy hunters; a crackling fire; a series of shotgun shots; a gun reloading; a conversation among some hunters; a truck door slamming followed by the hunters driving away on their way to the blind; and a hunting dog sniffing at our microphone.

You should devise your own system for keeping records of what tapes you've brought back, and the system should be keyed to plans for including the tape in the production. By repeated listening and making notes, you will become familiar with the material so that subconscious editing will begin to occur. Ideas for structure, and especially for links and transitions, will start to come into your mind—even in your sleep. Let your subconscious mind do a little work for you: find a quiet moment and juggle the material around in your head. A natural starting point will become clear. Eventually, the ending will become obvious as well. When stuck for a beginning, ask yourself what is the best piece of tape I have from the field? Put it first. Try to grab the listener right at the beginning and then structure the piece from there. This doesn't always work, however. News pieces, for example, are structured by the logical pattern of information.

During this process of reviewing your raw tape, you should check your notes and research material because you are into the difficult phase of deciding how much weight to give a piece of tape, a sound, a fact you've learned. This is the time to put a lot of tape on the editing room floor. If it doesn't fit, if it's not important, if it takes away from the main points of the story—*don't use it.*

There is always the danger of emotional involvement in the story, of liking a piece of tape too much. You may really think it is super material, needing just some editing and an introduction and a little script at the end to sum it all up. But you may really need to let go of it, for the sake of the overall story.

Outline Structure

One of those people who weighs such things once said, "There are no good stories, just good ways to tell stories." But how are you going to do it? You have now separated your tape into three categories, picked the best interviews and thrown away everything else. You now face a radio jigsaw puzzle.

One way to start is at the end. Find, in your tape or notes or research, an ending. Make it a good ending—not one that starts "And so, as the sun sinks slowly in the West, the issue is still undecided, only time will tell. . . ." If you have to restate what has been learned in the report, then something is drastically wrong with the report. At the end of our goose hunting piece, we used the sound of the killing of a goose.

Now back to the start. A simple way to structure production, was developed at the Canadian Broadcasting Corporation (CBC) as a means of training print journalists to be radio producers in a hurry: **Structure a piece in three-element sections—Sound, Script, Interview.** The first element, the sound, is always a full-up sound, a school bell, for example. The second element, the script, read over the [school] ambience, is the issue of controversy. And the third element, the interview, would be the teacher, explaining why it's necessary to hit the kids when they won't pay attention.

It is possible to put together long news features using no other structure than this simple, three–element device. And if you have to work very fast, not having to think about the structure can help a lot. Just do those three elements at a parent's home, and then do another three outside on the playground talking to the kids. It's a formula, but one that works.

Perhaps the CBC style is not your style, but do you *have* a style? Just when you figured out how to do a piece one way, you should be trying to figure out another way and then another. Keep on trying until you have a repertoire, a trick bag you can choose from to fit the material. It is always *content* that should be the determining factor in structure.

The best way, I think, to study structure for radio is to study other media. The opening and closing scenes of movies translate wonderfully into audio devices. Short story scene setting tricks, television commercials: these are often made by good people working in other media who are doing, every day and very well, exactly what you are trying to do in your radio story. *Tell the story, tell it right; but make it interesting, moving and memorable.*

When the story's done, edited, written, and almost finished, put it away for a while if you can. Go read a book or see a movie, or work on another project. And then, without listening to the tape again or reading the script over, ask someone to edit the piece for you.

This is your first chance to test the material on a listener. Read the script and play the tape cuts in your final production. *You* know the story well, but your "editor," like a radio listener, is hearing the story for the first time. Talk about the piece. Does it explain the story, is the tape interesting, what is missing, is anything unclear? Is the presentation too long or without details? Your editor's first impressions are important. Use those first reactions to clarify the story.

Putting It All Together

The goose hunting story was assembled as a series of scenes. We began by stating the premise of the story; every year thousands of geese come to the Eastern Shore of Maryland from Canada. Thousands of hunters come to the Eastern Shore every hunting season to walk in the woods, sit in a cold, dank duck blind all day and test their skill in bringing home a goose. Next we presented the high school goose calling contest. It explained that goose calling is an art in that part of the country.

We then used the interview with the hunter to explain why dogs are important to the process. Our hunter also gave a little insight into the character of the hunters, the locals, and the outsiders. Then it was on to the lobby of a local hotel as the hunter and his buddies gathered at 4 a.m., talking about the geese and the day's hunt. Next, the game warden revealed more about the character of the hunters and the conflict with managing natural resources.

The last scene took place in the duck blind with the hunters, a hunting guide, a dog, a couple of dead geese, and a beautiful morning sky. We used the sound of a shooting and an interview with the guide.

The production was a team effort. Noah Adams prepared the script and narrated the piece, Flawn Williams recorded sound in the field and mixed the tape in the final production, and I cut and structured the piece.

You are at the end of the process. You have structured your piece, cut it, mixed it, written and recorded a script, and had the piece edited. You're ready to put it on the air.

Listen to the way it sounds on the radio. It's always different from the way it sounds in the studio. If someone liked it, ask them what he or she didn't like about it, what could have been done better.

The final test should only come two or three months later. Get the tape out and listen—you'll probably like what you hear.

III
RECORDING, EDITING AND PRODUCTION

|| 8 ||
Field Recording: Equipment, Supplies and Accessories

by Flawn Williams

Introduction

One of the strengths of radio is its portability: not only the portability of the transistor radios listeners can carry everywhere, but also the ability to travel outside the studio to collect materials for creating radio programs. **Field recordings** (recordings made outside the studio) can give your audience a stronger sense of involvement, a sense of "being there."

The advances made in portable tape recorders over the last decade have made it much easier to get good field recordings. But field recording is still inherently less predictable than studio recording. It requires that you pay attention to *where* you're recording, *how* you're recording, and *what* your listeners will hear from the tapes you make.

This chapter will describe: a kit of basic equipment for field recording; how to operate it to your best advantage; how to analyze the acoustical environment you're recording in; and how to spot problems and know how to deal with them. The kit consists of a portable tape recorder, one or more microphones, and some helpful accessories and supplies. The kit should be kept small enough to fit into a briefcase or shoulder bag, to keep you truly portable.

Portable Tape Recorders

What's a portable tape recorder? For the purpose of your work, it should be a tape recorder weighing less than ten pounds, operable on battery power, and capable of recording sound on tape and playing it back with good fidelity.

Portable tape recorders can be divided according to the type of tape they record on: some recorders use **open–reel (reel–to–reel)** tape, while others use the

Flawn Williams has been involved in radio production for 15 years, and in public radio for 10. Prior to joining NPR's Technical Production Department he served as Director of the Democratic National Committee's Radio-TV Office. He has also run a music club and produced concerts; worked in commercial television; and taught radio production for five summers at the National High School Institute in Evanston, Illinois. He has previously written an article in TV Guide and numerous production handbooks.

now–familiar **cassettes.** Recording on open–reel tape has some advantages. It offers better fidelity due to wider tape and faster recording speeds; and when you bring your field recordings back to the studio you can work with the original tapes on studio machines. In contrast, field recordings made on cassettes must be dubbed, i.e., transferred in the studio to open–reel before editing.

But for the radio producer on a budget, cassettes offer many advantages for field recordings. With the recorders currently available, satisfactory recordings can be made on cassettes. Portable cassette recorders are lighter, easier to operate and cheaper. They also use less power than their open–reel counterparts. So we will concentrate on helping you get good field recordings with a portable cassette recorder. Most of what is said here, however, should still be useful if you have access to a portable open–reel recorder.

Basic Features of Portable Cassette Recorders

Almost all portable cassette recorders share some basic features:

- A *PLAY* **button,** a mechanically interlocking button for playing the cassette (i.e., you can't press *PLAY* and stop or a fast-motion button at the same time).

- Another mechanically interlocked button **marked** *RECORD,* for recording on the cassette (often accomplished by having to engage both the *RECORD* and *PLAY* buttons).

- **Buttons for fast-winding** the tape back toward the beginning (*REWIND,* sometimes marked *REVIEW*) or toward the end (*FAST FORWARD,* sometimes marked *CUE*).

- A *PAUSE* **button** or switch for momentary interruption of the tape motion during record or play.

- A **digital counter** to aid in locating particular sections of the tape (not a minutes–seconds readout, just a relative numerical reference).

- The ability to be powered by **disposable batteries,** and also (often with optional accessories) by house power, by rechargeable Nicad (nickel–cadmium) batteries, or by the electrical system in a car or boat.

- A **jack** where an earphone can be plugged in, to monitor what's going on during recording or playback.

- **Volume and tone controls** to adjust the loudness and crispness of the sound during playback.

- A **small loudspeaker** for field playback.

The exact operating details will vary from model to model. Consult the operating instructions for the particular machine you'll be using, to acquaint yourself with its capabilities.

Not all portable cassette machines offer adequate recording quality or the necessary features to make tapes which are useful for broadcast work. You can expect to pay $150 or more for a decent broadcast–quality portable cassette recorder. And what will you get that's different? Here are some features to look for:

There should be a jack provided for connecting a separate microphone to the cassette recorder (typically marked *MIC* or *MIKE IN*). Some recorders offer only recording with a built–in microphone. This might be acceptable for transcribing meetings, but it is not good enough for broadcast. We'll describe later what types of microphones you should use, but make sure at this point that your recorder has a jack to plug a microphone into.

There must be some means of controlling the volume "level" of what is being recorded. If the recording is made at too low a volume level, then the noise of the tape (hiss) will be objectionably loud compared to the recorded sound. If the recording is made at too high a level, the louder sounds will be distorted and unusable for broadcast. There are three systems for controlling recording level found in portable cassette recorders:

- **Automatic Level Control (ALC or AGC)** monitors what's coming in from the microphone or other sound source, and automatically adjusts itself up and down to ensure a safe average recording level. This is a good system for avoiding distortion and noise when you can't pay much attention to the recorder during recording. But there's a drawback: the resulting sound isn't as "natural" as with other techniques. The background sounds are constantly getting louder or softer in response to the nearer, louder sounds. This constant variation also makes tapes recorded with ALC harder to edit unobtrusively.

- **Manual Level Control,** found on better portable cassette recorders, leaves the control of recording level up to you. The recorder provides a meter to show how loud the sound being recorded on the tape is; your job is to set the record level knob at the proper position so that the loudest sounds you're recording move the needle on the meter to its highest recommended position, and no further. Some adjustment of the record level knob during recording may be necessary, but if you can find a good setting and leave it set for the duration of the recording, the resulting tape should sound more "natural" than one recorded with ALC.

- **Manual Level Control with Limiter** is available on some of the better recorders. This offers the sonic advantages of manual control, with an added protective feature. The limiter senses any sounds which would be loud enough to distort the recording at the setting you've placed the record level knob and it lowers the recording level very briefly, just long enough to prevent distortion.

The recorders which are most useful for broadcast field recording offer a selection of level control options. You can choose ALC for situations where you have to be away from the recorder, and can't monitor what's being recorded, but when you're around to monitor, you can make better recordings using the manual or manual-plus-limiter feature.

Other Convenient Features of Portable Cassette Recorders

Some portable cassette recorders offer other features that are useful for making field recordings. Among them are:

- **Automatic Shutoff and/or End–of–Tape Alarm.** This lets you know when you've run out of recording tape. Some recorders even warn you a few minutes *before* you run out of tape.

- **Variable Playback Speed (Varispeed)** can save some crucial recordings. If you record something when your recorder's batteries are weak, the tape may run at slower–than–usual speed during recording. Played back later with normal power or good batteries, the tape will run at normal speed—and the recorded voices or sounds will sound faster and higher–pitched than they should. With Varispeed, you can slow down the playback speed to match the errant recording speed, and transfer the recording to another tape at proper speed.

- **Cue and Review** are features which let you listen to what's on the tape during fast–forward and rewind, respectively; this helps rapid location of a particular section of the tape.

- **Off–Tape Monitoring** allows you to listen to the sound you're recording a fraction of a second after it gets recorded on tape. With an ordinary cassette recorder, the sound may seem fine going in during recording; but if there's some problem with the recording process or with the tape itself, you may not know it until you go back and play the tape after the recording is finished. If your cassette recorder has off–tape monitoring, you can listen to what's actually recorded on the tape, while recording is going on.

- **Noise Reduction,** such as Dolby, dbx, or ANRS, is helpful in making recordings with less of that objectionable tape noise. Typically, noise reduction is available only on portable *stereo* cassette recorders; these machines can, however, be used for monaural recording too. Some are equipped with a stereo/mono switch which places one microphone input on both channels in the mono position. Remember when using noise reduction that to get good natural sound and less noise, the noise reduction must be turned on during both recording *and* playback.

- **Ability to Use Higher–Quality Cassette Tapes.** If you've been shopping for cassettes, you've already run into a wide range of different types of tape. Greatly improved recordings can result from use of premium tapes, but *only* if your cassette recorder is capable of recording properly on them. Check your recorder to see if it has selector switches for different tape **bias** or **EQ** settings. (These are explained in greater detail in the next section.)

Decent quality portable mono cassette recorders with most or all of the above features are available in the range of $150–250. And for those seeking excellent performance from cassettes, higher quality units are available for under $1000. By comparison, a portable open–reel tape recorder might cost $1,000 to $6,000 or more (late 1982 prices).

Once you've acquired a portable cassette recorder, read the instruction manual to familiarize yourself with its operation. Follow the step–by–step directions for inserting a cassette, for playback and recording of tapes, and checking battery strength. You should be familiar enough with the "feel" of the recorder to operate its mechanical controls without looking at them.

Cassette Tapes

The "cassette" which the recorders we've been discussing use is a plastic housing that contains two spools, a length of recording tape, and various rollers and guides which permit smooth motion of the tape during recording and playback. When we say "cassette," we're referring to the "Compact Cassette" developed by Philips in the 1960s. The case measures 2.5 inches by 4.0 inches, and is 0.5 inches thick; it uses tape which is .150 inches wide (commonly referred to as *150 mil tape*).

More recently an even smaller cassette, called a "micro-cassette," has been introduced. Generally, recorders using these smaller cassettes do not make broadcast–quality recordings, and should be avoided.

The plastic housing encloses two spools. The one on the left is the **feed spool,** and the one on the right is the **take–up spool.** When you begin recording on a cassette, the tape should be on the feed spool. As recording progresses, the tape unwinds from the feed spool and passes by a series of open slots in one of the long sides of the cassette (Figure 8.1). First it passes over the **erase head** of the cassette recorder (where any previously recorded information on the tape is obliterated) then over the **record** and **playback heads** (which are often combined in a single head). The tape then passes between a metal rotating drive-shaft of the cassette recorder called the **capstan** and a rubber roller called the **pinch roller.** When the tape is pressed against the capstan by the pinch roller, it is propelled at a constant speed. The tape then winds onto the take–up spool.

When all the tape has been shuttled from the feed spool to the take–up spool, the cassette can be ejected from the recorder, flipped over, and reinserted with the other side of the cassette facing up. Now the tape is once again on the left–hand spool, and recordings can be made on the other half of the tape (referred to as a **side** of the tape even though both sides are recorded on the upper and lower halves of the same surface).

If you've made a recording on Side A of the cassette which you want to protect against accidental erasure, find the small plastic tab on the back edge of the cassette, on the feed–reel, or left, side (as viewed from Side A). Breaking out this tab will prevent the cassette recorder from being put into record mode when that side of the cassette is loaded into the recorder. If, later, you want to record new material on Side A of that cassette, place a piece of adhesive tape over the open slot where the tab was; the cassette should now record properly. The same procedure applies to the B Side.

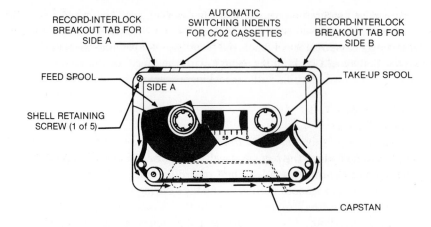

DETAIL OF STANDARD PHILIPS-TYPE "COMPACT CASSETTE"

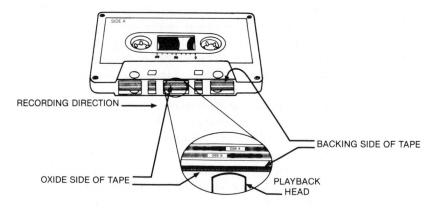

Fig. 8.1 The Anatomy of a Standard Philips-Type Compact Cassette.

There is, on most cassettes, a small scale of dots or lines marked 0–100 just beneath the clear plastic central window. This is a rough scale for locating positions on the cassette, and is *not* referenced to minutes or any other accurate estimate of time or tape length remaining.

Selecting Cassettes

Cassettes vary in the type and quality of tape they use, duration of recording time, type of housing and quality of construction. What's best for your purposes? Here's a guide to some of the variables.

Tape Types

There are four different types of tape currently being manufactured. To achieve good recording results, each must be used with a recorder which is capable of handling it properly. Most portable cassette recorders are only capable of handling *Type I* tapes, but many of the better recorders have switches to select the proper recording characteristics for *Type I, Type II, Type III,* or *Type IV* tapes.

Type I: Referred to as *normal* or *standard,* also as *low noise* and/or *high output* tape; requires normal bias and normal (120-microsecond) equalization (EQ); uses ferric oxide particles.

Type II: Often referred to as chrome type, since most tapes in this category are made with chromium dioxide (CrO_2) particles. Requires high bias and 70–microsecond equalization.

Type III: Called *ferrichrome* (FeCr) because it uses a combination of chromium dioxide and ferric oxide particles. Needs its own bias and EQ settings, usually called Type III or FeCr settings.

Type IV: The newest, called *metal,* requires yet another combination of bias and EQ, and higher than normal recording levels which only the most expensive machines can provide. Uses particles of pure metal instead of oxides.

Check the instruction manual for your cassette recorder carefully to find out whether it has a switch to select use of different types of tape. If it does, you can substantially improve the quality of your recordings by using one of the Type II or Type III tapes. If it does not, then use Type I cassettes.

Bias refers to a high–frequency signal which is added to the sound during recording, to make the magnetic patterns flow more smoothly onto the tape. **Equalization,** or **EQ,** refers to an electronic manipulation of the sound, which must be done in both recording and playback functions. Each of the four types of tape requires a different set of bias and equalization settings.

Type II and Type III tapes cost somewhat more than Type I tapes; and Type IV costs substantially more than the rest. But if your machine is capable of using II or III, the difference in quality will be well worth the difference in cost. (As of this writing, the same cannot be said for the Type IV metal tapes.) Remember, too, that you can reuse cassettes many times, so the cost–per–use of good tape isn't much more than that of mediocre tape.

Tape Lengths

Cassettes have a standard labeling system for length: the number is twice the recording time available on one side of the cassette. The most common are C–60 (30 minutes per side) and C–90 (45 minutes per side); other common lengths are C–30, and C–120.

It's hard to pack so much recording time into such a small package; to get their extra recording time, the C–90 and C–120 cassettes use thinner tape than the other cassettes. While results are usually good with cassettes up through C–90's, the C–120 is a risky proposition at best: it is more prone to jamming, tape tangling, and other mechanical problems, due to the extreme thinness of its tape.

Cassette Shell Construction

There are two ways of assembling a cassette: some are held together with five small screws, while others are welded together. This isn't all that important, until the need arises to disassemble the cassette. When the tape breaks or tangles, and it's necessary to get inside the cassette to repair or retrieve the tape, you'll find the job to be much easier with the screw–type shells. Screw shells are also an indication of better overall construction quality.

Cassette Quality

Just as with cassette recorders, there is a wide range of quality in the cassettes available for you to buy. For use with most portable recorders, the best *type* of tape may not be necessary, but you should still stick with the better name–brands: each makes tape of all types. The local drug store ads are always offering cassettes at ridiculously low prices, but you can be sure that the quality is just as ridiculously low. High–quality, name–brand cassettes don't cost much more, when you weigh the increase in sound fidelity and the decrease in heartache.

Tips on Using and Storing Cassettes

- *Avoid recording on the first 30 seconds or the last 30 seconds of each side of a cassette.* These areas are the most likely to have wrinkles or other anomalies in the tape surface which cause momentary "drop–outs" in the sound.

- *Erase old recordings which are no longer needed, before reusing the cassette.* This can be done with an accessory called a **bulk eraser,** or by running the cassette through the recorder set in the "record" mode, but with no sound being fed in; either way, it helps avoid a lot of confusion.

- *Store cassettes in a cool, dry location when possible.* Cars are not a good place to keep cassettes, because of heat, vibration, and dirt.

- *Don't try to splice cassette tapes,* except in a dire emergency to repair a broken tape. When material recorded in a cassette needs editing, transfer it to an open–reel tape before splicing or editing (see Chapter 11, "Studio Production").

Microphones

The microphone is one of the most critical components of your portable recording system. You may have to go to a bit of trouble to get a good professional–quality microphone to use with a cassette recorder, but the better recordings you get will justify the trouble.

What's a microphone? It's a **transducer,** a device which changes mechanical vibrations (sound) into electrical signals (or vice-versa, as with loudspeakers). In this sense, the microphone acts just like your ear, translating the mechanical energy in sound waves into electrical impulses which your brain can understand. Like your ear, the microphone can pick up nearby sounds, and more distant ones as well.

There are many different microphones available: some are useful in many different situations, while others have specialized uses. They can be divided several different ways: by *pickup pattern;* by *transducer type;* by *impedance;* and by *special features.* We'll examine each of these categories individually.

Microphone Pickup Patterns

The **pickup pattern** of a microphone is a way of describing the direction in which it is most sensitive to sound. Some microphones are equally sensitive to sounds from all directions; these are referred to as **omnidirectional microphones.** If you drew a picture of an omnidirectional microphone's sensitivity, you'd see something like Figure 8.2A: roughly circular.

Another popular microphone pickup pattern is **unidirectional.** Mikes with this characteristic are most sensitive to sounds arriving from directly in front of them, progressively less sensitive to sounds coming from the sides, and least sensitive to sounds arriving from the rear. If you drew a picture of a unidirectional microphone's sensitivity, you'd see a shape like Figure 8.2C, roughly heart–shaped. This gives us another name for the popular unidirectional microphone: **cardioid,** from the Greek word for heart.

There are other pickup patterns, too: **bidirectional** or **figure-eight** microphones are sensitive to sound from front and back but not from the sides; **hypercardioid** microphones are even more sensitive than cardioids to sounds coming only from directly in front; and **shotgun** or **line** microphones have extremely directional sensitivity. For the basic field recordist, however, the most versatile microphones are the omnidirectional and the cardioid.

Microphone Transducer Types

Microphones can also be described by the *way* they convert sound waves into electrical signals. Most common is the **dynamic** microphone, consisting of a metal

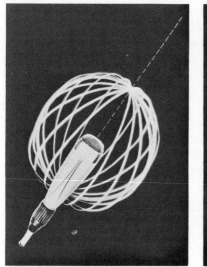

A: The omni-directional polar pattern.

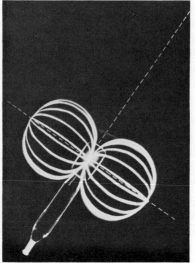

B: The bidirectional or figure eight pattern.

C: The unidirectional or cardioid pattern.

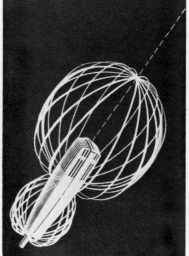

D: The unidirectional hypercardioid pattern.

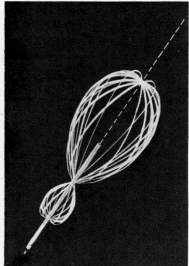

E: The shot-gun or line pattern.

Fig. 8.2. Three-Dimensional Representations of Microphone Pick-Up Patterns.

diaphragm moving in the field of a magnet; the small movements caused by sound waves striking the diaphragm induce an electrical signal.

Also fairly common is the **condenser** microphone, in which two metallic membranes (one of which is electrically charged) are suspended very close to each other. Sound waves striking one membrane cause it to move closer to or farther away from the other membrane, and this movement creates a variation in the electrical charge of the other membrane. This tiny electrical signal is then amplified in the microphone. There are two types of condenser microphones: **regular condenser** mikes require external power to charge the membrane, while **electret condenser** mikes have a permanently charged membrane. Both types require power from a battery or other source to run a small amplifier in the microphone.

Most microphones you'll encounter will have either dynamic or condenser transducers. Other types which you may occasionally see are **ribbon** microphones and **crystal** microphones. Ribbon mikes are generally too delicate for field recording work, and crystal mikes are extremely low in sound quality, so we won't explore them in any detail.

The only other type of microphone transducer you're likely to run into is one you've already been using for years: a **carbon** microphone. Never heard of it, you say? Well, that's the kind of microphone which is used in almost all telephones. Sound waves going into a carbon microphone cause the particles of carbon to jostle around and strike each other, modulating an electric current passing through them. We'll go into more detail about working with telephones in the next chapter.

Which microphone is best for your needs? There are many tradeoffs involved; and so far no one has built the "perfect" microphone. Some of the problems you'll encounter are:

- **Wind and blast noise.** Microphones are built to sense the tiny motions of air molecules caused by sound waves. When air strikes the microphone too hard—as is the case with wind blowing across the microphone, or a blast of air from someone pronouncing a "P," "B," or other plosive consonant near the microphone—the microphone produces a distorted signal, causing a loud noise on the tape which obscures the sound you're trying to record. Dynamic mikes are better than condenser mikes for outdoor recordings where wind is likely to be encountered, and omnidirectional mikes are less sensitive to wind and blast than cardioid mikes. In addition, some mikes are built with metal mesh or plastic foam screens to help break up wind. For extreme situations, you can get an extra foam wind screen to slip over the mike.

- **Handling and contact noise.** Moving your hand around on a microphone, or placing the mike on a surface where it can pick up vibrations or concussive sounds, will cause noise. Both dynamic and condenser mikes share this problem; it is a little less severe with an omnidirectional mike than with a cardioid. Some microphones are specially built to minimize this problem: their pickup elements are shock-mounted within the microphone casing.

- **Recording in a noisy environment.** In this situation, the cardioid mike can give you much better results than the omnidirectional. By pointing a cardioid microphone at someone who is speaking in a noisy room, and getting to within a foot or so of the speaker's mouth, you can get more direct sound from the speaker and less of the general room noise. To get the same ratio of direct-to-background sound with an omni mike, your mike would have to be within a few inches of the speaker's mouth, which may be close enough to make the speaker uncomfortable. It is the cardioid microphone *pattern,* not its *type* (dynamic or condenser), which makes it more suitable in noisy environments.

So far, we've presented a mixed case for choosing an omnidirectional or cardioid mike for your field recording kit, and a fairly strong case for choosing a dynamic mike over a condenser mike. Condenser mikes, in general, have greater sound fidelity than dynamic mikes, and better high–frequency response, but they are more difficult to use in the field. If you are limited to acquiring one or two mikes for field recording get dynamics. As to the choice of omni or cardioid: each is useful, and if your budget can handle it you should get one of each. But if you're restricted to one microphone, the omni is the safer, more versatile choice.

Other Characteristics of Microphones

There are still some details to know about your prospective microphone. One is its **impedance,** a measure of its electrical "resistance" which must roughly match that of the tape recorder input. Most microphones which you'll come in contact with are **low impedance** or **LO–Z** mikes; typical values you'll see range from 50 to 500 ohms. But there are some mikes which are **high impedance,** or **HI–Z,** which have values from 10,000 to 50,000 ohms. These will not function properly with most cassette recorders, and should be avoided.

Another factor is whether a microphone's output (the signal it is producing) is **balanced** or **unbalanced.** Most professional microphones are capable of operating in either a balanced or unbalanced mode; this has to do with how the mike is internally wired and externally connected to the tape recorder, *not* with how the mike responds to gravity. Almost all portable cassette recorders' microphone input jacks require unbalanced signals. Figure 8.4 shows how to connect a balanced–output mike to the unbalanced–mike input jack of a cassette recorder.

The last characteristic which we'll examine is the type of support required by a microphone. The most versatile mikes are designed to be hand–held, or attached to a stand or other support with an accessory clamp. Some mikes are so large and awkward, or susceptible to handling noise, that they should be used only when attached to a stand. And some specialized mikes are designed to be attached to the person whose voice you're recording: **lavalier** mikes hang by a strap around the speaker's neck, dangling at chest level; **tie–tack** mikes can be clamped onto the tie or other clothing. These mikes are usually omnidirectional, and can give quite good results when used as designed, but are not versatile for other field recording needs.

The Importance of Using Quality Microphones

When you acquire a cassette recorder, it will often come equipped with a small, built–in condenser mike, for which great claims are often made by the manufacturer. Or a separate condenser mike may be offered as an optional accessory, for which even greater claims are made. But for the exacting requirements of broadcast recording, most of these microphones are inadequate. Your field recording system requires a rugged, versatile, dependable microphone and those qualities don't come cheap. Professional microphones offer:

- *Good sound quality,* with sensitivity to a wide range of sounds from low bass to high treble. This is called good **frequency response.** Response should be both wide (covering almost the entire audio range, 50–15,000 Hz) and flat (without much variation through the range of frequencies).

- *Ruggedness,* in order to take the punishment of field work. Most professional mikes are made from die–cast aluminum or other metals, not from plastic.

- *Protection* from some of the problems of wind, blast, concussive noises and distortion.

- *Versatility,* the ability to be put where you need them, to record what you want your listeners to hear. A versatile mike can be hand–held, placed on a table stand or floor stand, attached with a clamp to other objects, hung in mid-air—wherever your judgment tells you would be a good perspective to listen from. This also may involve the use of long extension cables, so that the mike can be placed at a distance from the cassette recorder; this is easier to do with professional low impedance mikes.

Connecting the Microphone to the Cassette Recorder

Most professional microphones sold in the United States do not have a permanently–attached cable. Instead, they have a particular type of built–in jack for attaching the cable. (The cable connects them to the equipment they're being used with—tape recorders, microphone mixers, or amplifiers.) This jack has three pins, arranged in a triangular pattern, surrounded by a round collar of metal. The corresponding plug on the cable, which "mates" with this jack, has three holes in the same triangular pattern. The plugs and jacks are called **XLR connectors.** They're also sometimes referred to as **Cannon connectors,** referring to the original manufacturer; but currently many companies produce plugs and jacks which are compatible with the Cannon XLR series (see Figure 8.3A). Plugs or jacks which have protruding pins are called **XLR male;** plugs or jacks with holes are called **XLR female.** XLR plugs and jacks are sturdy and safe; when connected together, they lock with a spring latch, so that it takes positive action to disconnect them. They are also suited for carrying balanced connections (which require three wires, including a ground/shield wire) or unbalanced connections (which only require two wires).

Unfortunately, no cassette recorder under $500 has a corresponding mike–input jack of the XLR type. Most cassette recorders' mike–input jacks are of the type that accept "mini" or quarter-inch phone plugs only (see Figures 8.3B and 8.3C).

Fig. 8.3. Plugs Commonly Used in Connecting the Microphone to the Cassette Recorder.

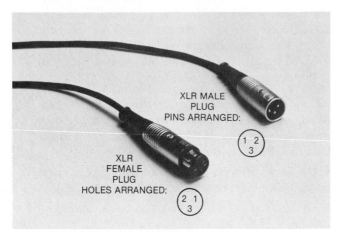

A: XLR or "Cannon" Connectors.

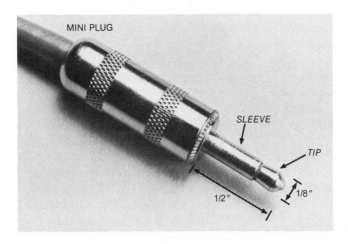

B: Mini Plug.

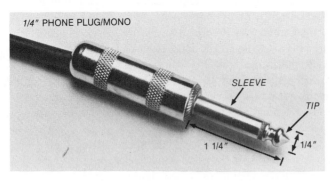

C: Quarter-Inch Mono Phone Plug.

To compound the problem, no major manufacturer makes a complete adapter cable with the necessary XLR female plug on the end for the microphone and mini plug on the other end for the cassette recorder. The manufacturer of the microphone will generally include a cable with the proper XLR plug on one end, and bare wires on the other end; once you have ascertained what type of mike–input jack your cassette recorder has, you'll need to purchase an appropriate plug to attach to the bare–wire end of the cable. This requires soldering the bare wires onto the terminals inside the plug. If you don't have the proper tools for this job, or don't want to attempt it, you can seek out an audio repair shop, broadcast maintenance engineer or radio hobbyist, and ask them to make one (plus a spare) for you. (See Figure 8.4 for the details of wiring the cable.) Often the adapter cable is made from scratch using a retractable "coily cord" with the appropriate connectors attached to each end. Once you have this adapter cable, your life is made much easier. If you need to move the microphone farther away from the cassette recorder than the adapter cable can reach, you can use additional cables with XLR plugs on both ends in between the microphone and your adapter cable, to extend the cable run as needed. These cables *are* commercially available.

Using More Than One Microphone

Some events can be better recorded using more than one microphone. But the typical monaural portable cassette recorder has only one microphone input jack. It is physically possible to construct a cable which can connect two microphones to one input jack; it looks like a "Y" and is called a **Y–adapter.** But this technique has many disadvantages. It alters the sound quality of both microphones; it doesn't give you a separate record level control for each microphone; and it's prone to pick up buzzes and other spurious noises.

A better idea, if you need to use two microphones, is to get a **mixer.** There is a wide variety of mixers available, from the small, simple kind which can mix two to four mikes, to the semi–portable ones which mix twenty or thirty mikes. Basically, they all perform the same function. You connect the mikes you want to use to the mixer, and adjust a separate level control on the mixer for each mike. The mixer then combines all the mikes into one signal, which you can connect to the **aux** or **line** input of your cassette recorder.

Another way to record two mikes on one cassette recorder is to use a stereo cassette recorder. The stereo recorder will have a separate mike input jack for each of the two channels; you can connect one mike to each jack, and record them on separate channels. Later, when you get back to the studio, you can mix the two channels of the stereo cassette down to one monaural sound. This gives you the additional flexibility of being able to vary the relative levels of the two mikes in the studio after the event, instead of worrying about getting an exact sound balance between the mikes while recording. There is one drawback to this method: the tape noise on the two channels of the recorded cassette will add together when the two channels are combined to make the monaural mix.

A: XLR female plug connected to mini plug or quarter-inch plug using single-conductor shielded cable.

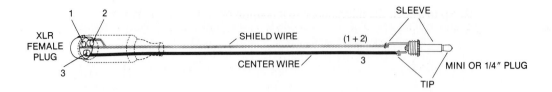

B: Same plugs connected using two-conductor shielded cable.

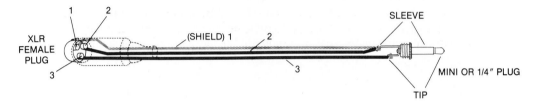

Fig. 8.4. Wiring for Cable Connecting Mike and Cassette Recorder.

Storing and Transporting Microphones

Even the more rugged professional microphones will last longer and make better recordings if they are properly taken care of. Keep mikes away from extreme heat, humidity, smoke, dust, and especially from iron filings (remember, there's a magnet in every dynamic mike). Whenever you don't need to have the mike handy and connected, put it away—in the box supplied by the manufacturer, in an old sock, a pouch, or some other protected place. If you're carrying a briefcase or shoulder bag for accessories and supplies, set aside a protected corner in it for your microphones.

Accessories for the Recording System

The following items will help you make better use of your cassette recorder and microphone(s) in making good field recordings of interviews, press conferences, speeches, or just the characteristic ambient sounds of a particular location or environment.

Accessories for the Microphone

• The all-important **adapter cable,** to connect the mike to the recorder. Don't forget to make, and carry, a spare adapter cable.

• A **desk stand,** which is a small support for the microphone, good for recording someone sitting at a table. Some look like small tripods, while others have a wide base and small pole.

- The **stand adapter clip** supplied with the mike by the manufacturer, which lets you attach the mike to a desk stand or other support.

- A **clamp** to attach the microphone to a podium or other upright support; some excellent clamps are made for supporting cameras (one is marketed by Rowi), and can be adapted to microphone–support use.

- A **gooseneck** for extending the height of the desk stand or clamp; it's a flexible metal tube, generally 6 to 18 inches long.

- Extra plastic foam **windscreens** to protect against wind noise or vocal blast.

- A **floor stand** and **boom arm** won't fit into the standard briefcase kit, but they can come in handy for some recording situations where you don't want to have to hold a microphone for a long period of time. Also, a mike on a stand placed close to someone is not as disturbing as a mike held close by someone; the inanimate stand doesn't violate personal space the way an aggressive arm does.

- A **microphone mixer** is useful for situations where two or more mikes are needed to get a better recording of an event.

Accessories for the Cassette Recorder

- **Extra batteries.** You should know how many and what size your recorder uses, and how long one set of batteries will last in the machine (in the record mode).

- **Rechargeable battery pack** for longer trips when there's time to recharge between recording sessions.

- **AC power cable** or **external power supply** for the cassette recorder, plus an **AC extension cord.**

- **Car/boat power adapter,** if your work includes driving or boating.

- **Earphones** for monitoring during recording and later private listening. The earphones supplied with the inexpensive tape machines are inadequate for this purpose.

- **Shoulder strap** and **carrying case,** to protect and support the recorder if you're not carrying it inside a briefcase or shoulder bag.

- **Accessory cables** for special needs: a mini–plug–to–mini–plug cable for connecting your cassette recorder to another cassette recorder for copying cassettes and other applications described later; a mini–plug–to–alligator clips cable for connecting your cassette recorder to a telephone (see next chapter).

- **Extra cassettes** of the proper type for your machine, up to twice as many as you think you'll need.

General Accessories

- **Pad** and **pencil** (even in this electronic age, print notes can be recalled more easily).

- **Adhesive tape,** such as the metallic-gray **gaffer's** or **duct tape,** for securing microphone, cables, etc.

- **Blank cassette labels** are helpful when you're reusing old cassettes.
- A **briefcase** or **shoulder bag** large enough to carry the cassette recorder, microphone(s), accessories, and supplies. Make sure there is room left over for printed matter and other materials you'll pick up in the course of making field recordings.

Maintenance of Your Cassette Recorder

The only item in your field recording kit which needs much routine maintenance is the cassette recorder. Check with the instruction manual for the recorder for exact details of maintenance, but here's a set of general guidelines and procedures applicable to most recorders:

Cleaning the Tape Path (after every 10 hours of use)
This small bit of maintenance can make the difference between noisy, distorted recordings and good ones.

- Use cotton swabs and *denatured* alcohol, which are available at drugstores. Ordinary rubbing alcohol contains water, which could cause heads to rust.
- Remove the cassette from the recorder, then lock the recorder in the *PLAY* mode for better access to the heads and other components.
- Clean everything which the tape comes in contact with—heads, guides, pinch roller, capstan.
- Don't use the so-called "head cleaner cassettes," which claim to clean the heads and tape path while running in the machine; they don't live up to their advertising.

Demagnetizing Cassette Recorder (after every 25 hours of use)
Heads and other metal parts which come in contact with the tape can become gradually magnetized. This can lead to loss of high–frequency sounds, and eventually gradual erasure of tapes which are played many times.

- Obtain a small hand–held head demagnetizer.
- Disconnect cassette recorder from power source, and remove batteries; then lock the recorder in the *PLAY* mode for better access to heads and other components.
- Following the instructions supplied with the demagnetizer, plug it into power while still a distance away from the cassette recorder. Slowly bring it close to each metal part in the tape path (heads, guides, capstan), pass over each part, and withdraw the demagnetizer. Disconnect from power again, at some distance from the cassette recorder.
- Take care that you do this procedure properly; otherwise, you may wind up with heads more magnetized than before you started.

Maintenance to Refer to a Technician

Your recorder should be checked at least twice a year (sooner if audible problems develop) by a qualified service technician. If you work at a radio station, the engineering staff there may be able to handle these needs; otherwise, cultivate the friendship of a repair person at your local stereo store. Things which should be checked:

- **Record bias and equalization.** Give the technician a sample of the particular type and brand of cassette you've decided to use. Have him optimize the recorder's performance for that tape, then continue to use that type and brand of tape for best results.
- **Head alignment.** Many problems of severe loss of recording quality can be traced to heads being out of alignment.

It's a good idea to buy a repair manual for your recorder, to help you or the person handling your maintenance know what's going on (or what's gone wrong) inside the recorder. They're available from the manufacturer of the recorder for a few dollars.

Other Suggested Maintenance

- Clean the metal contacts of your connecting cables periodically with *denatured* alcohol.
- Tighten set screws on XLR connectors on mike cables.
- Check adapter cables for loose connections.
- Check cable insulation for damage, replace damaged cables.

| 9 |
Field Recording: The Process
by Flawn Williams

Introduction

If there is one word that could guarantee you a better chance at success in field recordings, the word is *practice*. This involves not only the rudimentary practice of familiarizing yourself with how your tape recorder and microphone work, but also simulating interviews and other recording assignments. Once you've convinced yourself that you're ready to handle the recording apparatus by yourself, draft a coworker or friend to serve as a guinea pig and stage a mock interview. This should give you a better sense of what it takes to pay attention to both the interview and the recording process. Listen back carefully to your recordings of these mock interviews, and pay attention to the sound, which you may be able to improve with better technique.

Recording Checklist

Here's a list of reminders and helpful hints to prepare you for recording in the field. First, **before you leave** for the recording assignment:

- Load tape into the tape recorder.
- Attach the microphone to the recorder.
- Put the record in *PLAY* mode, and check the battery strength.
- Put the recorder in *RECORD* mode, and check the record meter or other visual indicator; also, listen to the recording with an earphone.
- Play back the test recording and listen to it through the built–in loudspeaker or the earphone.
- Rewind the tape to the beginning, then move the tape past the leader, zero the index counter, and turn off the recorder. You should now be ready to record.

Next, when you're **ready to start** recording a real interview:

- Set up the recorder as before, plugging into AC power if it is available.
- Start recording about ten seconds before you're ready to start asking questions. This gives you a bit of the "ambience" of the recording location; and if you're recording with an Automatic Level Control (ALC), it gives the ALC

sensor some time to sense what the average loudness of this recording will be. (Don't try to hide from the interviewee the fact that you're recording. Warn him when you're about to "roll tape.")

- During the recording, check the record level meter or other visual indicator, and adjust the record knob (if not recording with ALC) to make sure the highest meter readings fall within the range advised by your recorder's instruction manual.

- Monitor the recording with a good pair of earphones, listening for cable–banging, mike–handling or other concussive noises, wind blast, popping P's, etc. If necessary, adjust the mike position to eliminate the problem.

- Check visually to confirm that the tape is still moving.

- If your recorder has a separate playback head which allows "off–tape monitoring," occasionally throw the switch to monitor the tape to confirm that something is actually being recorded on tape.

- At the end of your interview or the event you're recording, let the tape run on for an additional thirty seconds or so with the mike held in the same place, but with no conversation. This gives you more "clean ambience," which will help you when assembling the final produced tape in the studio.

After the recording is completed:

- Rewind the tape a bit, and listen to some of the last part of the tape to confirm that the recording was satisfactory.

- If you're recording on cassette, and wish to protect the new recording from accidental erasure, break out the protection tab on the rear edge of the cassette. (See Figure 1A, Chapter 8.)

- Load fresh tape into the recorder before putting it away, so you can be ready to record again quickly if the need arises.

Recording Ambience in the Field

"Ambience," in acoustical terms, is the surrounding or pervading acoustic atmosphere, the sound environment around you. When you're making field recordings, ambience is the "sound" of the space where you're making the recording. Often, it's an important part of the story itself, a way of telling your listeners something about a place or an event without using words.

When you're out "on location" listen for *characteristic sounds* of the environment—airplanes, particular machine noises, birds, children playing, church bells, barking dogs, etc. Try to get recordings of these sounds with no conversation or interview going on nearby, and get recordings of these sounds from various distances and perspectives. It may be helpful to you to think in the jargon of film or television, and think of these perspectives as "close-ups," "medium shots" and "long shots." You can use a close–up recording of a sound to focus the listener's attention on a location, environment, or mood; then mix in medium and long–distance perspectives of the same sound behind narration or interviews. But you can't do any of this if you don't record different perspectives of the ambient sound in the first place.

When recording voices in their natural ambience—that is, someone speaking with audible background environment sound—it's difficult to get a good balance between the voice and the ambience. If your mike is too far away from the speaker's mouth, the background sound may obscure what the speaker is saying. Also, editing of the speaker's words may be more difficult, since the listener will hear abrupt jumps and changes in the background ambience at the points where edits are made. One solution to this problem is to record your interviews, monologues, narration, etc., in a quiet location (perhaps even in a studio), and mix them later with the recordings you've made of the appropriate ambiences for the story. (Modern film soundtracks are usually made this way.) [*Modern journalistic ethics would prohibit you from creating the impression that a studio recording was made in the field, through the use of mixed-in ambience or sound effects.—Ed.*]

Always record more sound ambience than you think you could ever use. It's much better to have too much of it when you're ready to assemble the piece than to have too little. Be sure to bring enough recording tape and batteries, and allow enough time to make recordings of ambience as well as voices.

Controlling the Environment

In many instances, you won't have any control over *where* something you want to record takes place. Many news events happen where they happen, or where the newsmaker wants them to happen. But often, in setting up interviews, you can have some effect on where you conduct the interview. Paying attention to the acoustic environment can result in tapes which sound much better and are easier to edit. In general, conduct the interview in the quietest, "deadest" place you can find. If the local sound is important to telling the story, record that separately and mix it in later. Interviews will be much easier to edit if they are recorded in a quiet ambience. Here are some acoustic traps to beware:

- **Fluorescent lights:** Most fluorescent lights emit a buzzing or humming sound, which may not be all that noticeable when you're in the room—but you'll hear it when you play the tape back in the studio. Buzz or hum makes tape harder to edit unobtrusively, and the constant noise is tiring to your listeners' ears; they'll lose interest in your program more quickly.

- **Air conditioning** or forced–air heating systems make a great deal of background noise, which again is fatiguing to your listeners' ears. Is it possible to turn off the blowers for the duration of the interview? Similar problems occur with office machines, refrigerators, space heaters, and other appliances which use motors or blowers.

- **Wind noise** can be a problem if you're recording out of doors. Try to find someplace which is sheltered from the wind, such as the leeward side of a building.

- **Outdoor traffic** is a bigger problem if you're recording out of doors; cars, trucks, trains, and airplanes may all be a part of your story, but they can be disruptive in an interview.

Be cautious also about recording indoors in rooms with lots of hard surfaces: linoleum or wood floors; stone; cinderblock or plaster walls; no carpets or drapes; etc. Rooms such as this have a noticeable reverberation, and the reverberation of one spoken word will carry over into the next word. This makes for noticeable jumps in the sound if you attempt to edit out words or phrases from a tape recording made in such a room.

Taking care to pay attention to the recording environment, and seeking out a quieter place to record an interview, can give your guests the impression that their particular interview is important to you. This can make them feel more important, and you may get a better interview as a result.

Microphone Placement and Handling

Much of your field recording will consist of holding the microphone in one hand, to record either your own voice, someone else's voice, or appropriate sounds. When "miking" your own voice, try to find a place to hold the mike which is close enough to make you sound "on–mike" but not close enough to cause "popping" when plosive consonants such as P, B, T, etc. are pronounced. If you're using an omnidirectional mike, you may be able to bring the mike as close as two or three inches from your mouth. In either case, don't hold the mike directly out in front of you, pointed at your mouth; instead, hold the mike below your mouth. Keep it close to your chest, pointed up, and talk *across* the front of the mike (see Figure 9.1A). This will help minimize breath noise.

When miking someone else in a situation where you and the other person are standing or seated together, many of the same rules apply. You'll be searching to find a happy middle ground between getting too close (where you'll get popping P's, breath noise, etc.) and too far away (where the voice will sound distant, less distinct, "off–mike"). But there's another factor to take into account: something the sociologists call "social distance." Pointing a microphone at someone, at close range, may be unconsciously or consciously interpreted as an aggressive act, an invasion of their personal space. Or you, being unconsciously cautious about invading personal space, may not want to hold the mike close enough to the person. The result is a tape that sounds "off–mike," and the only remedy is not to be afraid to place the mike in the best place for good sound. Push the limits of social distance a bit if you need to. As long as you keep the mike low and pointed up, rather than straight at the speaker, it will be less intrusive.

One decision you should make before starting to tape any particular interview is whether your questions, asked during the recorded interview, will be needed in the final program. If they're not, then you can concentrate on keeping the microphone aimed properly at the interviewee, thus producing a stable aural perspective which is easy on the listener. Your questions on the tape will sound fain-

Fig. 9.1. Miking Techniques

A: *Try Miking from this Angle,* close to the mouth, with the microphone off-axis relative to the mouth.

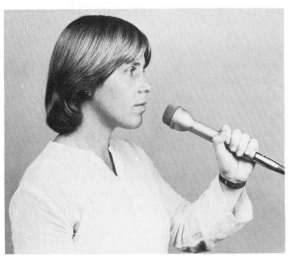

Photos by Phoebe Chase Ferguson

B: *But Not This Angle*—this position is the most likely to accentuate plosive pops and other breath noises.

ter and more distant than the interviewee's answers, but if only the answers are going to be included in the final broadcast version, that's not a problem.

Unless you're really certain that you won't need your questions in the final version, though, it's much safer to record both questions and answers. To record the complete interview—both your questions and the interviewee's answers—with equal quality, you'll have to move the mike back and forth. When doing this, you need to be even more conscious of social distance: you'll have a strong tendency to place the microphone closer to you than to your interviewee. Try to err a bit in the opposite direction, by overcompensating to make the interviewee sound a little bit closer than you. With practice, you can find the right balance.

When recording with a hand–held mike you should also listen for noises caused by moving your hand on the mike or bumping the mike cable. These noises can be intensified when you must move the mike back and forth between you and other speakers. But by listening with good earphones while recording, and by checking your tapes afterwards, you can train yourself to find the safest way to hold a particular kind of microphone without generating these spurious noises.

Recording with Stationary Mikes

In recording situations where you have the time to choose a quiet place to do a "sit–down interview," you can avoid most of the noise associated with hand–held mikes by mounting the microphone on some stationary object before starting the interview. When recording with just one mike, this technique is useful for getting a good recording of just the interviewee. If the interviewee is seated at a table or desk, use a desk stand for your mike; have the person talk while you test a few positions to find the best-sounding spot for the mike. If the person is seated in a chair, couch, etc., you may be able to use a clamp and gooseneck extension bar to position the mike where you need it. In this situation, a floor stand with boom arm can also be helpful. Keeping the mike in one stable position means that there will be no jarring shifts or acoustical perspective on the tape. But there's an inherent danger to watch for: your interviewee may move away from his/her original position, or may try to "talk around" the mike instead of into it.

If it's necessary to have both you and the interviewee on tape, and you have only one mike, this stationary miking technique is not recommended. But if you can set up two separate mikes—one for yourself, another for the interviewee—and record both of them, you'll get good results. Two mikes can be combined with a mixer and then recorded on a monaural recorder. Or two mikes can be recorded on a stereo tape recorder, and the resulting two–channel tape mixed together to mono later in the studio. (See "Using More Than One Microphone" in Chapter 8 for details.)

When two mikes are used, try to position yourself and the interviewee farther apart than you would be if you were conducting an interview with a single hand–held mike. One rule of thumb for placing yourselves and the mikes: the distance from your mouth to the interviewee's mike should be *at least three times* the distance from your mouth to your mike, and vice versa (see Figure 9.2). Even

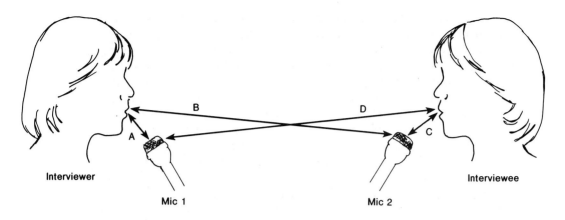

Interviewer

Mic 1

Interviewee

Mic 2

Fig. 9.2. *Distance Ratios for Recording with Two Mikes:* When recording two speakers with two separate microphones, the distance of the far microphone should be at least three times the distance of the closer microphone. From the interviewer's perspective, "B" should be at least three times "A"; from the interviewee's perspective, "D" should be at least three times "C."

more distance would be helpful, so that not too much of each voice picks up in the other person's mike.

Lavalier or tie–tack microphones can also be very useful in this kind of two–mike sit–down interview. If you use this kind of mike, you still need to pay attention to separating yourself from the interviewee by at least that three–to–one ratio of distances. Also, listen for noise from the microphone or cable rubbing against clothing, and for the sounds of the interviewee fiddling with the cable from his/her mike.

Recording a Speech or Press Conference

Generally, in this situation, one or more persons will be seated at a table or standing at a podium. If this is true, you should be able to get your mike relatively close to the person speaking by using a desk stand or mounting clamp. Often a gooseneck extension will be needed to get the mike into more convenient range for picking up the voice.

Add microphone extension cables to your mike if necessary, so that you can keep your tape recorder with you wherever it's convenient to sit. It's awkward to have to get up and run to the podium periodically to change tapes, and if you have to leave the recorder at the podium or press conference table, it's impossible to monitor recording levels, note index counter readings, etc.

Occasionally you'll need to record someone giving a speech who is not standing at a podium or seated at a table. The only way to get a good recording of this event is to get the mike close to the speaker. Try to convince the speaker to wear a lavalier or tie–tack microphone which you supply, or have the speaker hold your microphone. If the speaker doesn't intend to move around very much, he/she might be willing to talk into a stationary mike if you have a floor stand to mount one on; but if movement is indicated, the lavalier or tie–tack (with enough extension cable to give the speaker room to move) will give better results. In any case, make sure the speaker is aware that the microphone is for recording purposes, and not for the public address (PA) system; otherwise, confusion may result. If there is a PA system, locating your recording mike with the PA mike (by clamping or taping one to the other) is essential (see "Recording From a Public Address System," below).

If none of these options is practical, you may be able to get a usable recording by using a highly directional microphone such as a hypercardioid, shotgun or line microphone from a relatively long distance. You would probably need to hand–hold the microphone, get as close to the speaker as possible under the circumstances, and follow the speaker's movements with the mike.

Recording from a Public Address System

Recording a speech, press conference, or other event can be either helped or hindered by the presence of a public–address (PA) system. (These systems are also referred to as "sound reinforcement systems.") A PA system usually consists of a microphone, amplifier, and loudspeakers designed to reinforce a voice or other sounds so that larger numbers of people can hear what's going on.

In the simplest case, the presence of a PA system will mean that the people who are speaking will tend to stay close to the mike for the PA system. If you can position your mike next to the mike which is connected to the PA system, you stand a good chance of getting a usable recording. One difficulty of recording in the presence of a PA system is the same as recording in a reverberant room: the sound bounces around the room and takes a long time to die away, and some sound from one word will still be lingering when the next word is spoken. This makes the recording difficult to listen to and to edit. *The closer your mike is to the person speaking, the less of this unwanted background sound you'll get.*

In some cases, if you can locate the person operating the PA system, you may be able to attach your tape recorder directly to the PA amplifier: the mike for the PA system thus becomes the mike for your recording as well. To make this connection, you'll probably need some adapter cables which have on one end the proper plug to connect to your recorder's *AUX* or *LINE IN* jack. You'll also need a suitable (and probably different) connection on the PA system end, most often a **quarter–inch phone plug** or **RCA phono plug** to attach to the PA system's **record output.** The person operating the PA system may be able to help you make the connection.

If you're using a direct connection from the PA system to make your recording, be sure to make a test recording to check the sound quality you'll be getting. If there are problems with the sound quality of the PA system, these will become your problems, too. Also watch out for electrical buzz or hum on your recording; direct connection to a PA system often creates such problems.

If you can't attach a mike near the PA system's mike, or make a direct connection to the PA system's amplifier, try putting your mike close to one of the

PA system's loudspeakers. If necessary, you can use a clamp, stand, or adhesive tape to attach the mike to the loudspeaker. You won't get perfect voice quality with this method, but you'll often get a more intelligible sound than with certain other techniques, such as holding a mike somewhere in the audience.

Recording from a Mult Box

When an event is being covered by a number of press and electronic media organizations, often a **mult box** (sometimes called a **splitter box**) will be set up by one of the media organizations or by the organizers of the event. In this case, one microphone is set up for the newsmaker to speak into; this mike is connected to a large box with many jacks on it. Each reporter can then connect a tape recorder to one of the jacks on the box, and receive a signal from that microphone. This saves the trouble of everybody setting up their own mikes, and reduces visual clutter caused by a forest of mikes in front of the newsmaker.

When these mult boxes are designed to provide your recorder the same kind of connection and the same kind of electrical signal as a normal professional quality microphone, the boxes are referred to as operating at **mike level.** So you should be able to plug into the mult box with the same cable you'd use for your mike (the mult box replaces the mike). Sometimes mult boxes will have different connecting arrangements, however, so it's a good idea to bring along a variety of adapter cables such as those you'd use for hooking up to PA systems. You may want to check in advance with the event's organizers to find out what type of equipment, if any, will be available.

Recording the Output of Another Tape Recorder

If you have the proper connecting cables, you can transfer sound directly from one tape recorder to another. This provides much better quality than, for instance, playing a tape on one machine and aiming a mike from another recorder at the loudspeaker of the first machine—a practice definitely *not* recommended.

The direct connection is accomplished by plugging a cable into the *EARPHONE* or *LINE OUT* jack of the machine which is playing back the already-recorded tape; then plugging the other end of that cable into the *AUX* or *LINE INPUT* jack of the machine you want to make the copy on. Adjust the playback level and tone controls on the first machine to somewhere in the middle of their range; then adjust the record level control (if any) on the second machine to get proper peak readings.

Note that, in this arrangement as well as when recording from a PA system, you must connect to the *AUX* or *LINE IN* jack on your recorder, *not* to the *MIC* jack. This is because output signals from amplifiers and tape recorders are much stronger than the signal from a microphone. If you plug an amplifier or tape machine's output into a tape recorder's *MIC* input jack, the resulting recording will be grossly distorted.

You should, of course, listen to a sample recording—making whatever adjustments are necessary—before proceeding to record an entire event from some line level source.

If your tape recorder doesn't have an *AUX* or *LINE IN* jack—if it has only a *MIC*–level input jack—then in order to be able to connect your recorder to "line–level" sources such as the ones described above, you'll need a special cable called a **level–dropping cable,** which is available from electronics specialty stores. With one you can plug line–level sources into the *MIC* input jack of your tape recorder.

You can also use the technique of connecting the input of your recorder to the output of another recorder to help get good recordings of events in an emergency. For example, let's say you arrive at an event, and discover that you don't have enough microphone extension cable to reach all the way from the podium, where the newsmaker is speaking, to the area where you need to sit. But another reporter has already set up a mike on the podium, run his cable over to where you both will be sitting, and connected the cable to his tape recorder. If he's willing, and if you have the proper adapter cable, you can connect from the *EARPHONE* output jack of his recorder to the *AUX* or *LINE IN* jack of your recorder. In this fashion, as long as he is recording, you can also record through his microphone. *It is always best, however, to have your own microphone up on the podium as close to the speaker as possible.*

Transmitting Tape and Voice Over the Telephone

For "breaking news" stories—where it's important to get what you've taped on the air as quickly as possible—it may be worth trading a loss of some sound quality for speed of transmission back to your station by using the telephone. Telephones have a restricted frequency response (about 300 Hertz to 3,000 Hertz)—hardly high fidelity. Much bass, treble, and intelligibility are lost. There is also a lot of background noise and substantially more distortion than you'd get if you took the tape back to the station. But, in many cases, time is of the essence—so your station should have some way of taping what comes in on its telephone lines.

Head for the nearest telephone. But *don't* attempt, except in the direst of emergencies, to send sound over the telephone by holding its mouthpiece close to the tape recorder's loudspeaker. The inferior–quality carbon microphone in the telephone adds distortion; background noise from the room where you're using the telephone will leak in; and the resulting sound which reaches the radio station over the telephone will be virtually unintelligible.

There *is* a technique for connecting your tape recorder so that you can play tapes into the phone. Here's what you need to do:

- Have a cable which can connect your recorder's *EARPHONE* output to a pair of "alligator clips" (spring-loaded clips) (see Figure 9.3).

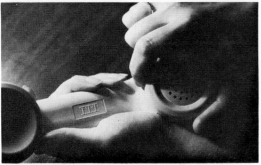
Unscrewing the receiver mouthpiece by twisting it counterclockwise. (Note: Many pay-phones are permanently sealed, and will not permit this.)

Removing the mouthpiece cover, revealing the carbon microphone.

Removing the microphone by lifting it out of the receiver.

Attaching the first alligator clip to one of the receiver's "tongues."

The alligator clip is attached in this fashion to provide the firmest connection. Its teeth grip tightly *across* the edges of the "tongue," rather than gripping the flat, smooth surface, from which the clip could slide off.

The second clip is attached in a similar manner. It doesn't matter which clip goes to which tongue, as long as the clips don't touch each other.

To prevent the clips from touching each other, rubber or plastic sheaths are recommended. This receiver is now ready for "phone-feeding."

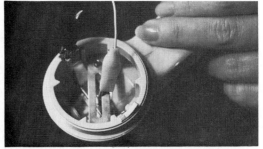
In some parts of the country, GTE style ("Automatic Electric") phones are found. They use two bars instead of "tongues."

Fig. 9.3. Playing Tape through the Telephone

- Unscrew the mouthpiece of the telephone. (You can't do this with some styles of telephone, or with pay phones whose mouthpieces are sealed. Go find another phone.)
- Remove the loose disc inside the mouthpiece. This is the carbon microphone. Underneath it should be two exposed metal posts.
- Connect the proper end of the cable to the tape recorder, and the alligator clips on the other end of the cable to the posts. It should not matter which clip goes to which post.
- Play the tape in your recorder. Listen through the telephone earpiece and adjust playback volume and tone controls for the loudest, clearest sound without undue distortion.

You may also be able to read live narrations through this setup, with better quality than by using the carbon mike in the telephone. With the tape recorder connected as described above, put blank tape in the recorder. Plug your mike into the recorder; set the recorder into *RECORD* mode, and activate the *PAUSE* control. If your recorder has "feed-through" capability your voice should be heard down the telephone line in this manner.

Conclusion

This chapter has presented a basic outline of the most typical field recording situations, and suggested techniques for getting good recordings. It's impossible to write down all the potential pitfalls and solutions, but in conclusion, let's recap the basic points you'll need to remember:

- **Prepare yourself.** Find out as much as you can about a recording situation *before* you set out to record. Check your recording equipment carefully, and keep the heads and capstan assembly clean. Knowing the capabilities of your recording equipment can free you to concentrate more on the content of the interview or event you are recording.
- **Pay attention to the recording environment.** Listen to the place you're going to record, with acute ears. Acoustic problems avoided in the field are problems you won't have to deal with later in the production process. Take the few extra seconds to do a quick test recording, and listen back to it. If you're well–practiced, you can accomplish this without making other people feel like they're waiting around for you.
- **Listen for sounds which communicate.** Spoken words, as well as characteristic sounds and noises, must be able to get a message or meaning to the listener on first hearing; few listeners get a second chance. Recordings that are clear to you (because you were there to see and hear) may be unintelligible to a listener. Use the intimacy of radio to take the listener close to an event, by getting good quality, close–perspective field recordings.

‖ 10 ‖
Tape Editing
by Jonathan "Smokey" Baer

Broadcast journalism is not a process of transmission but a process of synthesis. In other words, reporters don't simply play back whatever material they have recorded in the course of covering a story. You may spend three days on a story, record more than an hour of tape, and have to distill all this experience into a five–minute report. In radio, there is no more useful tool in packaging information than the skillful use of tape editing.

Before tackling the mechanics of tape editing, you should understand one thing. While *editing tape* is a physical task (cut the tape, join it together again), *tape editing* is a creative process that is as demanding and rewarding as fine writing. Like a writer attending to grammar, a tape editor must be careful to make clean splices that leave the listener unable to distinguish edited material from unedited material. An editor must also take professional (i.e., ethical) responsibility for content. The power to change someone's comments and leave the listeners with the impression that what they have heard is what the speaker said is awesome and easily abused. A good editor can listen to a passage, understand what is being said and then present the passage in a manner that is most accessible to the listener with the least possible distortion of the sense of the original material.

Sometimes this means leaving a passage of tape intact. Other times a great deal of cutting must be done. I once tagged along with reporter Howard Berkes as he did an interview with a member of the Klamath Indian tribe in southern Oregon. After forty minutes of rambling interview, Howard explained to her that, when the material would air, the woman would be a short portion of a seven minute report. She shook her head and wondered out loud why white people were always in a hurry. Why couldn't they leave things as they were?

I think she's right from her side. Ideally, people should experience events, be they interviews, ceremonies or ordinary activities, in *real time*. But real time is different from *radio time*. When Scott Simon produced his award-winning report for *All Things Considered* on an American Nazis' rally in Chicago, he condensed a six–hour event into 17 minutes. He selected the telling details, not necessarily the obvious ones. He described a warning patients in a nearby hospital received from hospital officials—a warning that prepared the patients for the unusual activity that they might hear but not see later in the day. Using short snippets of

Jonathan "Smokey" Baer first learned to edit tape at WBFO in Buffalo, New York in 1968 when someone came up to him, pointed at a tape on a machine, handed him a razor blade and said, "Here, kid. Put leader on that." He's been editing tape ever since, including six years with All Things Considered. *Smokey is now NPR's Associate Producer in Chicago. He describes his work with a paraphrase of a comment by A. J. Liebling: "I edit tape better than anyone who can edit tape faster, and edit faster than anyone who can edit better."*

tape gathered in the crowd interspersed with well–written, highly–detailed narrative, he built a sense in the listener of what it was like to be at the rally. Just as a painter or photographer carefully selects what to include inside their frame, he constructed a picture of that event. The only way to have become closer to that event would be to have been there for the entire day.

But people don't have entire days to immerse themselves in all the stories and issues pertinent to them. They must rely on media to transmit information to them in short, digestible bits.

Radio time is compressed time. Translating real time to radio time necessarily compresses information. When I worked on a program about the Americans held hostage in Iran, I selected a passage of tape acquired from an American who'd been living in Tehran at the time of the Iranian revolution. He'd recorded his thoughts as he stood on the roof of his apartment building surveying the revolution in progress. The sound of people shouting in the streets can be heard underneath the observer's monologue. This particular segment of tape provided very little practical information, such as economic or religious explanations for the Iranian revolution. What that material did provide was *an environment for the listener,* a context for understanding what was to follow in the program and an emotional experience which they could relate to. It ushered the listener into radio time where intelligence and imagination could be engaged during the "harder" segments which followed.

Imagination is the key to radio time. Radio takes place in the mind of the listener. The humorist Stan Freberg developed a now–famous promotion for a national radio sales convention. When asked the question, "What can radio do that television can't?" he replied that, on radio, he can turn Lake Michigan into the world's largest hot fudge sundae. Then, using a remarkable combination of sound effects and description, Freeberg drains the water from Lake Michigan, fills it with hot fudge, brings in a 500–foot mountain of whipped cream, and has the Royal Canadian Air Force drop a 10–ton maraschino cherry on top, all to the cheers of 25,000 screaming extras. "Try that on television!" is the tag line.

The conventions of radio allow the radio artist's imagination to interact with the listener's; there is a unique understanding between the producer and the listener that is at once both personal and distant. Ideally, the producer is able to share experience with many listeners and yet leave each listener with the sense that they've been communicating with a friend. Achieving this intimate relationship with the listener requires the balancing of a number of interacting choices and is difficult. Tape editing, the selection and arrangement of words and sounds on magnetic tape, goes a long way towards making radio a medium capable of aural magic.

Introduction to Tape Editing

A good way to view tape editing is that it is simply a technique for manipulating audio information—like written words on a page which by "cut and paste" can be excised and rearranged to form shorter paragraphs. It's the same with tape. Words, sounds—even breaths and pauses—all have locations on magnetic tape. A trained editor can mark the location of a sentence, word, or syllable and move or remove it.

An additional difficulty, not faced in print, challenges tape editors: preserving the qualities of speech which linguists call *suprasegmentals,* the cadence and inflection of the voice. This is all audible information you can't see in a transcript but is picked up and processed by the ear and the brain. Just listen to a bad edit. The text makes perfect sense, but your ear knows something is amiss. For example, there may be no breath where the speaker should have taken one. Abrupt changes in ambience can also be disturbing to the listener.

Tape Mechanics

No written guide to tape editing can *show* you how to make an edit. This chapter introduces you to the process. Your understanding of this process (not to mention your safety while working on a professional tape machine) would be best served by a practical demonstration along with some practical experience. Someone with access to a tape machine and knowledge of editing can give you an adequate demonstration in about ten minutes. Then, equipped with a reel of tape to practice edits on, this chapter and a few hours, you'll likely become an adept tape editor.

First, get familiar with the tape you'll be cutting (see Figure 10.1). Audio recording tape is made of plastic. It is ¼ inch wide and quite thin, usually 1.5 mil (.0015 inch) in thickness. Each side of the tape has its own distinct function and appearance. The **backing** provides structure for the tape. It holds the **oxide** which carries the material that actually stores the audio information. The oxide side faces the playback head, which senses the magnetic flux contained in the material on the tape. Sometimes, tape gets a twist in it and the backing side faces the playback head. You recognize this because the sound of the tape is "bassy;" the higher frequencies are absent from the signal. This can be corrected by removing the twist from the tape. In the unlikely event that the entire tape is wound on the reel incorrectly, simply wind it on to another reel, putting a twist in it so the tape rolls up with the backing side facing the outside of the reel. Though the two sides have different appearances, the variety of tapes on the market make it difficult to give an absolute rule for determining which side is which. For Scotch 176, the backing side is shiny brown and the oxide side is dull brown. For Ampex 406, the backing is a dull flat black but the oxide side is a shiny brown. Looking and listening to a tape while it is being recorded will make these differences immediately apparent.

The tape winds onto reels of 5, 7, or 10½ inches in diameter. The largest reels are the easiest to edit with because their hubs have the largest diameter. This makes them easy to rock back and forth. There are two terms that indicate the direction the tape is wound: **heads** and **tails.** A tape that is **heads out** is wound on the reel so that the beginning of the tape is on the outside of the spool of tape. **Tails out** means the end of the material on the tape is on the outside of the spool and the tape must be rewound before it can be played back.

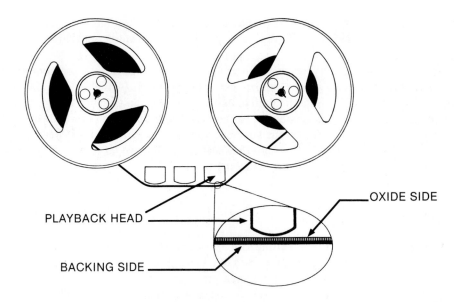

Fig. 10.1. Tape Structure

The tape machine is the device which allows you to record and playback information stored on magnetic tape. It consists of a **transport,** that part of the machine which moves the tape along, and the **electronics,** that part which takes the magnetic energy on the tape and transforms it first into a weak electrical signal and ultimately into mechanical energy that vibrates air and produces sound.

It's important to note here that both the transport and electronics work in tandem to produce sound. If there is no motion of the tape, then no sound will be produced. The first step in making the machine work is to thread the tape machine (see Figure 10.2). The reel of tape (if it is heads out) is placed on the left–hand, or **feed hub.** An empty **take–up reel** is placed on the right–hand hub. The tape is then threaded around the **idler arm** and **reel idler,** past the **tape heads,** between the **capstan** and **pinch roller** and finally around the take-up reel.

When the tape is secured in this fashion, the buttons will operate the machine, *if* the tension arm (which activates an interlock) is in the up position. Sometimes when you press *PLAY,* this arm will drop below the requisite angle and the machine will automatically stop. Be sure that the tape is tautly threaded and that the tape tension switches are correctly set. Professional machines have controls for adjusting the tension on the threaded tape. These controls select tensions for small reels (5 or 7 inches), large reels (10½ inches), or a combination of the two. It is always best to use the same size reels on both the supply and take–up reels. Proper tension settings will insure that the machine moves the tape at proper speed and prevents stretched or broken tape.

REEL

HEAD ASSEMBLY

HUB

TAPE

IDLER WHEEL

PINCH WHEEL

CAPSTAN

TENSION ARM

Fig. 10.2. Tape Path

Besides the tension–select switches, modern professional tape machines have buttons which make the machine play, stop, run at fast–forward, rewind, and operate in the **edit mode.** The functions of the first four buttons are self–explanatory. The edit button puts the machine in the play mode but instead of winding the tape onto the take–up reel, the machine continues to play while the tape spills onto the floor. Essentially, this button disables the take–up reel motor, engages the capstan and pinch roller, and overrides the tension arm switch which normally stops the machine when the arm drops down and the tape starts spilling. This function is a convenience to editors when deleting long portions of tape.

When going from either fast–forward or rewind, many modern machines have an automatic device called **motion sensing.** This slows the tape down before allowing the machine to apply its brakes. Without motion sensing, a sudden stop might break or stretch the tape. Unfortunately, motion sensing occasionally malfunctions. A simple method of preventing this is to operate the machine as if it did not have motion sensing and you have to slow the tape down manually. From high speed in one direction, press the button to send the tape in the opposite (high speed) direction (from *fast forward* to *rewind* or vice versa). Then, as the tape approaches the point at which it stops going in one direction and begins to go in the other, simply press "stop." Some day, this procedure will save a tape for you. Obviously, this technique should *always* be used with machines *not* equipped with motion sensing.

Reproduction of Sound

Once again, reproduction of sound from tape is made possible by motion of the tape past the **playback head.** The playback head is the device which senses the magnetic information stored on the tape. Professional machines have three heads (see Figure 10.3). From left to right, they are the **erase head,** the **record head,** and the **playback head.** For the purpose of this chapter, we need only deal with the playback head.

Again, motion of tape past the playback head is essential to the reproduction of sound, and the speed at which the tape passes the head is crucial. Seven-and-a-half inches per second (ips) is the broadcast standard speed of ¼-inch reel–to–reel tape machines. Other speeds occasionally used are 3¾ ips and 15 ips. The faster the speed, the higher quality the recording and the easier it is to edit. At higher speeds, a given amount of sound is stored across a greater length of tape making it less difficult to find the spaces between words. The drawback of working at 15 ips is that twice as much tape is needed to record the same amount of material, and thus more tape—and more reels—are consumed (at 15 ips, an hour–length program would require two 10½ inch reels, necessitating a reel change during broadcast. For speech, 7½ ips is an economical and convenient speed for recordings. When working with music, where fidelity tolerances are more exacting, it is highly desirable to work at 15 ips.

Finding an Edit Point

Imagine these three sentences are on tape, and you want to remove the middle one:

President Reagan spoke about the energy situation. His manner was grim but optimistic. He indicated there would be no gasoline shortage once the price per gallon reached two dollars.

Assume that between each sentence is a breath and the recording was made in a quiet studio.

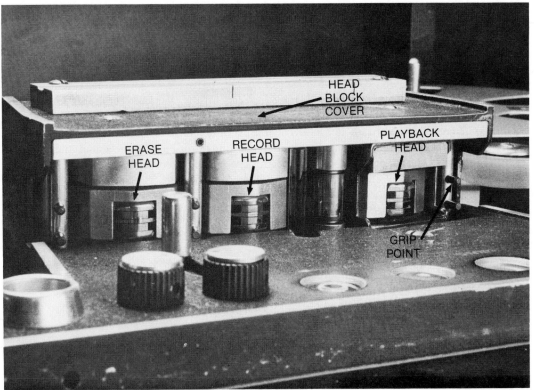

Fig. 10.3. Tape Machine Heads

Every sound you hear played back has a physical location on the tape. Since the tape head is in a sense "reading" the tape, you know that the instant you hear a particular sound, the point at which that sound is located is at that moment passing across the center line of the playback head. If you stopped the machine when the speaker began the second sentence, you probably would have stopped the machine in the midst of the "H" sound in the word "he." This is not the edit point, *yet*. There are two important skills you must develop to determine the exact location of the edit point: **rocking the tape** and **identifying phonetic sounds at low speeds.**

Rocking the tape enables you, in a sense, to take a magnifying glass to the passage you're editing. To do it, place one hand on each reel, then twist both reels first in a counter–clockwise then clockwise direction. This moves a small portion of tape forwards, then backwards past the head. It'll take a while to become comfortable with this motion. Practice it often. First rock the tape slowly and the words will sound like murky sludge. As you speed up the motion, whole words become clear: "situation. His manner . . . ," and then the same words backwards.

This brings us to the second skill: recognizing phonetic sounds at slow speeds (and backwards too). In general, hard consonant sounds (B, D, K, etc.) are the easiest to locate and cut between. Softer sounds, particularly vowels, are often more difficult. There is no simple trick for recognizing phonetic sounds. Experience is the key.

There are some pitfalls to avoid. The most common error is that when rocking the tape, some people become too cautious and intent on finding the sound and they slow the motion down. This results in the sound becoming lower in pitch, less distinct and, if the motion is slowed enough, inaudible. The best motion is one that is quick enough to make the phonetic sounds recognizable and yet slow enough to isolate the sounds. In terms of our example, instead of rocking slowly between the words "situation. His manner . . . ," the best motion would reduce the rocking to the point between the "n" in "situation" and the "hi" of "his." The "h" should then reveal itself as a distinct sound after the breath. Since you've narrowed the possible changes in sound to so few (only between the "n," breath and "h"), the one after the breath must be the "h." It also helps to look at the tape as you're doing this. Perhaps not at first, but eventually, you will sense the relationship between the sound and space on the tape it occupies at a given recording speed (see Figure 10.4).

EDITING CHART

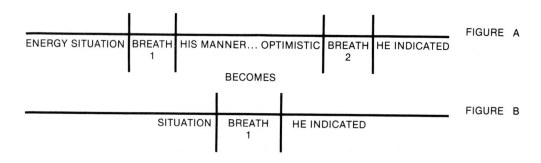

Fig. 10.4. Sample Edit Point

Marking the Tape

Once you've found the edit point, you will want to mark that spot on the backing side of the tape so you may remove the tape from the head and still know where the edit point is. For this, you need a **grease pencil.** This is really a china marker, a type of pencil capable of leaving marks on slick surfaces (Blaisdell 164T or equivalent). They are available at art supply stores. Use only bright colors, white or yellow, so the mark contrasts against the dark tape backing.

To make the mark on the tape, you need only lightly touch the grease pencil to the back of the tape, leaving a small dot, or draw a small line perpendicular to the tape (see Figure 10.5). Don't press too hard. The cumulative effect of pressing hard against the playback head with a grease pencil is substantial and could alter the critical alignment of the head relative to the tape. Pressing hard also leaves excess marker material on the tape which can get on the capstan and the oxide side of the tape as it winds on the reel. Too large a mark will leave a deposit of marker material on the playback head and reduce its high–frequency response, reducing the performance of your machine.

An alternate method of marking the tape dispenses with the grease pencil. It is better for the maintenance of the tape machine but may be slightly less accurate than using a grease pencil. Once the edit point is found, grasp the tape between your thumb and index finger at a point which is a specific distance from the head, the grip point. The edge of the head block is very convenient. Since the distance between your thumb and the edit point will always be constant, you can calibrate your edit block by making a mark on the edit block which is the same distance from the cutting channel as the grip point is from the center of the playback head.

Once you've grasped the tape at the grip point, move it to the edit block being careful not to allow your fingers to slide along the tape. Place the tape in the tape channel, positioning that part of the tape gripped by your fingers at the calibrated mark on the edit block. This should position the edit point in the proper location for cutting.

Making the Edit

Now we examine the edit block in detail, a sort of mitre box for carpenters of tape (see Figure 10.6). The block is a piece of machined metal with a specially designed channel that holds tape in place. Across the channel, at differing angles, are two or three slots which guide a razor blade as you draw it across and through the tape. The edit block was designed many years ago by Joel Tall, a CBS radio engineer during the early years of magnetic tape. Under his license, one manufacturer markets the EDITall, one particular brand of edit block. Mr. Tall's invention makes tape editing a simple, quick process which makes possible all sorts of programming alternatives that might not have existed without it.

Photo by Phoebe Chase Ferguson

Fig. 10.5. Marking the Tape with a Grease Pencil

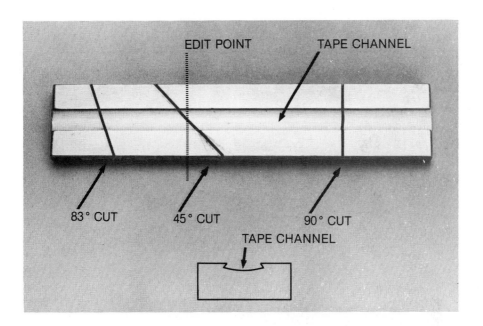

Fig. 10.6. The Edit Block

Looking at a cross-section of the edit block (Figure 10.6), you notice the channel that holds the tape is actually narrower at its top than at its bottom. This allows the block to hold the tape instead of lying there unfastened. To put the tape in this almost clamp–like affair, you place the marked portion on top of the tape channel, backing–side up, and, with one finger, gently press the tape into the channel. Then, sliding your finger along the entire channel, just press the rest of the tape into the channel (see Figure 10.7).

Once the tape is secured in its channel, maneuver the edit point in line with the appropriate cutting channel. If you've used a grease pencil, grasp the tape a few inches from the ends of the edit block, one hand to a side. Keeping the tape level with the plane of the top of the block, an easy tug will move the tape right or left and allow you to position your mark so the cutting channel will be directly underneath. If you don't use a grease pencil, you can grasp the tape between your thumb and forefinger at the right edge of the head block, place it down on top of the tape channel with your thumb at the calibrated mark on the block and press it into the tape channel carefully so you don't move the tape to the right or left. If properly done, the edit point should then be located over the cutting channel.

Edit blocks do wear down. If a tape won't stay secured in the channel, review the procedure for placing it down. If it still won't stay in place, you may need a new block or one of a higher quality.

On most edit blocks you can cut the tape at one of two angles. There is the ordinary cut, made at 45 degrees across the width of the tape. Older blocks also

Fig. 10.7. Placing Tape in the Tape Channel

have a vertical cut, 90 degrees across the tape. You should not use this cut, even for tight cuts where there is little or no space between words. The **bias tone,** which you can't hear but which is recorded along with the audio frequencies, cannot be cut at the 90 degree cut without the risk of leaving an audible click on the tape.

Besides the standard 45 degree cut, newer blocks have a **stereo cut** 83 degrees across the width of the tape. This is provided for cutting tape with two channels of audio information on it (see Figure 10.8). Even if a tape is monaural, it may be **two–track,** meaning audio information is recorded along two strips (upper and lower) of the tape. If the information is identical, the tape is mono. If the information corresponds to right and left sides of a stereo field, the tape is stereo.[1]

The stereo cut is useful when editing two–track tape because it reduces the amount of lag or lead between tracks at the point where the edit hits the playback

1. Occasionally, a tape will have completely different materials on each track, effectively doubling the amount of information that can be recorded on a given reel. Cutting tape with this *half–track* configuration also cuts the other track, at an arbitrary location and is therefore impossible without first dubbing each track onto a separate tape or section of tape.

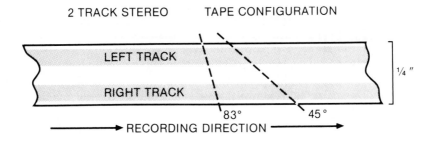

Fig. 10.8. Two-Track Stereo Tape Configuration

head. On a 45 degree angle, the material on the lower track arrives at the head an instant before the material on the upper track. Since each track is usually sent to a discrete speaker, the ear hears one channel of sound ever so slightly before the other channel. If you're working with stereo speakers, a 45 degree edit might seem to move from one speaker to the other. Cutting along the 83 degree angle, however, reduces the lead or lag to the point where the brain can no longer distinguish it.

At this point, with the tape properly placed in the edit block, you can reach for a single–edge razor blade and draw it through the slot provided. It should cut the tape very easily if you hold it at a 45 degree angle to the surface of the tape (see Figure 10.9). Do not try to saw through the tape perpendicular to it. If it binds or doesn't cut cleanly, you may need a new blade.[2] Get one, rather than be faced with having to fit two jagged edges together.

To complete the editing of the sentence we began with, repeat the above process, only making the edit point just before the "he" and after the "optimistic." Notice by making the edit here, you have taken the breath between sentences that naturally precedes the second sentence. As a rule, this should be normal practice when editing sentences or words with breaths in the middle. The reason that the first breath is preferred over the second is that reverberant sound from the end of the previous word carries into the sound of the breath. If you were to select the second breath instead of the first, the reverberant sound from the word "optimistic" (which was cut out of the resulting tape) would follow the word "situation" and the ear would perceive an artificial cut.

The joining of the two sentences into one paragraph on tape is finally accomplished with splicing tape. Like household "Scotch" tape, splicing tape is sticky on one side and slick on the other. It is slightly narrower than its corresponding–width magnetic tape, making it very easy to apply the splicing tape without having it slop over the sides of the magnetic tape. Before placing the splicing tape on, you must bring the two ends of the recording tape together with no space

---

2. Whenever you throw a razor blade out, cover the sharp edge with a piece of masking tape. This protects those who have to empty the wastepaper basket.

Fig. 10.9. Cutting Tape

in between the ends. The bright edit block surface is an aid. When you can no longer see metal between the tape ends, they should be matched up and ready to splice together. Apply the splicing tape centered left–to–right over the splice. (Some people stick the splicing tape on their razor blade and use the blade as a lever for proper positioning; see Figure 10.10).

This can be checked after the splice is made by inspecting the splice on the oxide side of the tape. To be certain the splice is strong, rub your fingernail over the splicing tape until all the air is forced out of the space between the adhesive and the tape backing. You'll know this has happened when the white color of the splicing tape resembles the color of the tape itself (see Figure 10.11). If for any reason the splicing tape should not be aligned with the recording tape and parts of the sticky side spill out over the sides, start again. To pry apart the splice, hold the tape, oxide side up, forming an upside-down "U" with the tape, then rock the tape with your fingers so the apex of the "U" rides back and forth across the cut. This should force one of the edges of the cut to loosen and this will give you enough tape to hold while you pull the splice apart.

Never reuse splicing tape. It's not worth the risk of a splice breaking. If, when reapplied, some adhesive from the first splice remains on the tape, be sure to remove it by rubbing it off with your finger. When wrapped on a reel, the adhesive could wind up on the front side of the tape and gum up your machine.

This, then, is *how* to edit. A far more important question is *what* to edit.

Fig. 10.10. Applying Splicing Tape with a Razor

Fig. 10.11. A Completed Splice

Organizing Tape

Making decisions about what to keep and what not to keep is, by definition, a subjective process. My rule of thumb has always been that you *take the bad stuff out and leave the good stuff in.* This is not as simplistic as it might at first seem. While I'm hesitant to offer any objective criteria regarding what's good and what's bad, I can suggest some methods that will help you decide.

Initial decisions about tape *can* be made at first listening. Don't be afraid to cut the tape for fear of locking yourself into an idea you may want to change. One of the wonderful things about tape editing is that you can always change your mind. The key to avoiding problems is *don't throw out your outtakes,* those sections of tape you think you don't want. You may want to put all those sections that sound interesting to you on a separate reel. This way, when you're done with the first listen, you have one reel for material to keep, another for **outtakes.** The **keeper reel** can then be edited to tighten, rearrange, and simplify the content. If you find you've edited yourself into a corner or left something important out, you still have your **outtake reel** from which to reclaim material.

The outtake reel can also be a great aid during the final editing process. Sometimes you need a pause, breath, or even a sound (like an off–mike telephone ringing) to throw into your tape to make an edit sound right. Consider your outtakes a reservoir of stock room ambience and speech effects (coughs, uhms, ahs, etc.) from which you can draw in order to maintain the natural cadence of a person's voice. You can't necessarily mix outtakes, though. The ambient sound of a certain place is closely related to microphone placement. A person's voice recorded, say, during a tour of a very large room, might change timbre as he or she moves through the room. Taking a breath or a phrase recorded in one part of the room and editing it into a portion of tape recorded in a different location may or may not work. Try it. Your ears are the final judge. If it sounds natural, leave it in. If it doesn't work, take it out and look for another section of tape to help you solve your problem.

An outtake reel is also a defense against the most common error in editing: **upcutting.** An upcut results when you've cut off a bit of the sound or word you intended to keep. "He," for instance, might sound like "e" if you upcut the "H." This is easy to repair, as long as you've kept what you cut out. Simply splice on the original material, find the correct edit point, and resplice the tape. (Little pieces of outtake tape, too small to splice on to an outtake reel, should be retained in or near the splicing block until you are sure that the splice "worked.")

This advice regarding outtakes is not to say you should keep every last bit of tape you remove from your keeper reel. Outtake reels are probably something you'll only want to use if you're working on something quite long and you'll be removing sections of tape which are 30 seconds or often much longer. Once you have your tape pared down, and the bits you're taking out are short sentences and phrases that you're certain you don't want, just toss the material in the garbage.

Frequently, you'll be undecided about a clip of tape. If it's long, put it on the outtake reel. If it's short, you can use masking tape to stick to the wall or some other convenient place, such as the tape recorder top. Be sure to stick the masking tape at the "heads out end" and on the backing side of the tape so no adhesive gets on the oxide side. You can label the clip on the masking tape.

Another way of dealing with tape on your first listen is just to take notes. Logging the tape is a more time–consuming approach, though for some people it may shorten the effort in the long run. A good way to log the tape is to index it relative to its running time. With a watch started when you begin playing back the uncut tape, you note particular phrases, questions, or ideas along with the relative time into the tape at which they occur. This requires you to either *not* stop the tape and watch once they've begun or, if you must pause while listening, stop both, then restart the two simultaneously. Some recent machines, such as those made by Studer, Ampex, or MCI, are equipped with electronic counters which measure the elapsed time of a tape from any point at which the counter is zeroed.[3] Since these devices keep track of the elapsed time of a tape, even in high speed going forwards or backwards, they are a great aid to logging your tape and later retrieving the material you want. Just remember, the counter must be reset to zero precisely at the beginning of each new reel, which is best denoted by leader tape. When you're done, you have a rough outline of the tape. Using the log of your tape, it should be easy to pick out, locate and order the segments of tape you want on your keeper reel. This leaves all your accumulated outtakes on the original reel. Which method you choose depends on the amount of time and patience you have, and is ultimately a matter of personal style.

There are times when an edit cannot be made with a razor blade because of an ambient discontinuity between two passages you want to put together. Your ear will alert you to these cases. It may be a worthwhile edit to make anyway, if the program material is vital enough to override audio–esthetic considerations. **Content always takes priority over form.**

Simple dub–editing techniques, using two tape recorders and a mixer, can help you make this more difficult edit. Using one machine to playback and the other to record at unity gain (see Chapter 11, "Studio Production"), play the first passage and at the point you want the sentence to end, quickly fade down the tape. Stop the record machine. Cue up the next passage of tape and record it. Now edit the two dubbed sections together in rhythm. The dub-edit can now be spliced into the tape from which it was made. This scenario assumes the first

3. Some older machines, especially those made by Ampex or Scully, can be equipped with an accessory, mechanical elapsed–time counter made by Lyrec (Denmark) and distributed by Gotham Audio Corporation of New York. They cost about $500 and will pay for themselves in the production time they save.

passage has a quiet background. If the situation is reversed, or if both passages are noisy, you can fade up on the second passage or fade down the first and fade up on the second.

Fine Editing

Not enough can be said about the value of maintaining the pace and cadence of a speaker. This does not mean that everybody on the radio should speak flawlessly. On the contrary, they should speak *characteristically*. The editor should be sensitive to a speaker's speech pattern and work to preserve it, despite editing. Listen to where a speaker pauses, how often they say "ahh." Do they run on their sentences? Are they given to multiple metaphors? Taking advantage of a speaker's traits can help you hide an edit. A well placed "um" can make a shift in conversation seem absolutely normal. If the interviewee tends to jump around conceptually in real time, you can use that to your advantage when editing real time to radio time. If the speaker builds arguments with tight logic, then the editing must reflect that. You can't leap to a conclusion after cutting out the keystone of the person's argument. The most important thing to remember is *let your ears be the judge*. Experiment until the tape sounds right. Your worst enemy is boredom. Tape is a lot of fun to work with, so don't let yourself become bored. Use your imagination to find the answers to editing problems.

Special Effects

Tape editing does not end with interviews and reports. You can edit music, sound effects and background sounds. Creative editing can produce an abstract whole from diverse sounds and words. Once you become facile at editing, you'll probably start to play games with it. For a lark, splice together coughs, um's, ahh's. Cut together in rapid succession people's responses to a single stimulus— like an audio pie–in–the–face. Create a narrative by cutting together a series of sounds. When you can edit tape well, you can arrange time in ways to suit your fancy—within the constraints of journalistic ethics.

Music editing is probably the most exacting kind of editing. To shorten a song or lengthen it to fit your production needs is difficult to do without leaving an audible sign that you've been there. The key is staying with the beat. Like speech, every song has a rhythm. This rhythm cannot be violated. The best way to follow the beat is to concentrate on the drum track of a song (for pop music). You can usually hear the downbeat and drums provide sharp, clear edit points. The problem, of course, is that other instruments are playing at the same time, often overlapping the beat you can cut. Sometimes you can just concentrate and hear the drum. Other times you may have to follow a different instrument. The piano is a good one. Editing music is so complex my best advice is to record some music onto tape and practice. Your ears are the best guide.

Tape loops are endless circles of tape. You can take a sound, music, or even a sentence, splice the ends of the passage together so you have a loop, and play it, round and round, continuously. The section of tape must be long enough to fit around the head assembly, but once threaded around the heads and between the capstan and the pinch wheel, all you have to do is keep tension on it so it is tight and flat against the playback head. This can be done by holding the tape outstretched but in the same plane as the tape deck, with a pencil.

Loops are particularly useful in lengthening background sounds for mixing under interviews. If you need the sound of an outdoor scene under a conversation that lasts three minutes, 20 seconds of outdoor sounds can be looped to make do. The danger resides in any identifiable sound that may occur in that 20–second passage. It will repeat six times in three minutes and even though it is under other material, it will be noticed. The best ambience loops are made from something nondescript. Music loops, on the other hand, can take a particularly catchy four–measure phrase and transform it into a rhythm bed for something you want to lay on top of it. You have another option: recording the section to be repeated as many times as desired, then rejoining that tape to the rest of the song. This way you can make instrumental segments large enough to drop additional material into, and still keep intact the complete song you've looped from. (See Chapter 11, "Studio Production," for more on tape loops.)

Housekeeping

Leader Tape

Leader tape is used for visual identification of sections of a reel of tape, such as the head, tail, or internal sections. Leader tape has no oxide, and thus cannot be recorded on. It is manufactured in several colors (e.g., white, yellow and red), or in white and colored stripes. Each production facility has its own convention for the meaning, if any, of the different colors. One common convention:

Color of Leader	Denotes
White	head end of reel; or internal tape segment
Red	tail end of reel
White with red stripes	head end of stereo reel

NPR stores tape tails out (even temporarily), and uses white head leader, no tail leader, and narrow red adhesive tape to attach the tail end of a reel to one outside face of the reel. The possibilities are endless. Establish whatever conventions you need and stick to them. *Note:* Most leader will bring to a stop machines that use photoelectric end–of–reel/broken tape sensors. This effect can either be used advantageously during editing, or can lead to disaster during broadcast (the tape will stop somewhere in the middle).

Reusing Tape and Reels

It is best to use only virgin tape and new reels when recording. Obviously, many stations and independent producers cannot afford to do this and must reuse tape from outtakes or recorded programs. There are several pitfalls to this practice that should be avoided:

- *improper splices:* will cause **dropouts** (lost instants of sound) when recorded over;
- *sticky splices:* with time, the "stickum" from most splicing tape will bleed onto one layer above, causing the tape to stick to a capstan or guide, or to the next layer of tape on the reel; the resulting "burble" will be perceived as a low "wow" in the speech or music; it will be most objectionable to the listener;
- *hidden internal leader:* if short lengths of leader tape are buried within a reel of used tape, nothing will be recorded on them as they pass the record head; possibly crucial information will be lost as a result; long lengths of leader tape are visible looking through one of the flat sides of a transparent reel;
- *bent or cracked reels:* metal reels can be bent out of "true;" plastic reels often crack. Don't use either—you may lose an entire reel of tape in rewind or fast–forward mode. Tape may also get momentarily stuck in a crack in a reel and also "burble" as it passes the record head.

Storage of Tape

Completed programs designated for medium to long–term retention should always be stored "tails out," uniformly wound onto reels or hubs (see below) under controlled conditions of temperature and humidity. Most machines cannot produce uniform winds at fast-wind speeds. See tape manufacturer's literature for further information.

Hubs

A **hub** is the plastic center of a 10½ inch metal reel. In some facilities, tape is handled without use of a feed or take–up reel, or both. Rather, the tape is tightly wound onto the hub, usually with one side of a metal reel (called a platten) underneath to guide the wind. Tapes wound onto hubs are sometimes called **pancakes.** *Never* rewind or fast–forward *onto* a hub—your tape will likely end up all over the room. Virgin tape is often ordered on hubs by large studios, who often buy reels and boxes separately (a reel and a box are not needed for every consumed reel of raw tape).

Added Considerations of Editing Tape

Once the mechanical skills of editing tape become second nature to you, editorial concerns will blend in with the technical process. Some people mistake the preference for smooth editing as a clear preference for style, or form, over content. What should be clear is that at the level of editing, the two are the same. When making editing decisions, you are the sole arbiter of how someone's comments are going to be presented. The act of editing is balancing style and content. It is not an either/or question.

By editing tape, you can control a person's ability to express themselves to others. This is a heady responsibility. Within the constraints of working with what's given you, there is still a lot of leeway for determining what somebody means to say, what needs to be said, and what remains to be said. I believe editors must be certain that their work does not distort the intended thought of the speaker. *Don't* edit a tape to turn it into something you think the speaker *should* have said. You should aim to make it into something they *would* have said. The highest compliment a tape editor can receive is to have someone hear themselves on a highly edited tape, and turn to the editor and say, "I thought you were going to edit this." Occasionally, this does happen.

‖ 11 ‖
Studio Production
by Skip Pizzi

Introduction

A good radio producer must first be a good radio listener. The craft of producing for the radio must always have as its primary purpose communication to the listener. Production techniques we will look at here are merely tools used to enhance that communication.

Radio production can be better understood when compared to another art form—wood sculpture, for instance. First, a piece of wood must be found; this compares to the gathering of raw materials for the radio production (field or studio recording). Next, the most desirable part of the wood must be selected and the rest discarded; this, of course, is similar to the editing process. Finally, the artist's technique is applied to the selected wood, and it is shaped and reshaped through the use of tools until the artist is satisfied that the wood reflects the desired artistic concept; the analogous procedures and tools in the art of radio production are the subjects of this chapter. Their purpose is to put the already gathered and selected pieces of sound together in a manner that will aid in the communication of ideas to the listener.

A couple of caveats before we begin: artistic techniques can be discussed here, but the essence of "radiophonic art" cannot be taught. The true art comes from within you, the producer, adapting and developing these skills and others to make good radio. And, finally, most importantly, be aware that radio production is purely a means to an end. Even the most experienced radio producer can fall prey to the temptation of having production *form* overwhelm *content,* which serves only to defeat the purpose of production: enhancing the presentation of information and entertainment to the listeners.

Skip Pizzi is Training Coordinator in the Technical Production Unit of NPR's Engineering Department. He started working in broadcasting and recording in 1972 as a volunteer at WGTB-FM at Georgetown University. Receiving a B. A. from there in 1975, he went on to work in music and theater performance, concert production, record and hi-fi sales, commercial radio (as a disc jockey), announcing, radio and recording studio engineering, and theater tech before joining NPR in 1977 as a broadcast recording technician. Skip now serves as both a trainer and consultant on radio production and music recording for NPR staff, member station personnel and independent producers nationwide.

The Elements of Radio Production

All basic radio production can be separated into four categories:

1. **Level (or "Loudness") Control**
2. **Mixing**
3. **Transition**
4. **Timing**

On a conceptual level, these four areas are the tools through which the desired effect can be presented to the listener. Later in this chapter we will discuss the actual nuts-and-bolts production processes and ways to apply them.

Level or "Loudness" Control

All art is appreciated by human beings through one (or more) of our senses; all artists should know something about the workings of the senses through which their work will be appreciated. So, discussion of a few things about the human ear is in order, especially in the area of the *perceived loudness* of sound.

The Perception of Loudness: The ear is quite a complicated and amazing instrument. Its parameters of "sound sensing" are far more advanced than the best of our sound recording and reproducing equipment, and this will probably always be true. We are constantly challenged to fulfill this hungry sense with interesting sounds.

Handicapping us right from the start is the fact that we may begin with real, live sounds; what the listener finally hears are approximations of those sounds. Most of the sounds go through a replication process a number of times before they finally reach the listener's ear. Each step in that process degrades the sound. These steps include recording, playback, and rerecording (sometimes several times), and final playback by the listener (see Figure 11.1). It is crucial, therefore, that the highest quality equipment available be used in each step in order to minimize the degradation of the sound. (We will discuss later on ways of reducing the number of steps as well.) Unfortunately, the greatest degradation usually takes place in the last step—in the equipment of the listener, over which we have no control. Nevertheless, with any equipment, the better it sounds going in, the better it will sound coming out. Today's consumer equipment standards are constantly improving, which provides yet another challenge for us to preserve the integrity of the original sound. With these things in mind, let's go back to the ear, and the way it determines the loudness of sound.

There are several factors involved here. First, look at an oscillograph of a sound (Figure 11.2A). This is a graphic representation of the electrical impulses produced by a microphone responding to sound waves. Note in this example that the peaks or highest electrical values occur at the oscillograph line marked +10. Figure 11.2B is an oscillograph of another sound; the maximum values also reach +10, but note that more of the other (non-maximum) electrical impulses' peaks come closer to +10 than those in Figure A. What this means is that the *average*

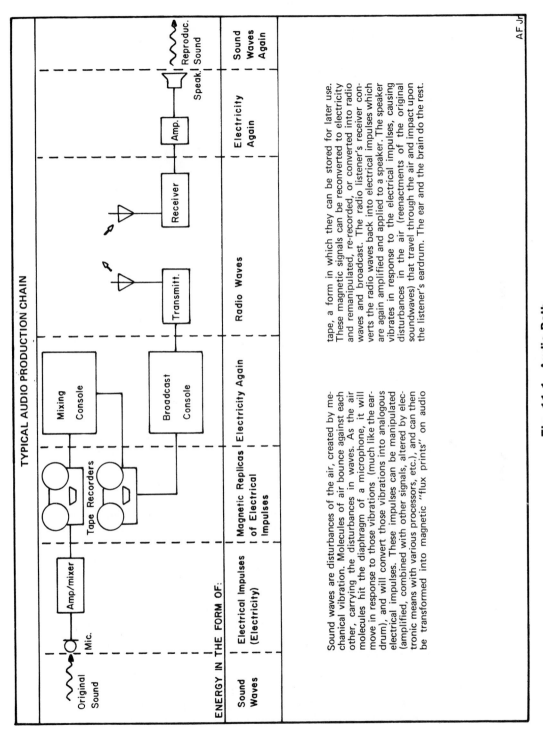

Fig. 11.1. Audio Path.

AF Jr

143

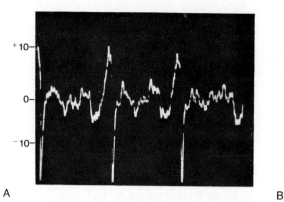

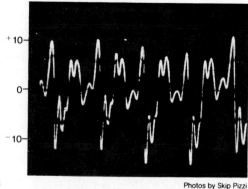

A   B

Fig. 11.2. *Oscillographs*. *A:* Oscillograph of a sound whose maximum peak energy reaches the value arbitrarily called +10. *B:* Oscillograph of another sound whose maximum peak energy reaches +10, but whose *average* intensity is higher than that of the sound pictured in A. In most cases, the sound depicted by oscillograph B will be considered *louder* by the human ear.

level of Figure B is higher than Figure A, since higher valued peaks occur *more often* in B. The ear translates this as Figure B's voice sounding louder than the voice in Figure A, even though their maximum electrical values are equal. This is the heart of the concept of "subjective loudness," or the ear's quantitative judgment of sound intensity.

Spectral Density: Another important factor is known as the **spectral density** of sound. Sounds as they occur in nature are combinations of **fundamentals** and **harmonics.** The fundamental is the lowest and loudest frequency component of a sound. Harmonics are multiples of the fundamental frequency, and occur at lower levels than the fundamentals. For example, a given piano note has a fundamental frequency of 440 Hertz (Hz) or cycles per second, meaning that the piano strings for that note vibrate 440 times each second. Secondary vibrations occur on those strings at 880 Hz (440 × 2), 1320 Hz (440 × 3), 1760 Hz (440 × 4), 2200 Hz (440 × 5), and so on. The number of these harmonics that occur, and their respective intensities, determine the **timbre** or tonality of the sound, while the sound's **pitch** will be determined primarily by its fundamental frequency. The harmonic or spectral density of the sound is the amount of harmonic energy that the sound contains. The loudness of a sound is also affected by its spectral density. The higher the spectral density (i.e., the more harmonics contained in the sound), the louder the sound will seem to the ear. Meters or other level sensing devices are not sensitive to this effect. A flute (which has relatively few harmonics) and a violin (which has many) recorded at the same "level" on a tape recorder's meters will have different loudnesses. The violin will sound significantly louder, due to its higher spectral density.

The only way to determine how loud the listener will think a certain sound is, is to listen to the sound yourself. We will encounter various meters and other level sensing devices, but none of them are able to truly judge subjective loudness as accurately or as simply as the ear itself. One of the cardinal rules of radio production, therefore, is *to accustom your ear to a particular volume in your monitor speakers or headphones, and leave the volume there for the duration of your production session.* The listener will not want to make frequent adjustments in the listening level, so the producer should listen at one constant and comfortable level and adjust the levels of the production's contents to please his or her ear at that listening level. This will ensure a consistent overall listening level for the program. When a voice is followed by music, or even by another voice, care must be taken to match the subjective loudness of the two elements, avoiding a sudden jump or drop in the apparent level. The listener's attention can be lost by abrupt changes in loudness. Often when program level variations would cause listeners to adjust their volume controls, they will adjust the tuning knob to another station instead.

Monitor Volume: Not only is it important to keep the monitoring level constant, but the absolute volume at which the producer listens is critical. Another phenomenon of human hearing is at work here. Many studies have shown that the ear's sensitivity to sounds of different frequencies is not the same at different frequencies. In other words, at a given volume the ear usually cannot hear bass or high treble sounds as well as it hears "midrange" (voice range) sounds. In addition, that frequency sensitivity changes with the volume of the sound; the louder a sound is, the better the ear hears the low (or bass) frequencies of that sound, and vice versa. For example, if you are listening at a very loud level when producing a radio piece, you may think there is too much bass content present, whereas to the audience, listening at a moderate level, the bass content will be normal.

The loudness button on some hi–fi equipment is designed to compensate for this effect; when it is turned on, more bass is automatically applied as the volume knob is turned down.

There is, of course, more to the ear's appraisal of loudness than the items just mentioned, but these are the major areas of concern for radio producers.

Loudness as a Production Tool: There are situations where a change of loudness is desired to achieve a certain effect. An example we have all encountered occurs when the musical portion of a radio, TV, or film soundtrack swells suddenly to heighten the emotional impact of a scene. The same scene might fall flat without that music loudness change. Another occasion is when an element of surprise is desired. Here, an abrupt loudness change can provide an attention–riveting shock. But these are special cases; unless such an effect is desired, a program's loudness must remain comfortable and consistent.

The control of the loudness of sounds in radio production is, therefore, both a useful artistic tool and a prerequisite to production of a piece that will attract and hold a listener. *But no meter will tell you how loud something really is. You must use your ears.*

Mixing

Radio production can be thought of as a *dynamic artform,* meaning that it exists not as an object in space (like sculpture), but as an event in time. In this respect it is akin to music, which also exists in the temporal, rather than the spatial, dimension.

In fact, radio production is really a diverse craft, bringing together parts of the disciplines of literature, music, speech, and theatre, blended with an aural artistry peculiar to itself. And it is a highly technical artform, requiring a good deal of hardware and skill of operation. Mixing, and the remaining two areas of production, **transition** and **timing,** all bear heavily on this dynamic form of expression.

Mixing as a Tool: The power of the concept of sound mixing in radio production is enormous. Two or more events recorded at separate times and/or separate places can be presented to the listener simultaneously. Things that happened independently can be brought together to provoke thought. Contrasts or similarities can be markedly illustrated. Ideas can be emphasized or paraphrased. Vast distances or gaps of time between two events can magically disappear. The possibilities for manipulation and juxtaposition of time are literally endless. *[However, journalistic ethics limit the amount and kinds of manipulation permissible in news radio; you may not use these techniques to create a reality which never existed.—Ed.]*

In addition, the relative loudness or levels of the sounds that are mixed can be varied so that one is louder than the other(s). This lends emphasis to the louder sound, of course, but the various levels can be continuously adjusted to shift the listener's primary focus from one element to another, while keeping the other sounds in close aural proximity. Moreover, this can be done in a discreet way so that the listener is not distracted by the mixing effect itself, but is engaged by the content.

Another effect of mixing (one most people are familiar with) is its use in the addition of music and sound effects to the spoken word for dramatic or comedic effect. These effects, usually mixed in at a lower level relative to the voices, can add immense reality and listenability to otherwise dry readings. Much of the success of the so–called "Golden Age of Radio" can be attributed to the early mastery of this technique, to the stimulation of listeners' imaginations. Suspense, humor, pathos and other emotions can be evoked with even a minimal use of these effects, along with a great deal of believability. In some sophisticated productions, literally dozens of **effects tracks** will be mixed in at different levels in a layering technique to create surreal or convincing radio tableaux. And in non–dramatic productions, effects can add to the understanding or involvement of the listener. Obviously, then, mixing is a key element in radio production.

Transition

The popularity of amusement parks and their thrill rides attests to the fact that people enjoy being transported in thrilling and surprising ways. Successful radio production takes this into account when it transports the listener from place to place or idea to idea with transitions in sound. We will examine some specific techniques for performing these transitions. Bear in mind, however, that *where* the transition occurs in any production is as important as the transition itself. Care must be taken to ensure that the listener isn't left in any one place too long.

On a more basic level, transitions are instrumental to the proper presentation of complex ideas on the radio. An orderly sequence of different sounds can aid in the comprehension and the attention span of the listener. The importance of certain ideas can be stressed by transition from one sound to a reinforcing one, avoiding any overt repetition. An example is the common news reporting technique of an announcer's description of an event followed by an eyewitness account. In this case, the transition should be simple and abrupt. In more involved production, transitions may be slower or more complex.

Timing

Closely related to transition is the element of timing. As tempo is to music, timing is to radio production. The overall length of a radio production should be appropriate to the subject. *A good rule of thumb: when in doubt, make it shorter, or faster.*

Creative use of timing allows for the reordering or telescoping of events to better present them to the listener. Again, ideas can be reinforced by the properly timed intertwining of sounds. Listenability is greatly enhanced by a good sense of timing in production. Usually the listener is only subconsciously aware that the element of timing is influencing their interest in a program. This is as it should be, since any overt notice of technique means that form has overtaken content, the scourge of any artform. In longer or highly produced programs, production techniques can be used to establish a *motif*. An effect can be introduced gently and subtly intensified or enhanced as the program continues. The first occurrence of the effect should serve not to shock, but to entice, the listener. Subsequent occurrences can employ more radical treatments, and build to a climax, as a good work of fiction does.

Finally, the overall pacing of a radio production must be *consistent* as well as appropriate to the subject matter. The flow of ideas must come at a rate that the listener can feel comfortable with; once established, it should not be disturbed. A balance must be struck between the boredom threshold and the sensory overload point of the listener.

Production Techniques

The real workplace for radio production is the production studio. The specific equipment and functions of a studio are not standardized. In fact, there are probably no two production studios exactly alike. So the producer must be able to tailor the production to the studio's capabilities. To a good producer, changing studios is no more difficult than changing cars, if the studio is adequately equipped and in good working order.

Another variable involves who actually operates the equipment: in many studios, the producer does everything—both the mental and the manual work. This is usually referred to as **combo** operation. In some studios, an engineer operates the equipment according to the producer's instructions. In either case, the producer must understand the basic workings of the studio to perform or explain the procedures necessary to accomplish the production. We will explore both the **combo** and **separate engineer** situations, but the concepts and production designs are the same in either case.

Preparation for Production

The first step in any radio production is preparation for the studio. Studio time is extremely valuable; preparation can literally save more studio time than any other production technique or short-cut. In most cases, the producer should have clearly in mind the exact nature and order of the work to be done (and, especially in the combo situation, exactly *how* to do it) before entering the studio. This includes a prepared script and prepared sound sources, already edited (and leadered, if on tape), in the proper order, and if necessary, timed. The production should be planned to be done in the simplest possible way, not just for efficiency in the studio, but because that usually results in the most effective production. Nevertheless, some production sessions can be rather involved, so it's often worthwhile to work out a plan on paper beforehand, exploring various options and making decisions. The final work plan or **production script** should come with you into the studio. (See Appendix C, "Sample Production Script/Plan.")

One of those decisions to be made before entering the studio is whether the piece will be **mixed** or **cut-together.** The latter is a quick and simple method of putting uncomplicated radio pieces together by splicing the elements together. If this is to be done, the subjective loudness of all the elements must be nearly equal, to avoid objectionable level jumps from occurring at the splices.

If the piece is to be **mixed,** all the elements will be run through the console and rerecorded, so matching of their *original* levels is not as critical. The criteria for this decision is usually determined by the complexity of the production and the time available to do it. In the case of a news spot, an announcer reads a script, followed by a piece of tape from an interviewer or on–location recording (an *actuality*), after which the announcer reads a conclusion. This piece could be cut together, if the actuality has been properly recorded. **Cutting-in** requires both less time and less equipment. If, however, the producer wanted a **sound bed** underneath the entire spot, using sound recorded at the scene, the spot would have to be mixed together.

It is important to assess the capabilities of your particular studio and what is feasible in it before beginning production. The number of sound sources (playback machines) available at any one time is one important consideration. (See Appendix B, "Assessing the Studio.")

Setting Up the Studio

Assuming all preparations have been made, the first step upon entering should always be to set up the studio. This includes cleaning all tape recorder heads, capstans, pinch rollers, tape guides, and other parts of the tape path (see Figure 10.2). Next, tape machines must be **lined up** to the console. This means that a "0 VU" reading on the console meter must show up as a "0 VU" reading on all tape machines' meters (see Figure 11.3). To accomplish this, an **oscillator** is required. The oscillator produces an electrical signal at a steady frequency (or pitch) and at a constant level. Both of these parameters can be controlled by the studio operator. A frequency somewhere in the center of the audio range is selected, usually 1000 Hz (cycles per second) also called 1 kilohertz (1 kHz), although anywhere from 400 to 2000 Hz can be used. The output of the oscillator is sent into the console (on some consoles it is a built–in feature), where it is adjusted to make the console meter(s) read "0 VU." Then each tape machine's monitor switch is set to *SOURCE* or *INPUT* or *REC* (depending on the brand of tape recorder). The input level, or record level (or "gain") is then adjusted so that the tape machine's meter reads "0 VU." (If the tape machine is two–track or mul-

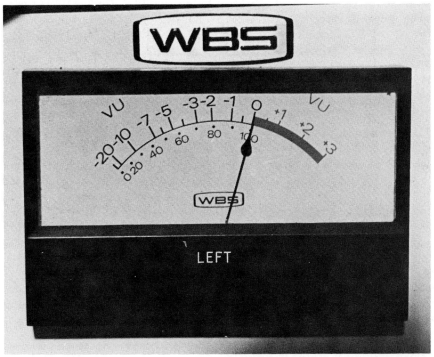

Fig. 11.3. *0 VU Meter Reading.* A "0VU" reading on the standard VU ("volume unit") meter. Note that the scale above the line is calibrated in db (decibels) above or below "0" or "reference level," and the scale below the line is calibrated in percentage of modulation for broadcast transmitters. "0 VU" equals 100% modulation.

titrack, these procedures should be followed for each channel.) The tape machine is now *lined up* to the console. This process should be performed on all tape machines in the studio that are hooked up to record from the console. Now, the operator need only observe good level on the console VU meter, and can be assured that the same level will be observed on the tape machines recording audio from the console.

Unity Gain

Next, the producer should set the output of the tape machine in the calibrate position (*CAL* or *SRL*). (For machines without a calibrate function, see Appendix D.) With the oscillator still sending a "0 VU" level, record a minute or so of the tone from the oscillator onto blank tape *of the type the machine is set up for.*[1] Record at the tape speed that will be used in the production. Professional broadcasters in the U.S. use 7.5 inches per second (19 centimeters per second) for most voice recording and 15 ips (38 cm/s) for music. As the tone is being recorded, change the monitor switch to respond to signals coming off of the tape (*TAPE* or *PB*). This will not affect the recording, but only changes the point to which the meter and output are connected. When the switch is made, the meter should remain at "0 VU," or at least stay between –1 VU and +1 VU. If the meter moves by more than this when switching from *SOURCE* to *TAPE,* or *INPUT* to *PB,* etc., and the output is in the calibrate position while recording a mid-frequency (1 kHz) tone, then the tape machine is improperly set up or malfunctioning, and authorized service personnel should be notified to correct the problem. If the meter does not stray excessively from "0 VU" after switching to *PB* or *TAPE,* the *RECORD GAIN* or *INPUT LEVEL* should now be adjusted slightly to return the meter to exactly "0 VU." Any adjustment of the knob will take a half–second or so to show up on the meter, since the knob you are adjusting is changing the level going *on* to the tape via the record head, but what you are watching on the meter is coming *off* the tape from the playback head (see Figure 11.4). The delayed reaction is caused by the time it takes for any point on the tape to travel from the record head to the playback head. (This phenomenon also provides for some interesting special effects—see Appendix G.)

Now you have recorded a bit of **0 level tone.** This should be done on each tape machine, and the tapes should be rewound to the beginning of the tone. The oscillator should now be switched off, or disconnected from the console. Next, play back a tone tape on one of the tape machines. The tape machine meter(s) should read "0 VU." The console fader (also known as a **pot,** short for potentiometer) that the tape machine is playing back through should now be adjusted

---

[1]When a tape machine is "set up" (performed by an electronics engineer or maintenance technician, and checked frequently), its *playback* electronics are adjusted to an industry–standardized test tape. Then, any tape will play back properly on this machine. Next, the technician records tones from an oscillator on to blank tape, and adjusts the *recording* functions of the machine to adhere to the same standard. These adjustments will only be proper on the type of tape being recorded on when the adjustments are made. Therefore, that is the *only* kind of tape that should be used for *recording* on that machine, but any kind of tape can be played back with proper fidelity.

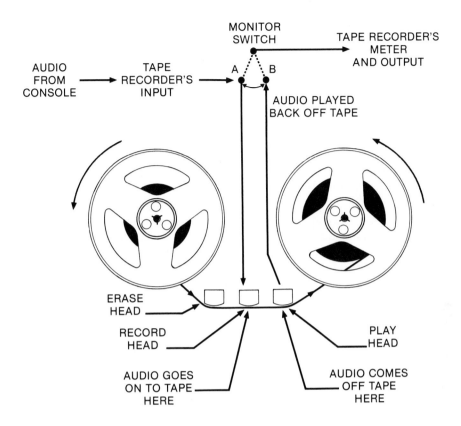

MONITOR
SWITCH

TAPE RECORDER'S
METER
AND OUTPUT

AUDIO
FROM
CONSOLE

TAPE
RECORDER'S
INPUT

A   B

AUDIO PLAYED
BACK OFF TAPE

ERASE
HEAD

RECORD
HEAD

PLAY
HEAD

AUDIO GOES
ON TO TAPE
HERE

AUDIO COMES
OFF TAPE
HERE

Fig. 11.4. *Tape Monitor Switch Position:* The monitor switch selects the point at which audio is sampled and sent to the meter and output. In position *A,* meter and output get audio as it comes from the console. In position *B,* meter and output get audio as it comes *off the tape.* For playing back a tape, monitor must be in position *B.* For recording, switch can be in either position. Position *A* is called SOURCE, INPUT or REC on different tape machines; Position *B* is called TAPE or PB.

until the console meter once more reads "0 VU." This process should be performed on each machine in turn, and each fader marked in some way at the point at which the "0 VU" tone tape makes the console meter read "0 VU." A wax pencil, magic marker on white masking tape, colored adhesive tape or any other non–defacing mark on the console will allow you to reset the fader to the same point at any time. When the fader is set to this mark (at which a "0 VU" level on the tape machine meter causes a "0 VU" level on the console meter), the condition called **unity gain** exists. Nothing is added or subtracted from the level of the signal as it travels from one tape machine to another, through the console. Hence, we use the term **"unity,"** which in mathematical terminology means "multiplied by a factor of one," i.e., equivalence. By the way, the unity gain point should fall between 12 o'clock and 3 o'clock on rotary faders, and around the −10 mark on linear faders (see Figure 11.5). If this is not the case, the console is not set up properly, and requires adjustment by electronics maintenance personnel.

POT

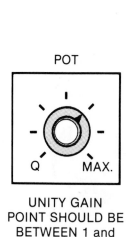

UNITY GAIN
POINT SHOULD BE
BETWEEN 1 and
3 O'CLOCK

FADER

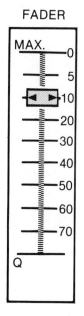

UNITY GAIN POINT
SHOULD BE AT 10 to 15 MARK
(10 to 15 dB BELOW MAX.
GAIN AVAILABLE.)

Fig. 11.5. *Unity Gain Point on Pots and Faders:* The unity gain points are shown in their appropriate positions for rotary pots or linear faders.

The preceding set up procedures may seem rather complex in this written form, but after performing them a few times, they become routine. Here is a brief review of the set up procedures:

1. Using an oscillator, set console meter to "0 VU" with approximately 1 kHz tone.
2. Set tape monitor switches to *SOURCE* or *INPUT,* and adjust record levels to "0 VU" on tape machine's meters.
3. Place tape machine's outputs in *CAL* position.
4. Record about 60 seconds of tone onto blank tape of proper type.
5. Change monitor switches to *TAPE* or *PB,* and readjust record gain to "0 VU" on meters if necessary.
6. Turn off oscillator, and rewind tapes.
7. Playback each tape, setting each console fader for "0 VU" on console meter.
8. Mark console at each fader where "0 VU" point occurs.

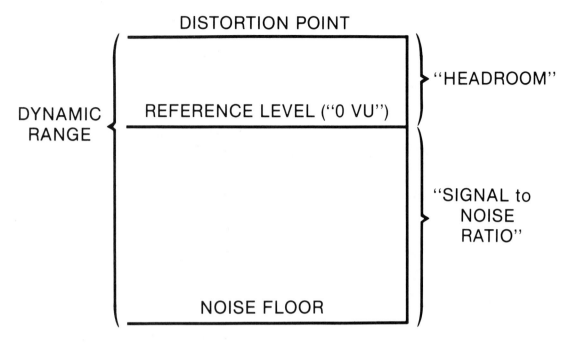

Fig. 11.6. *Dynamic Range Chart:* This is a conceptual diagram of the limitations in volume extremes inherent in all audio systems. Too high a level causes distortion, too low a level causes the audio to be masked by system noise. A happy medium or "reference level" is selected, which has both sufficient "headroom" (15–20 db) between reference level and distortion, and sufficient signal-to-noise ratio (60 db or more) between reference level and the system noise level or "noise floor."

Not only do these procedures provide great operational conveniences, to be discussed shortly, but they insure that optimum fidelity will be obtained, since all systems are arranged to be operating at what is known as **design center.** Due to the limited dynamic range of even the best equipment, compromises must be made to incorporate natural sound into electronic circuitry with a minimum of audio quality loss (see Figure 11.6).

Preparing to Mix

Once the set up is complete, the next step should be the dubbing of any material from disc onto tape. This procedure not only saves time during retakes but saves records as well. Repeated plays of the same section of a disc in a short period of time will cause serious and irreparable damage to the record surface. This is especially disturbing on sound effects records, where the dramatic impact of a sound effect is seriously compromised by the easily recognizable clicks and pops of record surface noise. A thorough cleaning of the record is imperative before dubbing it. When dubbing the disc, make sure the level going to tape is optimum—that is, peaking the VU meter between −3 and 0 VU. (If your console is equipped with peak reading meters instead of or in addition to VU meters, see Appendix E.)

Now, the various elements should be placed on the tape machines or cart machines, according to your production plan. A **cart** or cartridge machine is a tape deck that uses tape contained in a plastic cartridge, similar to the commercial 8–track cartridge. The tape is wound into a continuous loop inside the cartridge. The major advantage of the cart is its ability to "recue" itself, by means of an inaudible tone put on the cart when it is recorded. If any carts need to be recorded, they should be done at this time. Carts are especially useful for inserting sound effects. A wide assortment of them can be kept on hand, and dropped into a mix quickly and conveniently, since they do not require cueing or threading, and have a fast start–up.

There are disadvantages to carts, however. Their wow and flutter (speed variations) can be quite audible, especially on music. Their noise and distortion performance is usually inferior to reel–to–reel recording, and their high–frequency response is often deficient as well. (In stereo work, an even greater problem is created by tape–skewing, an up–and–down motion of the tape as it passes the heads. The resulting variation in tape–to–head contact can cause phase cancellation of the high frequencies for the mono listener. See Appendix I).

Recording Voices

Voice tracks should be precisely recorded, edited and leadered for complex productions. For simple sessions in combo operations, you may be able to record your voice tracks live as you produce your piece. In the separate engineer situation, the producer gives the engineer in the control room tape elements with a script to follow, then goes into the studio to read the voice tracks. (By the way, the term "studio" is often used here to denote both the control room and the studio *per se*. The control room is where the console and tape machines are located; the studio is the adjacent room used only for microphone pick–up of acoustically produced sound—voices, instruments, etc. In the combo situation, the control room also serves as a studio.)

When **tracking** (recording voice), the voice level and loudness must be matched to the level and loudness of other principal elements. If the piece you're producing is going to be cut (as opposed to mixed) together, play the actuality cut(s) at unity gain (adjust the tape playback fader on the console to the mark you made during set–up), and match your voice level (by ear) to the tape level by adjusting the microphone fader.

The meter should be observed to insure that you are not exceeding any electronic parameters, but the **level matching** process should be performed by listening. This may be difficult in the combo situation, when listening live to your own voice on headphones. Do a little trial and error, playing a first sentence sample recording back at unity gain and checking its loudness against the actuality at unity gain. Once the levels are balanced, just record your voice tracks onto blank tape, and assemble the piece by intercutting them with your previously recorded actuality.

There is no need to rerecord the actuality in this case, unless it is not in suitable condition, and needs fixing. In that case, or in the case of more complex productions, *mixing* the piece is required. For mixing, especially if the work is to be done combo, it is usually advisable to prerecord all voice tracks. When doing so, be sure to get a good level, since the tape you are making will be played back and rerecorded at least once more, so optimum fidelity in this first generation is required.

Beware of **plosives,** also known as **p–pops.** These can be avoided by positioning the microphone off to one side of your mouth rather than dead center in front of the speaker. You can feel the "plosive region" by placing your open palm two or three inches in front of your mouth as you say the letter "p." You will feel the sudden burst of air hitting your palm, but if you continue to make that sound and move your hand gradually to one side, you will find that the wind–burst is quite limited in width, and is hardly noticeable over at the corners of the mouth. This is where a microphone should be placed.[2] A windscreen on a microphone may help a bit, but it will not eliminate plosives—only proper placement can do that. You should normally place the microphone from three to six inches from your mouth for announcing, but this will vary greatly with microphone types and room acoustics.

Consistency in sound and pacing is important when reading. If it requires several takes, make sure you haven't moved between takes, or haven't changed your delivery. Avoid having to make a lot of edits in your voice tracks. Also, try to make your pacing compatible to that of your actualities, since they also contain voices speaking. Don't rush through your voice tracks, only to have your actuality's voice slowly stumble through a few sentences, whereupon you return with a flash and race along to your conclusion.

Sibilance is another related problem. It is the excessively sharp whistling sound associated with the letters C, F, and S caused by the forcing of air through very narrow mouth spaces formed when speaking words containing them. Although this sound is accentuated by close–miking, moving the microphone slightly will usually not eliminate the problem as it will with plosives. Sibilance will only be significantly reduced by moving a microphone one foot or more from the mouth. This is usually not acceptable for normal voice tracking. In this case, an electronic device called a **dynamic sibilance controller,** more commonly known as a **de–esser,** must be used (see Appendix G).

Mixing Techniques

Once you are ready to mix, just follow your plan, remembering to set a comfortable monitoring level and leave it there for the entire session. When fading sounds down, take them down smoothly and decisively, and leave them at a level that doesn't fight with the new sound introduced over them, but also not so low that they are indistinguishable.

---

[2]Other consonants are plosives as well. The letter B makes a plosive burst in the same area as the P, but it is usually much less severe. The T and the K can be a problem, but their plosive region is located below that of the P. Using the open palm again, the rush of air from T or K can be felt out in front of the chin, as it proceeds at a downward angle from the mouth. This is another reason for the selection of the corner of the mouth as the "plosive–free" area for mike placement.

Get into the habit of using the *RECORD SAFETY* or *SAFE* switches when putting tapes onto decks for playback. These switches insure that the record function on that machine cannot be accidentally engaged, which would cause erasure of the signals on the tape. In fact, it's best to leave all tape decks in the *SAFE* mode normally, and only place the machine you will record on into the *READY* mode when preparing to record.

A/B Reels

If you have five elements to be placed consecutively with a bit of overlapping of each, they can be set up on **A/B reels,** where elements #1, #3, and #5 are on one reel, (the A reel) and elements #2 and #4 are on a second reel (the B reel), all separated by two or three seconds of leader. Each reel goes onto a different tape machine, and the cuts are simply alternated. As cut #1 is ending on the "A" reel, cut #2 (the first cut on the "B" reel) is started on the other machine. Meanwhile, the first machine is stopped and cut #3 is cued up in the cue or audition channel of the console. As cut #2 runs out, the first machine is started again with cut #3. Cut #4 is now cued on machine two and so on (see Figure 11.7).

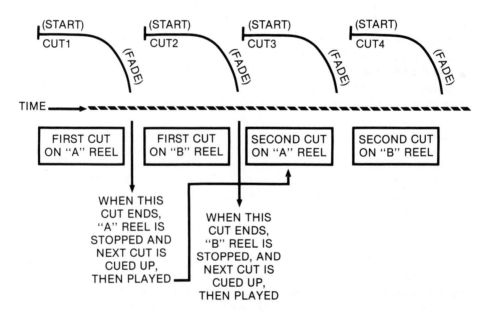

Fig. 11.7. *A/B Reels:* As shown, odd-numbered cuts are assembled onto the *A* reel, and even-numbered cuts go onto the *B* reel. When played back from two tape reels through a mixing console, the cuts alternate between reels for the proper sequencing, with short mixes between them.

Pick–Up Edits

In long or complex mixes, it is often impossible to perform all the required operations in one take. At these times, the **pick–up edit** becomes an invaluable technique. Here, instead of attempting to mix an entire five–minute section, for example, the mix is performed in several shorter sections, which are then edited together to form the complete five minutes. To do this, the producer must select **pick–up points** in the mix; these are places where the short sections can be edited together.

For example, if a piece begins with a mix of several elements, followed by a voice track (on tape), followed by more mixed elements, the voice track can serve as the pick–up point. This means that the producer can record the first mix adding the announcer track, then stop. The producer notes the position of the fader on which the announcer track was just played, then prepares for the second section (assuming the first mix was acceptable). Now the producer begins to record the second section, starting with the *same* announcer track the first section ended with, played at the same level as the first section. The second mix is performed, and the section is concluded. If this take is satisfactory, the producer now rewinds the recordings just made, and finds a suitable edit point in the voice track at the end of the first section. (A good place is a hard consonant sound at the beginning or even in the middle of a word; see Chapter 10, "Tape Editing.") Next, the exact same point is located in the announcer track that begins the second section, and the two sections are spliced together at that point. The entire piece now exists as a whole, continuous work, yet it was constructed in two parts that each shared a common element; they were later attached to each other by splicing their common element and creating a unified whole (see Figure 11.8).

Overlapping

A related technique is called **overlapping.** Consider a case where a 30–second section in the middle of a long program must be repaired or replaced, and can't be just cut out and a new section cut back in because of an extended mixed passage that starts several minutes before the bad part and continues through to several minutes afterwards; assume this mix is otherwise perfect except for the 30–second section.

The procedure of overlapping begins with playing the master tape and rerecording it onto blank tape about 15 seconds ahead of the problem area, with the playback machine's console fader at the unity gain mark. At this point, you are really just dubbing. When the problem area is reached, the "fix" can be performed in whatever way is necessary (new elements mixed in, levels changed, etc.).

When the problem area has passed, and you are back into the good territory of the original mix, bring back the master tape's playback fader to unity gain (if it was moved during the fix), make sure that all other input channels are faded

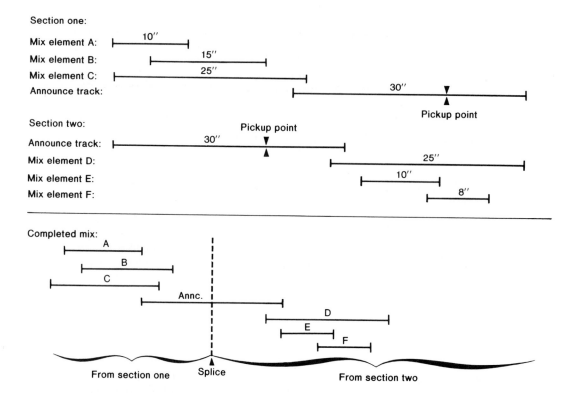

Fig. 11.8. *Pick-Up Edits:* This is a timing plan of a two-section mix with a pick-up edit in the announcer bridge between them. Mix elements *C* and *D* are ambience tracks or sound beds for each section; *C* fades out under the beginning of, and *D* fades up under the end of the announcer bridge. The pick-up point is any loud consonant in the announcer track where the announcer's voice is "in the clear," i.e., without any other elements mixed with it (after *C* fades out but before *D* enters.) The producer / engineer was careful to have the announcer's voice level be exactly the same during the recording of both sections to avoid any level jump at the pick-up edit.

down, roll about 15 seconds, then stop both the record and the playback machines. Those last 15 seconds were also just dubbing. Corresponding points can now be found on the original master and new recording in those 15–second long sections before and after the "fix," where you were really just dubbing. The flawed original section can be replaced with the new, fixed recording, without noticeable change since both are identical at the splice points selected, but different in between (see Figure 11.9).

When picking edit points for overlaps, select a good, loud, transient or percussive sound, since even at unity gain, the change of tape generations at the splices will change the hiss level and the splice would be noticeable or even objectionable if a soft passage were chosen as the splice point. If a splice point is at a loud event or word, it will mask the slight hiss change.

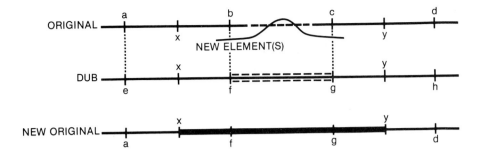

Fig. 11.9. *Overlapping:* Original has problem between points *b* and *c*. Dub is made at unity gain starting at point *a* and running through point *d* on original, but with original levels changed and / or new elements mixed in between points *b* and *c* on original. Dub is virtually identical to original between points *e* and *f*, and between points *g* and *h*. Between *f* and *g* is a new, fixed section. Points *x* and *y* are found (easy edit points in the unchanged section) on both the original and the dub, and the section between *x* and *y* on the original is removed and replaced by the same section from the dub. New original is one generation down between *x* and *y* but is changed and fixed between *f* and *g*.

The Art of Mixing

Mixing makes it possible for radio production to ascend to true art: subtle effects can be discretely introduced and removed; layers of ambience can be added for realism; and music can provide emotional impact. It is important that entrances and exits of elements be made slowly and carefully, without abruptness. An operator must become familiar with the **taper** of the console faders, which determines how much volume change occurs with a given movement of the fader. Developing a feel for this is the essence of mixing ability.

Even in a simple news piece, with announcer studio voice tracks alternating with location actualities, a quick fade up and fade out of the ambience at the beginning and end of the actuality adds a bit of listenability and "class" to the piece, as opposed to abrupt cuts in and out.

The Montage

Another mixing transition technique is the **montage.** Here, several short sound elements are played one after another, with the first fading into the second, the second into the third, etc. The transition between elements can either be a true cross–fade where the first element fades out as the second fades up (see Figure 11.10) or the second can start at full level as the first fades out (see Figure 11.7). The latter is especially effective with voice montages, often referred to as **vox pops,** meaning a collection of short cuts from person–on–the–street interviews. (See Chapter 1, "The Rules of the Game.") Subjective loudness matching of the different voices is also important here.

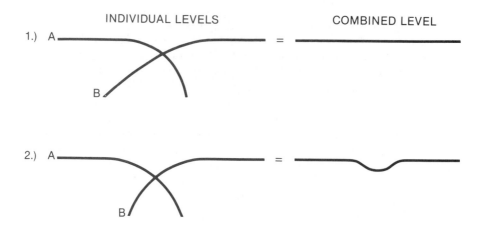

Fig. 11.10. *Crossfading:* Item 1 above shows the correct way a crossfade of two voices or sound elements should be done. Notice that the second element *B* is introduced and faded up partially before element *A* has begun to fade. Usually *A* is completely gone as (or just after) *B* reaches full level. This creates a stable overall sound level, as shown in the combined level diagram.

Yet another technique is to use ambient sound mixed under a voice montage to mask noticeable edits or ambience changes in the voice recordings. This is called **edit covering** and can be used also in live music productions to mask edits between songs, where significant ambience changes are created by the editing.

Entrance/Exit Covering

A more subtle technique called **entrance or exit covering** is used to conceal the final fadeout exit or initial fade–in entrance of a sound effect mixed in under voice, by timing the exit or entrance to occur under a group of closely spaced words, rather than happening "in the clear," that is, in a pause in the speech.

Multiple Elements

When mixing one or two tracks,[3] it is advisable to mix all the desired elements at once, rather than mixing two elements, then taking that mixed recording, playing that back and adding two more elements and rerecording, and so on. The first two elements have gone down an additional generation, and thereby lost fidelity unnecessarily. The preferred method—if you have the machines—is to mix all four elements simultaneously. Although perhaps more difficult, the sonic quality of the end result is well worth it. Moreover, you have total control of all the relative levels in the mix as you hear them together, and you are not stuck with premixed balances.

[3]Multi–track mixing—4, 8, 16 or more tracks—requires an entirely different technique and is beyond the scope of most facilities in public or commercial radio, and therefore beyond the scope of this book.

If dubbing alone is required and the original need not be listened to or in any way adjusted during dubbing, the dub may be made **tails to heads.** This means that the original is played back backwards, (from tail to head) and a recording is made of it. The advantages are two–fold: the dub can be taken off the recording machine from the take–up reel, without rewinding, and it will be heads–out, ready to play. Moreover, on most tape machines, the dub will be electronically superior to the original in its **phase linearity,** a measure of the synchronization in time of all the audio frequencies (a problematic area inherent in the tape–recording process). The dub will still be noisier than the original, and have slightly less high–frequency energy, but in at least one respect it will exceed the quality of the original. The reasons for this go beyond the scope of this text, and some are not even fully understood by experts in the field.

Normally, all dubs should be made with the original played back at the speed it was recorded. Frequency response errors will be introduced if dubs are made at higher speeds in an attempt to save dubbing time (except on equipment especially designed for that process).

Sound Effects

When using sound effects in a production, significantly better results will be achieved when you record the sound effects yourself on location, although many are available commercially on disc or tape. "Rolling your own" is almost always worth the extra effort required.

In dramatic productions, sound effects are crucial to the credibility of the program. Some studios which specialize in sound effects use something known as **"Foley–work" equipment.** Named after a well–known sound effects man from the "Golden Age" of radio, it usually is set up in the form of a multiply–sectioned sandbox, on the studio floor, with each section containing a different walking surface (flagstone, dried leaves, grass, twigs and branches, gravel, sand, etc.). Someone walks in place in the appropriate box, to create the effect of movement of the characters within their aural environment. Another typical accoutrement of such a studio is a small portable door and frame (about 2′ × 4′, usually), that is used to denote entrances and exits of characters. Portability is important, since placement in the studio and proximity to the microphone(s) are quite important to the aural *perspective* of the sound effects.

It is critical that effects appear to be in the same "space" as the characters, and in the correct proximity. *Off–stage* sounds should not be miked as closely as the *on–stage* actors' voices, for example. This is another problem encountered when using prerecorded sound effects, since their acoustical space is predetermined, and may not be proper for the effect desired. If these "canned" effects must be used, however, there can sometimes be a way to place them in the proper perspective. If, as is often the case, the sound effect as it comes off the record is close–miked and "dry" sounding, and the desired effect is for an off–mike sound, the effect can be rerecorded by playing it through a speaker in the studio, and picking it up through a mike (or mikes) arranged in the studio in such a way as to place the sound in the proper space. The acoustics of the studio are now being added to the sound. Artificial reverberation can occasionally be helpful in these cases, as well.

Use of Music

Music plays an important role in radio production, of course. As with any effect, it should always be appropriately styled, and not used gratuitously, or just for the sake of the effect. The way in which it is used is also a factor. A proper level ratio between the music and other elements is critical. A speaking voice over a singing voice (voice–over–vocal) should usually be avoided.

Backtiming

Voice–over–music often works well when the voice–over takes place over an instrumental intro and ends just before the vocals of the music start. This is a traditional but effective timing technique, and can easily be achieved by a process called **backtiming.** There are several different ways of performing a backtime, but the fastest and most accurate method employs a technique referred to as **reverse threading.** This can be done on most tape machines, as long as the capstan and pinch roller are exposed and not enclosed within the head assembly housing (see Figure 11.11).

Instead of the tape passing straight through the capstan and pinch roller in the normal way, Figure 11 shows how the tape is rerouted through them. When the *PLAY* function is engaged, the tape is pulled in the opposite direction from its normal, forward movement, but at the same approximate speed. The tape machine is operating in the normal way, but due to the modified threading, the direction of tape travel is reversed. Tape–to–head contact is often radically impaired in this mode, so no critical playback or dubbing should be attempted in this mode; it is purely a timing technique.

This process should only be performed with professional standard thickness (1.5 mil) tape, since the extremely sharp turns of reverse threading place undue stress on the tape, and can stretch thinner tapes. However, if backtiming must be performed on 1.0 mil or thinner tape, or if the tape machine does not have an exposed capstan and pinch roller (such as Revox, Studer, or Technics machines, or the Ampex ATR–100) backtiming can also be performed by exchanging the supply and take–up reels, and using the normal play function to roll the tape; the machine will be rolling forward, but the recording will actually be rolling in reverse. After the **backroll,** the reels are exchanged again, which replaces the recording in its forward direction.

Figure 11.11. *Reverse Threading:* This shows one method of reverse threading a tape for backwards playback, used in the backtiming process. Arrows show the direction of motion when PLAY function is engaged if the tape is threaded around capstan and pinch roller in the fashion shown. To accomplish this alternate threading, pull a little tape slack off the take-up reel, make an S-loop out of the slack, and slip it around in *front* of the capstan and around *behind* the pinch roller, instead of the usual threading straight through between the capstan and roller.

An example: Assume you have a piece of music with a 15–second instrumental introduction followed by vocals. You also have a voice track (more than 15 seconds long) that you want to mix over that introduction, and have the music's vocals start just after the voice track ends. Cue the voice track tape up to the end of the last word, set up the tape for reverse threading, push play, let it roll 15 seconds, and stop it. The point on the tape at the play head of the machine is now 15 seconds *before* its end.

Better still, instead of timing the intro of the music with a stopwatch, then backrolling the voice track by so many seconds, the processes can be combined into a quick and easy single step. The cueing and reverse threading process described above is performed, but instead of backrolling and watching 15 seconds tick off, *play* the music (forward) on another tape machine or turntable simultaneously. As the music's intro starts, hit play on the reverse–threaded

Figure 11.12. *Wax-Striping a Tape:* To draw a wax-stripe on the tape, line the wax-marked cue-point up to a tape guide, head-lifter or roller (*not* a tapehead), then press the wax pencil onto the mark, holding it as shown, in a sort of sideways method. With the other hand, slowly turn the feed reel clockwise, while pressing the pencil against the tape. (It is advisable to scrape any excess wax off the tape with the thumbnail after drawing the line.) When playing this tape back, the line serves as a visual warning to prepare for the passing of the cue-point, which follows at the end of the line.

(voice–track) machine; when the *vocals* start, stop the voice tracks. Now mark the voice *tape* carefully with a wax pencil against the playback head, and undo the reverse threading around the capstan and roller. A wax stripe should now be added on the tape, just ahead of the wax mark (see figure 11.12). Both machines can be recued and set up for mixing now. When the operator sees the stripe on the voice track tape coming, the music tape machine is readied, and as the tail end of the stripe passes the play head, the music tape (cued to the start of the intro) is started. The music can now be mixed in, and as the voice track *ends,* the vocals of the music will *start*.

Sometimes the pacing isn't quite right, and a bit more or a bit less space is required between the end of the voice track and the beginning of the vocal. This can be achieved by redoing the mix, this time starting the music tape a bit *after* the end of the stripe passes the playhead (if more space, or a looser cue is desired), or starting the music tape while the stripe is still passing over the head (for a "tighter cue," or less space). This is the basic technique behind most timing effects in radio production, and is simpler to perform than it is to read about. After a few attempts, one becomes comfortable with it, and develops variations as necessary. (Don't forget to clean the playback head of accidentally applied wax, *before* you begin your mix.)

Deadrolling

Another timing trick that comes in to use when producing a program that must fill in exact time is called **deadrolling.** Suppose you want to end a program with a piece of music or sound. The program must be timed without the ending music or sound, and of course, should be shorter than the program time allotted. The *deadroll* or closing music must be longer than the difference between the body of the program and the time allotted for this technique to apply. In other words, for a 29 minute program, if the body of the show is 27 minutes long, the close theme must be longer than 2 minutes. For instance, with a closing theme of 2:30 (2 minutes, 30 seconds), as the body of the 27 minute program is aired or mastered, a clock is run on it, and as the clock reaches 26:30, the close theme is *deadrolled*—meaning that it is started, but its fader is not opened, so it is not heard at first. Then, about 15 or 20 seconds later, as the program begins to wrap up, the closing theme is faded up and brought up full as the program ends. As the clock reaches the required 29:00 endpoint, the music will end exactly on time (see Figure 11.13).

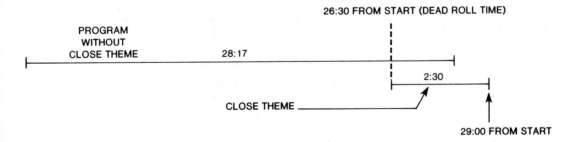

Figure 11.13. *Deadrolling:* Assume that a program must be produced to a 29:00 length. The program without closing music is 28.17. The close theme is known to be 2:30 long. A clock is started when the program begins (or the tape timer available on some machines can be used) and when that clock reads 26:30, the close theme music is started, but not mixed in yet. As the program body ends, the already rolling music is faded in, and since it is 2:30 long, and was started as 26:30, it will end at 29:00 on the clock.

Tape Loops

Another technique in common use in radio is the **tape loop.** Here, one end of a short piece of tape is spliced onto its other end, forming a continuous loop of tape. This can be done with a piece of ambient sound recording, when a longer bed of ambience than that which was recorded is required. It can also be done with music or sound effects, to create a rhythmic, repetitive, or hypnotic effect.

The loop itself is not difficult to make, but it must be selected carefully. For an ambience loop, the chosen section must be free from any sounds that stick out noticeably, such as coughs, shouts, clatters, etc. And the level or tonal quality of the ambience must not have changed from the beginning to the end of the section. For music loops, proper timing must be observed so the beat or *meter* of the music is not disturbed. When playing back a loop, since the tape is not on a reel, tape tension must be provided in creative ways, depending on how long the loop is, and how much slack needs to be taken up. The tape length of a given loop can be doubled (or halved) by dubbing to the next higher (or lower) tape speed.

The loop has to be long enough to at least make it around the head assembly. Slack can be taken up with a vertically held pencil, or a soda can (see Figure 11.14A and B). If the loop is long enough, it can be placed around a reel hub, on the take-up spindle. It is usually advisable to keep the take–up reel stationary either by holding it, or by using the *EDIT* function of the machine (if the machine has one) instead of the *PLAY* function (see Figure 11.14B). For longer loops, a plastic 5 or 7 inch reel can be used to take up slack, and hung over the edge of the tape deck (see Figure 11.14C). Or, a stationary reel on another adjacent machine can be used, or a reel on a pencil in mid–air, or whatever. The tension applied must be enough to provide good tape–to–head contact, but not too much, or the tape speed will be slowed and the tape may stretch. Obviously, music loops are most critical where speed is concerned, since pitch changes are quite noticeable to the ear. A music loop is best set up without any sharp turns (soda can or reel hub rather than pencil), with a very short piece of splicing tape on the splice, and with fixed tension corners (i.e., not hand–held devices providing tension). If a reel hung over the side is used, it is best to attach the reel to the side of the machine to keep it from turning or bouncing.

Working with an Engineer

Any of these techniques can be performed in the combo situation, or by a separate engineer following your instructions. In the latter case, your relationship with the engineer is an important factor in the production process. A good working rapport between the two partners in production can create great radio in short order, as two specialists in their fields cooperate. In many cases, each can learn from the other in the process. (Larger efforts can bring more people such as production assistants into the process.) Teamwork then becomes even more important. At the risk of mixing metaphors, the left hand must know what the right

A: Tape loop held with pencil.

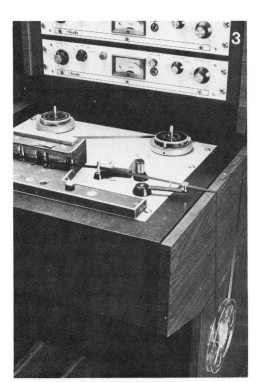

B: Tape loop held with soda can and reel.

Fig. 11.14. Tape Loops.

C: Longer tape loops can be handled by using a five or seven inch reel hung over the edge of the tape deck.

Photos by Phoebe Chase Ferguson

hand is doing, if two heads are to be better than one. A lot depends on the two people involved and their attitudes; without a good working relationship, the production session can be inefficient and frustrating.

The producer can help things get off to a good start by being completely prepared, with materials and a production plan. All tapes should be properly leadered, labeled, and heads out. The sequence of work should be clearly established. Don't confuse the engineer by overwhelming him or her with excessive detail all at once, or with unnecessary information. Show engineers that you are well aware of the production process, but don't try to impress them with your knowledge of the studio. Try to maintain a professional attitude at all times, even if things aren't going well. If you're stuck, ask the engineer for a suggestion, or feedback on the content—not just the technical stuff. The engineer's ear may hear something that you don't, or may have the objectivity that you lack after spending three weeks in an edit booth with this material.

But the responsibility remains with the producer to make the final decisions. The criterion for inclusion of any production idea or any sound element is its *meaning*. Does it have one, and if so, is it appropriate? Nothing should be included if it doesn't have a purpose, or if it doesn't fit in. The pacing and flow of a production is also quite important, and constitute a major aspect of the art of radio production. Getting the right "feel" is essential. And finally, as with any other skill, practice makes perfect.

IV
THE LAW
AND
THE MARKET

12

Basic Legal Concepts for the Radio Producer

by Janice F. Hill

Ignorantia eorum quae quis scrire tene tur non excusat.
"Ignorance of those things which one is bound to know excuses not."

Introduction

Radio producers should be aware of certain legal principles in communications and entertainment. Ignorance of legal restrictions could cost independent producers and stations valuable time and money. A station's very existence may be threatened by failure to recognize the legal areas treated in this chapter. Initially, the producer's legal responsibilities may seem overwhelming. The law is constantly developing; case law in the areas of libel and slander, for example, grows almost daily. It would be difficult for anyone other than a working attorney to keep up to date on all developments in communications law.

The purpose of this chapter is *not* to enable the producer to act as an attorney, but to illustrate potential pitfalls to help the producer avoid some of the most obvious legal mistakes a producer of news and public affairs programming might make. With a basic understanding of the legal principles described in this chapter, producers should, at the very least, know when to seek assistance from station management and legal counsel.

Throughout the chapter there are references to federal law covering radio broadcasting services, specifically, parts 70–79 of Title 47 of the *Code of Federal Regulations*. These will be referred to as "FCC Rules and Regulations (FCC R&R) 73. . . ." The *Code of Federal Regulations* is revised annually, and all stations should have a current copy of the relevant section on hand. All stations should also have a current copy of the Communications Act of 1934, the federal statute through which the Federal Communications Commission derives its regulatory power and under which it regulates broadcast services. For information on how to obtain copies, consult the bibliography at the end of this book.

Janice F. Hill was Deputy General Counsel for National Public Radio for 4½ years; she is now West Coast Counsel for Westinghouse Broadcasting and Cable and Business Affairs Counsel for Group W Productions in Los Angeles. A graduate of Princeton University and the Georgetown University Law Center, Ms. Hill is a member of the Federal Communications Bar Association, and chaired the Subcommittee on Public Broadcasting of the Patent, Trademark and Copyright Section of the American Bar Association. Ms. Hill is also an active member of American Women in Radio and Television (AWRT).

The Federal Communications Commission

The Federal Communications Commission (FCC) was established by the Communications Act of 1934 to license and regulate broadcasting in this country. The FCC's regulatory powers fall into three major categories:

- Common carrier services (telephone and telegraph)
- Non-broadcast radio services (safety and special, including amateur and CB)
- Broadcast or program services (radio and television)

FCC regulation of radio broadcasting includes the allocation of frequencies, assignment of call letters, and the licensing and regulation of stations and operators. Generally, broadcast stations are licensed to serve the "public convenience, interest, and necessity."

While the FCC is prohibited by law from censoring program content, it does have many regulatory responsibilities in the program area. It enforces regulatory policies on fairness in the presentation of controversial issues, "equal opportunities" for political candidates, and rules on personal on–air attacks. Licensees who violate FCC rules or policies are subject to sanctions including loss of license and fines up to $10,000.

The Fairness Doctrine

Because of its broad application to broadcasting, the "Fairness Doctrine" is a worthy first topic of discussion. The Fairness Doctrine grew out of case law and evolved into FCC policy. It is codified only en passant in Section 315(a) of the Communications Act of 1934, which provides that broadcasters have an obligation to afford reasonable opportunity for the discussion of conflicting views on issues of public importance.[1]

The "Fairness Doctrine" is often confused with the law on political broadcasting (see below). Both lay and professional broadcasters sometimes think the phrase "equal time" is triggered under both principles. A helpful way to distinguish these principles is to remember that the Fairness Doctrine applies to *issues,* and the political broadcasting rules only to *persons.* Operation of Fairness Doctrine does *not* require "equal time" or the providing of "equal opportunities."

The Fairness Doctrine does require: 1) that the broadcaster devote a reasonable amount of time to the discussion of controversial issues of public importance; and 2) that if one side of such an issue is presented, "reasonable opportunity" is given for the presentation of contrasting views on that same issue. Note that "reasonable opportunity" does not mean "equal time." There are no specific requirements that the same format or identical amounts of time be devoted to each side of an issue.

The station need *not* present contrasting views in a single broadcast, or even in the same series of broadcasts, provided the station presents them *somewhere*

[1]FCC R&R 73.1910

in its overall programming. Thus, if a commercial station presents an editorial favoring one side of an issue, it need not present a specific "counter–editorial," as long as it presents contrasting views elsewhere in its overall programming.

The Fairness Doctrine does not give individuals or groups, under any circumstances, the right to demand time on the air or the right to specify who should present contrasting viewpoints. A station may solely determine how to cover important issues. Imagine, for example, that during a teachers' strike the head of the local school board demands "equal time" in response to a program which contained interviews with local teachers. The station planned to air a follow-up program to report on the school administration's position without interviews. Must the station interview the school board head under the Fairness Doctrine?

No—as long as the station covers all sides of the issue in its overall programming. Remember, too, that for the Fairness Doctrine to apply the topic in question must be a **"controversial issue of public importance."** Often advocates feel their cause is of paramount public importance. However, the radio station's good faith determination of what is or is not a controversial issue of public importance will be accepted by the FCC unless there is a pattern of abuse of discretion, indicating that the station has an apparent bias, or a demonstration (documented by reference to other media sources) of the public significance or controversiality of the issues.[2]

Political Broadcasting

FCC regulations on political broadcasting, however, are more specifically defined than the Fairness Doctrine. In general, political broadcasting law requires that a station give all candidates equal opportunities to describe and defend their candidacies, equal opportunity being defined in broadcast terms as *equal time plus comparable audience.* The following programs are **exempt** from the equal opportunity requirement:

- *Bona fide* newscasts;
- Regularly–scheduled *bona fide* news interview programs (such as "Face the Nation");
- *Bona fide* news documentaries in which the use of the political candidate is incidental and on a topic other than his or her campaign.

In all other non–exempt programming, any legally qualified candidate whose voice is identified or identifiable prior to or during an election has made a **use** of your station. Each use triggers "equal opportunities" providing every other legally qualified candidate the right to *use* your station to describe or defend his candidacy in a similar manner for the same position or office.

The responsibility for requesting "equal opportunities" air time lies with the candidate: he or she must contact the station within one week of the day on which

[2]See FCC Public Notice, "Fairness Doctrine and the Public Interest Standards," 39 Fed. Reg. 263F2 (see Bibliography).

his or her opponent made "use" of the station's facilities for broadcast. Remember that as a prerequisite, the candidate must show evidence of legal qualification within the meaning of the FCC requirements.[3]

Special political call–ins and other such non–news programs can be designed to limit the station's exposure to equal opportunity requests. The key is careful planning and the artful use of releases.

For example, imagine an election is approaching. A station has decided it can produce four call–in programs, one for each of the three major candidates and a fourth for all remaining candidates. Candidate A agrees to speak on the program and a date is set. To keep Candidates B and C from demanding "equal opportunities," it is best to approach Candidates B and C before airing Candidate A's program and offer the same treatment and services provided to Candidate A. Have B and C sign a release setting out the terms, conditions and format of the program the station envisions for them. Signed releases can help prevent any later allegations that the contemplated program did not live up to B's or C's expectations. In a release, a candidate should agree that the proposed program satisfies any equal opportunity right he or she may have to respond to the first (Candidate A's) program. Any candidate who does not want to appear should sign a release waiving his or her equal opportunity rights.

Political debates usually trigger equal opportunity requests unless the debate is completely outside the control of the broadcast station *and* is broadcast in its entirety live or within 24 hours of the debate. The FCC considers coverage of debates which meets the above criteria to be "on–the–spot coverage of news events," and thus exempt from equal opportunity requirements. This interpretation made possible the broadcast of the 1976 and 1980 presidential debates produced by the League of Women Voters, a non–broadcast, non–station–related organization.

A producer or station cannot censor equal opportunity political broadcasts, including spot announcements. The only legitimate complaint a station may make is in regard to the length of the material, if it disrupts the station's daily programming. Since a station has no right to censor the content of political spots, the station is exempt from liability caused by the content, such as libel, or which may arise due to personal attacks made on the air. The *candidate* may be responsible, however.

The Personal Attack Rule - *Give them a chance to respond. No comment*

The FCC has ruled that if, during the coverage of a controversial public issue, there is an attack on the *"honesty, character, integrity, or like personal qualities of an identified person or group,"* a station must take the following steps within one week after the attack is broadcast:

---

[3]For a detailed explanation of what constitutes a "legally qualified" candidate and other aspects of the law of political broadcasting, see *The Law of Political Broadcasting and Cablecasting: A Political Primer,* published by the FCC (see *Bibliography*).

1. Notify the person or group attacked of the date, time and title of the program on which the attack was made.
2. Send the "attacked" person a script or tape of the attack, or an accurate summary if neither is available.
3. Offer a "reasonable opportunity" to answer the attack on air. (Note: a station has the discretion not to permit an actual on–air response so long as the station reads the attacked individual's response.)

The personal attack rule does not prohibit the broadcast of personal attacks. Furthermore, it does not apply to attacks made by candidates or their campaign associates on other candidates, or to attacks on anyone else if made during a candidate's "use" of a station's facilities. Attacks made during newscasts, news interviews, and on–the–spot coverage of news are also exempt. However, station editorials are subject to the personal attack rule.[4]

Defamation: Libel and Slander

Libel and *slander* are common law claims (as contrasted to rules imposed by government regulation, such as the previously discussed Fairness Doctrine and rules of political broadcasting) that can directly involve producers and broadcasters in time–consuming litigation, possibly resulting in money damages. Generally, libel is a written defamation and slander an oral defamation; for the purposes of this discussion the two terms will be considered interchangeable.

A station may be accused of libel if it makes a *false* statement about someone which is published (i.e. made to a third person) and which injures that person's reputation or good name. Examples of libel include *false statements* which:

- accuse one of being mentally ill or of having a loathsome disease like leprosy, plague, or syphilis;
- accuse one of a criminal action;
- accuse one of business impropriety or bad business management;
- imputes unchastity to unmarried women.

Assume a station has falsely reported that a local politician and a school bus driver were both leaders of an organized crime ring. The politician would have a more difficult time proving a case of libel because public officials and public figures must prove that those making the false statement, knew or should have known, that the statement was false *or* that the producer or station didn't care whether the statement was true or not. This "actual malice" standard requires that the speaker, reporter or station had actual knowledge that it was a false statement or one made with a reckless disregard for the truth. All the school bus driver has to prove as an ordinary citizen (not a public figure or public official)

[4]FCC R&R 73.1920.

175

is that the speaker, reporter or station was negligent in making the false statement. By looking at what a libel plaintiff has to prove, one can gain insight into minimizing the potential for libel litigation.

Elements of Libel

To prove libel, the plaintiff must show that the allegedly false and damaging statements referred to him, i.e. he must be identified in name or by reference. There must be enough detail to identify the person or group. In the case of groups, if the group is small enough, all members may be libeled. For example, if a reporter were to falsely report that "some members of the police department are crooks," it would be difficult for any one of the officers to sue. Of course, if the "details" more clearly indicate specific individuals, such potential plaintiffs would have a better case.

Defenses Against Libel

A review of available defenses can demonstrate appropriate forms of precaution. These defenses include:

a. *Truth.* Truth is an absolute defense to claims of libel. Confirm and be able to prove that any potentially injurious statements are true.

b. *Testimony taken during court and legislative hearings.* Stations can safely rely on making a full, impartial report of official judicial and legislative proceedings. Statements made by those participating in their official capacity may be published. It is usually considered reasonable to assume the truth of statements made in the conduct of official capacity.

c. *Opinions are not libel.* It is possible to criticize someone without running the likelihood of a successful libel suit if the criticism is cloaked in *opinion* and it is made clear that fact is not presented. The facts on which the criticism is based and the tone of the criticism should be objective, not antagonistic.

d. *Consent is a defense.* If the prospective libel plaintiff has consented to the making of statements, knowing they were for broadcast, the station has a defense. However, consent may be good only as far as it goes if a station is careless. If consent is conditioned upon review, then only those statements which have been reviewed by the speaker or his/her agent may be broadcast. It is much wiser to secure pure consent in writing. Certainly avoid agreeing to let participants review material before it is aired. Remember, *the defense of consent is lost if the material is distributed outside the conditions of the consent.*

e. *Statute of limitations as defense.* There is a time limit on how long a plaintiff can wait before bringing a libel suit, or any other tort action. The "statute of limitations" varies (from state to state) between one and three years. However, each time the false and damaging statement is republished or restated, the clock starts ticking again. Failure to sue within the period of the statute of limitations is an absolute defense. In other words, if someone is libeled on a program and the statute of limitations is one year, and the libeled party only brings suit on the 366th day after broadcast, the lawsuit will be dismissed. However, if the program has been repeated, then the statute of limitations begins again—a note of caution.

If someone is possibly libeled, the station or producer should attempt to mitigate damages by issuing a carefully worded apology or retraction to the audience which heard the libel. Legal counsel should review retractions or apologies to preserve legal defenses, in case of suit.

If what is reported is true, be able to prove the truth as stated previously. All prudent journalistic techniques of substantiating and corroborating information are necessary. Certainly, document as much as possible.

Confidential and other sources are often an integral part of libel litigation. If a source is reliable, at least two options are available to the producer. He or she may report what a person said is fact or merely couch it as that person's opinion.

In sum, the area of libel is one with which all journalists should be familiar. Often the best legal position derives directly from the application of sound journalistic principles:

- thorough investigation;
- corroboration of damaging material, particularly if non–public officials are involved;
- knowing the trustworthiness of sources;
- quickly redressing mistakes with a carefully worded retraction.

Obviously, it is best not to be sued. All litigation is expensive.

Invasion of Privacy

Broadcasters should also acquire a tacit understanding of the laws against invasion of privacy. Four distinct invasions of privacy are recognized by the courts:

1. *Intrusions into an individual's solitude or seclusion.* It may not matter that what is described is true—if a description violates one's reasonable right of personal privacy, liability may arise.
2. *Placing an individual in a "false light."* If half–truths cause listeners to infer wrong or damaging conclusions, liability may arise. For example: If, hypothetically, a station reports: "Ralph Nader never fastens his seatbelt," but the station fails to mention that his VW Rabbit has automatic passive restraint seatbelts, which are not actually fastened, the station placed Ralph Nader in a "false light."

3. *Use of an individual's name or voice for commercial purposes.* The typical example is use of a well–known name to endorse a product, *without permission.* Stations and producers should avoid splicing tape of voice segments creating a seeming endorsement of the station or product or any service without first obtaining written permission.
4. *The airing of sensational material.* A suit under invasion of privacy laws is likely if a station publicizes private, intimate, non–newsworthy matters; someone's personal habits regarding hygiene or sexual conduct falls in that category.

Again, one defense to a claim of invasion of privacy is **consent.** This always is especially useful in the commercial appropriation claim of invasion of privacy. In general, the defense is simply that the individual permitted the station to broadcast the statements which are claimed to be an invasion of privacy.

Another defense to invasion of privacy is that of "newsworthiness." The public may actually have a legitimate interest in what was being said—especially about public figures. The public life of public figures is open to reporting and even some aspects of a public figure's private life may be of public concern in a particular circumstance.

It is much more difficult to successfully use the newsworthiness defense in claims brought by private individuals. Private individuals must be directly involved in a *newsworthy event* before the defense is available. For example, it is not an invasion of privacy to report that a private individual who saved the President's life is a homosexual.

Obscenity and Indecency

The areas of obscenity and indecency are ones which are misunderstood by many producers. With the courts becoming increasingly restrictive, many producers search for guidelines on words or images which may be legally aired. The Supreme Court has held the definition of obscenity is to be determined by local standards. Obscene material is that which appeals to the purient interest, i.e., is sexually titillating. Indecent material is merely offensive and may include four–letter expletives which are not obscene.

The "seven dirty words" in the so–called Carlin case (FCC v. Pacifica Foundation) were not found to be obscene but were classified as *indecent* (i.e., offensive). During the Carter administration, then FCC Chairman Charles Ferris stated that the Carlin case would be held to its facts. Therefore, in determining whether language is obscene one must look to the *time of day the program is broadcast.* In Carlin, the program aired in the early afternoon *when children were likely to be in the audience.*

However, it would be a mistake for a station to believe it could broadcast potentially obscene or indecent material freely at night. However, under Carlin, it is *less likely* a station will be brought before the FCC or to court if it broadcasts this material late in the evening. A word of caution: Some communities may feel there is no appropriate time of day or night to air Carlin–like material. And there has been at least one local prosecution of a radio broadcaster (WAIF–FM, Cincinnati, Ohio) for alleged on–air obscenity. Under the Carlin decision, the Supreme Court left the final determination of what is indecent or obscene to the community.

Releases and Performer Permissions

Releases are agreements between a station or producer and a person being broadcast, and are critical to legal protection. They may serve any one or a combination of the following purposes:

1. To document the consent of a person participating in a program, and/or;
2. To protect the station by making only the participant responsible for what he/she says, and/or;
3. To grant the producer rights to the material.

It is highly recommended that a release be obtained in connection with programming treating sensitive issues, such as interviews with unwed mothers, minors with drug problems, or criminals. In the first case, a release would document the consent of women to broadcast their remarks and thus prevent later assertions of invasion of privacy.

If a station contemplates doing a live studio broadcast and therefore is not able to edit what is said, a release may be essential to clearly state that the guest will compensate the station for any damage arising as a direct result of the broadcast. This release will not relieve the station of FCC requirements, should the speaker trigger a right of reply under the personal attack rule, but such an agreement may be helpful if the station is sued for libel.

If a station wishes to broadcast a speech or other performance for which the speaker or performer is normally paid, a release should be signed by the speaker or performer which indicates the station's rights in the broadcast material and spells out what compensation, if any, is to be paid to such speaker or performer. (For information on interviews and related issues of consent, see Chapter 3, "Interviewing.")

Anyone who is not an employee of the radio station and performs as a musician, singer or actor should sign a performer permissions form. These forms should contain:

1. The names of all parties.
2. The purpose of the document ("Performer X grants station Y the right to broadcast . . .").
3. Nature of permission, including frequency of use (one–time, multiple, in perpetuity) and extent of distribution (local, national).

4. What fees, if any, are to be paid the performer, and whether these fees cover one-time use or multiple use (i.e., are they to be paid again if program aired more than once).
5. Whether the likeness of the performer can be used in station/program promotion. For example, if a station taped Herbie Mann and wanted to use his photo as part of a promotional campaign, the station would have too have written permission to do so, to avoid legal difficulties.
6. The understanding regarding disposition of the station's tape of the performer. Stations may wish to retain a copy of the tape for archival purposes, a fact that makes some performers nervous: the permissions form should spell out the station's right to do so, even if permission has been granted for one–time use only.

Copyright

In general, producers of *performance* (music and drama) programs face copyright issues more often than producers of news and public affairs. But all producers should know something of the basics of copyright, since music and drama may be used to illustrate public affairs issues. Copyright also protects a producer's original work.

Copyright is a form of protection provided by U.S. law to authors of original works, including literary, dramatic, musical, artistic, and certain other intellectual works. The copyright owner has exclusive rights to (and may authorize others to) do the following in reference to the copyrighted work: reproduce; prepare derivative work from; distribute copies or phonorecords of; perform; or display such copyright work.

Under the Copyright Act of 1976, copyright is secured automatically when work is created, and the work is "created" when it is fixed in a copy or phono-recording for the first time. Copyright protection is available for both published and unpublished works.

When a work is published under the authority of the copyright owner, a notice of copyright should be placed on all copies. Use of the copyright notice does not require advance permission from, or registration with, the Copyright Office. The notice in and of itself indicates the owner's copyright in the work. The notice appearing on forms of sound recordings should contain the following three elements:

1. The symbol Ⓟ (the letter "P" in a circle)
2. The year of publication of the sound recording
3. The name of the owner of copyright

Examples: Ⓟ 1983 Joe Doe
Ⓟ 1983 National Public Radio

Even though registration is not required, the federal copyright law provides several advantages which encourage copyright owners to register their work. For example, special statutory damages for infringement are available to copyright holders who have registered their works. For information and application forms, contact the Copyright Office, Library of Congress, Washington, D.C. (see *Bibliography*).

Employees of radio stations produce material which is generally considered "work for hire." The station is considered the "author" of the work under copyright law. If material is being specifically created for the station by an independent producer, it is important to execute a written contract that states that the material is a "work for hire" so there is no dispute about copyright or ownership.

If a station wishes to read or adapt a literary work for radio, it is best for the station to contact the publisher for permission. In the case of music, most stations have blanket licenses (from ASCAP, BMI, or SESAC) to broadcast all music except "dramatic" music such as operas or staged choral works. Dramatic music requires the clearance of what are called *grand rights* before a station may broadcast them. If the material a station wishes to use is in the public domain, or was created by the Federal Government, no copyright clearances are needed.

Rebroadcast Consent

In order to use material off–air from another U.S. television or radio station, the FCC requires the consent of the originating broadcaster. By the same token, if another station wants to use your material, you must be asked.[5]

Other Areas to Watch For

While by no means exhaustive, the following is a brief summary of other kinds of program considerations that have legal implications for radio producers:

Staging of News Stories: The FCC requires that an announcement be made at the beginning of any news segment where the public may be misled into believing that *recorded* events they hear are occurring *live*.[6] The staging of recorded events in such a way as to make them appear live is frowned upon by the FCC. Good journalistic practice should help avoid trouble because the "FCC will not commence action on complaints or distortions, faking, staging, investigation, or falsification of news unless it receives extrinsic evidence (evidence apart from the program content) of such deliberate conduct on the part of the licensee involved."[7]

[5]FCC R&R 73.1207
[6]FCC R&R 73.1208.
[7]FCC Publication 8310.100.

Lotteries: The Federal Criminal Code prohibits the broadcast of ads for, or information concerning, lotteries.[8] A lottery is defined as a game, contest, or promotion that contains all of the following: 1) a prize; 2) an element of chance in determining winners; and 3) consideration—the entrant must pay for his participation or buy something of value. The only exceptions are state–run lotteries: lists of prizes or other information may be broadcast by a station within that state or within an adjacent state if both states have state–run lotteries.

Commercials: Non–commercial broadcasters are prohibited from "promoting the sale of a product or service" over the air. Hence, non–commercial broadcasters should not use commercials without seeking a waiver from the FCC. Waivers may be obtained by writing a brief description of the reason for including the commercials and the length of the commercial message to the FCC Broadcast Bureau, Washington, DC 20554. (If a station is represented by an FCC attorney, such requests should be submitted through its attorney.) As are often included in old–time radio shows, commercials for fictional or defunct products do not require a waiver. A waiver is also not necessary if the commercial name is directly linked to the title of an event. Then the full title (commercial name included) may be used without a waiver. Because federal law bars the advertising of cigarettes and small cigars on the air, the FCC cannot grant waivers for these products.

A Word to the Wise

Many court actions or those which result in revoked station licenses started with a casual unthinking act or statement on the part of uninformed station employees. Know the underlying law of your profession. Think before you act. A lot of money and possibly a license may be saved.

[8]FCC R&R 73.1211.

13

Funding, Marketing and Distribution

by Dave Creagh

Introduction

In this chapter, I'll try to provide an overview of what can be done with a radio program once it has been produced—that is, to get it used by radio stations. Ideally, this will result in the producer getting paid. Some of the information in this chapter relates to specific organizations or programs in existence as of this writing, late–1982. This information may change as the radio industry does, as different patterns of use and funding of radio programs develop, and as changes in the economy affect an individual's ability to earn a living making radio programs. The fundamental principles outlined here will undoubtedly endure. This summary is intended to help you get started.

Funding

Most audio producers start by working either as a volunteer at a radio station, or by working individually as an independent producer, attempting to create short works that can be sold to any number of markets. If one wishes to undertake a larger project—a series of half–hour–long programs for example—it is almost always necessary to secure production funding in advance of actual production. This could come in the form of an advance contract from a radio station or network, or in the form of a grant. Traditionally, only a few organizations have been in the business of providing funding for radio production, but *it is possible* to receive such a grant.

Public Funds

Each state has a council or commission on the arts, and one on the humanities. These offices give small–to–medium–sized grants to individuals and organizations to produce works of special interest within that state. A state arts council, for example, might be very interested in a well–produced series of sound portraits

A native of Washington, D.C., Dave Creagh started working for NPR in 1971 as an engineer. He held numerous positions within the organization, as: editor, director, producer and executive producer of All Things Considered; *director of the National Training Project; station liaison for the National Program Service; and as the first director of the Satellite Program Development Fund. Creagh left NPR in 1981 to become General Manager of an NPR member station, KLON, in Long Beach, California.*

of jazz artists who were born in or have performed widely in that state. A humanities council might typically fund production of an oral history program on a particular city or region within that state. These agencies are generally located in state capitals. They will all happily provide more specific information on their current funding policies and guidelines.

At the national level, you should contact the **National Endownment for the Humanities (NEH)** and the **National Endowment for the Arts (NEA),** both located in Washington, D.C. (Addresses for the Endowments, as well as all other specific organizations mentioned in this chapter, can be found at the end of this chapter.)

Within NEH's Division of Public Programs, the Media Program in the Humanities provides support for innovative television, radio and cable projects. Types of grants include planning, scriptwriting, and production grants. Producers of news and public affairs should be aware that projects presenting current affairs in a "purely descriptive way" are not considered eligible for NEH funding. The emphasis should be on *interpretation,* placing events in the context of history and showing their relation to U.S. society. Therefore, coverage of a single political debate would not be eligible for NEH funding, but an examination of the impact of political debates over the last two decades might be.

The NEA assists individuals and organizations involved in radio through the Radio Project division of its Media Arts Program. The NEA has supported projects that demonstrate innovative approaches to the use of the radio medium in supporting the arts and awareness of radio as an art form. The kinds of projects funded include documentaries, classic or experimental drama, audio art, children's programming and the presentation of literature and music.

Because the federal funding picture is everchanging, you should always write to NEH and NEA for the most recent guidelines and application forms. Both Endowments require very specific information in applications, and have only one or two funding rounds a year.

National Public Radio also makes grants available through its **Satellite Program Development Fund (SPDF).** SPDF grants are made on a competitive, peer–review basis to support projects using innovative techniques in production or exploring subject matter previously unavailable to public radio stations. The intent of the SPDF program is to encourage new talent, and to provide initial funding for larger projects to enable them to attract outside funding. Any individual or organization, whether principally in business to produce radio programs or not, may apply for a SPDF grant, with the exception of NPR and its regular full–time employees. In the past, grants have been made to NPR member stations, non–member stations, individual and corporate independent producers and various groups and associations.

NPR Acquisitions

You can also sell pieces to NPR's **National Program Service (NPS).** Historically, NPR's news magazine programs have been actively interested in acquiring short pieces for radio, ranging from 45–second news spots to fully produced stereo half–hours. If your program is accepted for broadcast, NPR pays according to established rates. NPR maintains strict editorial, production and technical standards, and normally will acquire exclusive rights to the program.

All Things Considered is interested in three-to-eight-minute reports on the day's breaking news. Because of its format, *Morning Edition* broadcasts reports that are considerably shorter, averaging three to four minutes in length. Material can also be submitted to the daily news magazine programs through NPR's specialized reporting units, such as the Science Unit, Arts Unit, History Unit and Sports Unit. *Listen carefully to the particular program you're interested in working for prior to attempting to produce any material for it.* **NPR Acquisitions** has specific guidelines available that outline in great detail how to submit your work; these can be obtained by writing or calling NPR Acquisitions.

A word of advice here for aspiring radio producers: be prepared to have much of your early work rejected or heavily edited. Often producers attach quite a bit of ego to their work, and have felt hurt when rejected. It is a difficult relationship, working with an editor by long–distance telephone. But with patience and hard work on both sides, it can be a rewarding one.

Private Funds

Private funding from both foundations and corporations has been available for radio production. Foundation support can be a very capricious thing; a foundation may choose to support radio for a time, then change its mind. Traditional foundation support is targeted to programs on subjects consistent with the foundation's field of interest. For example, when a foundation is concerned with issues in nutrition, it will likely only fund programs which pertain to nutrition. There are many thousands of foundations of all types, but only a handful have been interested in funding radio production. There is a resource organization called the **Foundation Center,** located in several major cities, which compiles data on past patterns of giving for U.S. private foundations, but not for government agencies or corporations. Use of this service would help considerably in locating foundations interested in funding public broadcasting in general, or radio production in specific content areas. For a fee, the Foundation Center can provide computerized reports on funding patterns in many areas, including, most pertinently one entitled, "Television, Radio and Communications."

Most large corporations have non–profit subsidiaries or departments that act very much like foundations, or, in some cases, are called foundations. In the past, oil companies and other corporations have seen fit to underwrite costs or production for public television programs and for occasional public radio programs. This is to their advantage for two important reasons: there often is a tax advantage for contributions to non–profit organizations, and they get on–air funding credit at the end of the program(s). Many corporations like the idea of audiences associating their corporate name with a high–quality program. Identifying likely corporations will require some detective work and persistence on a station or producer's part. One caveat: corporations almost never fund individuals.

Marketing

Broadcast Marketing

Marketing involves: 1) deciding what outlets a radio program is intended for; and 2) convincing decision–makers at these outlets to use the program. In the radio broadcast sector, we're speaking of radio stations. At this writing, cable radio and direct–to–home broadcasts from satellites are not yet viable markets for radio producers.

Radio stations are autonomous in their program decision–making; by law they have the right to reject network or any other programs. Commercial stations are generally not interested in acquiring programs, except for programs in subject areas which closely related to the station's format. The vast majority of commercial radio stations in this country are tightly formatted, and play a single type of music almost exclusively. These stations will have little use for a highly–produced radio drama or documentary. The Federal Communications Commission has in the past required all radio stations to air a certain amount of public service–type programs, but many did so at little expense and at very early hours on Sunday mornings. This requirement has now been eliminated as a result of "radio deregulation." For a serious public affairs producer seeking to get a program aired widely, public radio stations would seem to be a better market.

Getting your program *to* the stations is relatively easy; getting *on* the stations is often difficult. The cost of delivery via satellite is relatively low, in the neighborhood of $50 to $90 an hour. The real hurdle is convincing radio station decision–makers (generally program directors or station managers) that they should use your program.

Public radio stations are a very diverse lot. Some have eclectic interests and flexible formats. Many of them are actively looking for new and interesting programs. A few others have primarily jazz formats, or broadcast public affairs or all news. But the majority of public radio stations are limited to a fine arts format, which means almost exclusively classical music. From a marketing standpoint, this means the programs most likely to be selected for broadcast by these stations are those which complement classical music programs, be they performances, documentaries, or perhaps sound portraits of classical composers or performers. In general, the most strictly classical music–oriented stations are not among those most receptive to new or diverse offerings from the outside.

The most important bit of marketing advice I can provide is to remind you that a program must be *listened to* by the appropriate station staff before a decision can be made. It is my experience that these decision–makers at the local level tend to be woefully overworked. Aside from distributing an audition feed to stations which are satellite–equipped, I recommend the mailing of audio cassettes to all of your target stations. Cassettes are inexpensive to make and mail, and are the handiest way for a program manager to be able to audition your product. This is not, incidentally, a good place to economize. Use good quality cassettes and a reputable duplication service. It is a good idea to check the audio yourself on as many of these cassettes as practical before mailing.

A package of attractive graphic material should be included in any mailing to prospective stations. This serves a dual purpose. First, you'll want it to catch the eye, and with luck, the interest of the person receiving it. Second, this material must be useful to the station in promoting the program to the public. Almost every public radio station publishes a regular monthly program guide, which often includes illustrations. In addition, a station may choose to purchase a newspaper or magazine advertisement for the program, for which some sort of eye–catching art would be most appropriate. The graphics package should include all of the appropriate information about the program: duration; mode (mono/stereo); number of programs if it's a series; format (interview, montage, music with interview, etc.); cost to the station (if you are asking using stations to pay for their use of it); rights or restrictions on use (if any); and the like. Press clips or any other prior acclaim or critical review is most appropriate.

It should be remembered that most program decision–makers will receive many more program offerings than they can possibly use, and that only the most interesting offers will receive any real scrutiny. The more attractive a package is, or the more persuasively-described, the greater the likelihood that the program will get a serious audition.

Some producers have found that following up this type of mailing with a telephone call has worked. It is wise to be cautious pursuing this strategy for at least two reasons: the cost of phoning up to 260 stations from Alaska to Puerto Rico would be formidable, and the risk of annoying program directors is considerable. Often, though, phone calls are the only way to break through the pack. The level of management at which scheduling decisions are made actually differs from station to station. Sometimes a printed package to both the station manager *and* the program director will have the desired effect.

The process of marketing a radio production can also be an opportunity to do market research. In any marketing campaign, all of the information you receive back from stations should be retained, so that you might obtain feedback which might be applied immediately to future projects. If station KXYZ says it *is* interested in science–related programs but never longer than eight minutes, that might imply that this station prefers shorter pieces. Thus marketing strategies, as well as production strategies, can be more closely based on real market information.

There are many commercial and not-for-profit syndicators of radio programs, whose users include public as well as commercial radio stations. Many of these syndicate only concerts; others have a broad range of programs from which stations may choose, including some public affairs programs that have been used by commercial stations to fulfill the public service requirements mentioned earlier. These syndicators offer a wide-ranging package of programs and services to the station and to the producer. The Longhorn Radio Network, for example, is operated by the Communications Center at the University of Texas at Austin. It distributes programs of all types to hundreds of stations nationally, and its mailing list includes every radio station in the U.S.

The advantages of seeking a distribution agreement through such a service are obvious. It does not follow necessarily that a gifted producer of radio programs will be either a successful or a willing entrepreneur. If he or she is not, it might be advisable to use the services of one of the many marketing and distribution concerns which operate quite successfully in many major U.S. cities.

Non–Broadcast Markets

There are other ways to distribute a radio program than by broadcasting it. Many producers sell tapes of their programs to individuals or institutions. If a production is of potential interest to either the general public or to educational institutions, you might well investigate the non–broadcast market. A wide variety of programs have been successfully sold directly to the public on cassette, either through program guides, by direct mail, or in stores.

There is a large and potentially lucrative market in education. School systems need good audio learning materials for all grade levels, and colleges and universities spend large sums of money for audio/print packages, which can be developed and sold to them. This is a very sophisticated marketplace, and it would obviously be very difficult for an individual to attempt to market a series to thousands of institutions of higher learning. The major textbook companies also market and distribute radio programs that they believe they can sell. Be warned that most publishers pay producers less than ten percent of the proceeds, *after* the production costs have been paid.

In summary, there *are* markets for radio programs, but they are scattered and must be addressed individually. Seldom will a single program or series be of interest to commercial radio stations, *and* to public radio stations, *and* directly to listeners, *and* to the educational market. A producer should consider carefully what market(s) his or her product should be designed to serve prior to production. Specific research should be done regarding the best way to make your program attractive to the widest possible spectrum of potential users.

Distribution

Distribution is the means of getting a radio program audio from its producer to the radio stations which might choose to broadcast it. In the recent past, the most common distribution medium was tape, via surface transportation. A master tape was taken to a duplication service, where many copies were made, often at high speeds. These copies were then packaged and either mailed or shipped by UPS. or some other carrier to their destination. This form of distribution is alive and well today.

Alternatively, large radio networks, such as NBC, lease special lines from the telephone company to enable the simultaneous distribution of a program to many places *live*. These lines, however, are generally of mediocre technical quality or worse, and tend to be expensive. Tape overcomes the technical problem, but is obviously unsuited for live or very timely programs, and is rather expensive. If a program is intended for many stations, and is not timely, distribution by disc (records) is often a cost–effective alternative to tape. Overall technical quality can be better than a high–speed tape copy. Approximately 400–500 stations is generally regarded as the break-even point for distribution by record.

Fig. 13.1. This drawing shows how programs are distributed over National Public Radio's satellite interconnection system. Programs are transmitted to the WESTAR communications satellite from NPR's main origination terminal near Washington, D.C. and from 17 other origination points around the country. The satellite amplifies and retransmits the programs for reception at ground terminals serving each public radio station.

Satellite Distribution

Satellite distribution can be less expensive than tape distribution, depending on the number of stations wanting to use the program and whether these stations are satellite-equipped or can make arrangements to use a satellite transmission. The more using stations you have, the more cost-efficient satellite distribution becomes.

National Public Radio was the first radio network to construct satellite receiver terminals for its members, and in 1980 became fully satellite-equipped. Using transponder capacity on Western Union's Westar I satellite (since replaced by Westar IV), 18 transmitter terminals (called "uplinks") and over 200 receiver sites (called "downlinks") are now installed. Satellite capacity is used in such a way that a number of stereo and monoaural programs can be distributed simultaneously, in real time, at the highest fidelity.

NPR operates another satellite distribution system called the **Extended Program Service (EPS),** that is a marketplace for programs produced by other than NPR producers. Producers wishing to distribute via EPS must have at least one public radio station among the program's intended market stations. Other, non-downlink-equipped public radio stations can use these transmissions by arranging for special telephone lines from the nearest equipped station, or perhaps through an arrangement where the downlink station would tape the program.

In using EPS, the producer alone decides what stations may use his or her programs, the distribution arrangements, and other distribution decisions: time of day, day of week, conditions of availability. The producer must pay for use of the satellite system, but these charges may be assessed to stations using the feed. A producer may charge other costs (such as production costs) to using stations, but producers are reminded that radio stations, particularly public radio stations, don't have a lot of money with which to acquire programs.

Rates for placing a program transmission on the public radio satellite system change from time to time, as may policies regarding the use of the system. Contact the NPR Distribution Center in Washington, D.C. for current information.

Satellite distribution will undoubtedly expand in the future: there are now commercial radio satellite networks, such as the Mutual Broadcasting System. In addition, there are now also syndicators offering full-time programming via satellite: these will perhaps provide program outlets for producers of short features on compatible subjects.

Tape Distribution

Many non-commercial, and most commercial radio stations are not yet equipped with satellite receiver equipment. Unless one wishes to pay the very high costs of leasing land lines from the telephone company, the sole remaining option is tape.

If a program is only going to be used by a small number of radio stations, it may be feasible for a producer to make tape copies at a radio station, at home, or in a small studio. For larger distribution jobs it is well to seek the services of either a commercial duplication service (which will simply make multiple copies of the tape) or of a distribution service.

Several of these services exist. The tape services of the **National Federation of Community Broadcasters** and the **Pacifica Program Service** offer such services, generally distribute only to non-commercial radio stations, and often without financial compensation to producers. As I mentioned before, policies change, so check with the staff of each for current information.

As with audition tapes, it is important to check the audio quality of as many tape copies as possible before mailing. Often a distribution service will do this for its clients, but if you intend to make your own copies, check as many as you can yourself. Many radio stations using taped programs will not check the audio before broadcast; on-air technical problems often yield poor relationships between producer and consuming station.

After broadcast, the physical tape itself may be required to be returned to the producer or the distribution service by the station. This allows the tape to be re-used as often as is desired. In other cases, the tape may be purchased as raw stock by the station. This ensures the station a continual supply of new tape for recording or production needs, and saves time and postage for the tape's return trip. Any combination of these arrangements can be worked out. In any form of distribution, however, it is well to remember the fact that *there are many more programs available to a radio station than it can use.*

International Distribution

From time to time foreign broadcasters will buy programs produced in the U.S. Sometimes the government-run radio systems in these countries will pay generously (by U.S. standards) sums for rights to broadcast programs they like. A few independent radio producers have managed to make a living working as freelancers for The Canadian Broadcasting Corporation (CBC). The British Broadcasting Corporation, and the Australian Broadcasting Commission have all purchased broadcast rights to U.S.–made programs. These organizations have offices in New York and Washington, D.C.

Final Advice

In this chapter I've attempted to outline some of the suggestions available based on real experience in the securing of funding and audiences for radio programs. As I said at the outset, situations change rapidly. The coming of cable, of direct broadcast satellites, and of ever–less expensive cassette distribution all present challenges and opportunities which will be fascinating to watch in the years to come.

The final word of advice I'd offer is this: listen to a lot of different radio stations, inquire about the sources of the programs you hear and the costs to the stations, and seek advice from producers at the state and national level who are actively involved in pursuing grants, in doing research, and in producing programs for wide distribution.

The best thing aspiring radio producers in this country can do is to keep trying different things, keep asking questions, and to keep sharing information with one another. Whether a producer is at a station or works as an independent, the continuously-growing body of knowledge about the industry (largely unwritten) and how to get into it is one of your greatest potential assets. I encourage you to get to know some good and experienced radio producers and to learn directly from them.

Addresses: Funding, Marketing
and Distribution Entities

1. Humanities Projects in Media
   Division of Public Programs
   National Endowment for the Humanities
   Mail Stop 403
   806 15th Street N.W.
   Washington, DC 20506

2. Media Arts: Film/
   Radio/Television Program
   National Endowment for the Arts
   2401 E Street N.W.
   Washington, DC 20036

3. *The Foundation Center*
   888 Seventh Avenue
   New York, NY 10106

4. *Satellite Program Development Fund*
   National Public Radio
   2025 M Street N.W.
   Washington, DC 20036

5. *NPR Acquisitions*
   (same address as above)

6. *NPR Distribution Center*
   (same address as above)

7. *National Federation of Community Broadcasters*
   1314 14th Street N.W.
   Washington, DC 20005

8. *Pacifica Program Service*
   5316 Venice Boulevard
   Los Angeles, CA 90019

V
EPILOGUE

14

Epilogue: New Technologies and Your Future

by Larry Josephson

The American telecommunications environment is, at this writing, rapidly changing. A new technology or new piece of *hardware[1]* is announced almost every month, along with a fresh claim for each that it will revolutionize the production, distribution, financing and consumer use of news, information, and entertainment *software.* The major new distribution technologies include **cable** (television and radio); **DBS** (Direct Broadcast Satellite, from satellite to home at frequencies far above the present AM and FM bands); the **video tape recorder** (VTRs) and the **video disk;** and the **microprocessor,** which forms the basis of many intelligent machines, from industrial robots to home computers.

The home computer, when tied to a central data bank by telephone lines, optical fibers, two–way cable or other means, becomes the basis of a system of electronic information retrieval, transmission and display of "print"—anything from hard news to stock prices to recipes. Some futurists claim that the paper–and–ink newspaper, which has been with us since Gutenberg, is obsolete and that someday we'll all "read" the morning newspaper on our television sets.[2]

In the same vein, the decline of broadcasting as it has evolved over the past 50 years has been widely predicted. The most important feature of cable, satellites, optical fibers and other new means of electronic dissemination is that they vastly increase the number of channels of audio, video and print information available to each consumer, and to each producer or distributor at the *head end* of each of these systems. Therefore, futurists and entrepreneurs claim that a flood of new products (including news) will emerge to fill these newly–liberated channels. The Cable News Network and a competing service planned by Westinghouse are examples.

---

[1]At the level of the average radio reporter/producer, new production technology has so far affected video more than audio. While television has mini– and microcams, sophisticated computer–assisted editing, and small lightweight videotape recorders, to date audio hardware has, for the most part, just been refined or miniaturized. The Sony TCD5M, mentioned in Appendix A, is an example of that process. The communications satellite is the only new technology which has profoundly affected radio, mostly in marketing and distribution. Satellites are also being used in production for transcontinental or intercontinental interviews and feeds at the highest technical quality. Digital audio and computer editing, to cite two examples, are too expensive at this point to justify their use in the economics of radio.

[2]However, economic or political shifts can delay or abort a technology. Television was perfected by 1939 but its mass marketing was delayed by the coming of World War II. A severe recession or depression would radically alter every futurist scenario.

Even a cursory glance at the history of applied technology in the 20th century does not support such sweeping, and often self–interested, claims. Very few of the myriad new technologies offered to the patent office ever catch the public fancy, let alone transform the way we live. Most fall by the wayside along with the messianic claims made for them. In this century so far, only the automobile, radio, television, "the pill" and the atomic bomb have profoundly altered our lives—for better or worse.[3] Microprocessors (silicon chips) and bioengineering may turn out to be the most revolutionary technologies of the late 20th century.

Another lesson of technocultural history is that new technologies do not always displace old ones. Some, of course, do. The automobile destroyed black-smithing and buggy–whip manufacturing. On the other hand, television did *not* destroy radio; its coming caused radio to adapt to a new reality and devise new programming for a new market. The old network shows went to television, some with more success than others. Radio then ceased to be a *broad–based mass medium,* and instead fractionated and specialized. By 1951 Jack Benny had left radio for television and was replaced by Alan Freed, the prototypical rock 'n roll disc jockey.

Since the early 1950s, radio has further divided itself into hundreds of formats and variations on them, including: all–news or news–talk; beautiful music; contemporary/MOR (middle–of–the–road); country and western; progressive rock or AOR (album–oriented–rock); disco; jazz; religious; and, of course, public radio (in several varieties)—just to name a few formats, each appealing to its own demographic segments of the total audience. In a major market a commercial radio station with an overall "nine share"[4] is a runaway success. Station owners can make money with a three or four share, depending on their audience de-mographics (the age and sex of the dominant group of listeners). In television, a prime time program needs at least a 25–30 share to survive.

The most important factor in the success of any technology is *the availability of software that consumers want and can afford to buy.* Programs, or streams of information and entertainment, are the software of electronic information dis-semination technologies. *The limiting factor in the production of programs is the shortage of good ideas, talent, money and facilities.* This has not changed since Shakespeare's time (1564–1616), a period that somewhat predates the video disk.

Most electronic communications technologies—new or old— require an audio track (the major exception being teletext). Since spoken language evolved thou-sands of years before written language, the audio track of any medium employing the moving image is almost always the primary form of information transfer. If you doubt this, try watching television by turning the sound up and listening from another room. Then go back to the room and watch the same program with the sound *off.* Which form of information (aural or visual) is indispensable to the process of communication?

[3]The telephone and telegraph, which certainly have had a profound impact, were 19th–century in-ventions.

[4]A "nine share" is nine percent of those using radio across all rated "dayparts" (a daypart being a defined portion of time on a specific day), Monday through Sunday, 6:00 a.m. to midnight.

The point is, then, that there will always be a demand for talented, imaginative, energetic, interested and well–read producers, reporters or editors—whatever the changing fashions in technology. The predicted addition of high–quality stereo to television (already a reality in Japan) can only reinforce this trend.

To summarize:

- Only a few new technologies are ever accepted by the public; fewer still have a profound impact on society.
- Mature technologies are not always replaced by new ones; the old, adapted for new uses, often continue to exist side by side with the new.
- Software, not hardware, is usually the limiting factor in the acceptance of any communications technology.

To reassure:

- Talented people will always be in demand, whatever technologies or distribution systems may be in vogue.

Almost all of the principles and techniques set forth in this book can be applied not only to radio, but also to the audio components of television news, industrial video shows, film strips or slide shows, Broadway theater or even commercials—any medium which requires the creative use of sound. The films of Steven Spielberg ("Close Encounters of the Third Kind," "E.T."), Francis Ford Coppola ("Apocalypse Now"), and George Lucas ("Star Wars") all use a highly elaborate sound track as an integral dramatic element.

You now have the wisdom of some of the best people in radio journalism at your fingertips. From now on its up to you. Go to it—and good luck.

APPENDICES

Appendix A

Buying Equipment

There are many different sources for the equipment and accessories described in Chapter 8. Much is available through your neighborhood stereo store, or through a local sound system (PA) contractor. Prices will range from list price down to 50 percent off list price, depending on where you buy, but discount stores are not necessarily the best places to buy. If you value good advice, the availability of a service department or a better selection of equipment, you might consider spending a little bit more money and getting a lot more in return.

Many mail–order establishments sell cassette recorders, microphones, accessories and tapes at discount prices. You can find their ads in the classified sections of stereo magazines. With a bit of detective work, though, you may be able to do as well in your local area. One source of up–to–date information on where to buy equipment is the National Federation of Community Broadcasters (1314 14th Street N.W., Washington, DC 20005; telephone—202–797–8911).

Cassette Recorders

Top honors for portable cassette recorders have been dominated by the Japanese manufacturers: *Sony, Nakamichi, Superscope, Technics, Panasonic,* and *Marantz* all have established reputations in the field. The first "broadcast–standard" reporter's cassette machine was the Sony TC–100; its successors, the TC–110 and 110B have also been popular, as has their TC–142 (all now discontinued) and the premium quality stereo machine, the TC–D5M. Many reporters are now using Superscope recorders such as the C–206LP and C–207LP, now no longer made. The corresponding new model numbers are PMD210 and PMD220. But there are many machines with the quality and features needed for broadcast work.

Microphones

American and European microphones have the strongest reputations among U.S. broadcasters. Japanese mikes have offered good sound specifications, but until the last few years have suffered from durability problems.

Among omnidirectional mikes, the industry standards seem to be the Electro–Voice 635A and RE–50 (the latter is essentially a 635A with additional mechanical shock isolation built around it). Both are dynamic mikes. Electro–Voice also has a series of popular cardioid dynamic mikes, including the RE15, RE16 and RE18. Shure Brothers' cardioid SM54 and SM58 are also widely used. In a higher price bracket, the Sennheiser MD421U dynamic cardioid is an excellent general purpose mike, although a bit too susceptible to mechanical handling noise and to physical damage. Its case is made of plastic. The Japanese manufacturers have been improving the ruggedness of their microphones, and some of them offer excellent performance and value. Their electret condenser mikes have met with best success. Sony's tie–tack ECM–50PS (balanced output) or the cheaper, unbalanced ECM–150 is widely used in broadcasting, particularly for TV audio.

Accessories

Most accessories described in this chapter are available from the same manufacturers and distributors as the main pieces of equipment. But there are exceptions: the best microphone–mounting clamps, for example, are made for cameras, not microphones. Check with your local photo or motion picture supply store for Rowi or Capro clamps. If you can't find them locally a few major stores such as Ritz-Brenner (11600 Route 1, Beltsville, Maryland 20705), or Standard Photo Supply of Chicago, Illinois, will sell them via mail order. Some vendors sell these clamps already adapted to fit the standard 5/8-27 microphone clamp thread.

Appendix B

Assessing the Studio: A Checklist

1. *Number and Type of Sources Available:* Reel–to–reel tape machines, cart machines and erased carts, cassette machines, mike inputs, phone patch, turntables?

2. *Quality and Format of Mastering Recorders:* Full track, two–track, four–track, other? Machines and heads clean and up to spec? Machines biased for [which] tape stock?

3. *Quality of Playback Sources:* Cart noise, turntable rumble, wow and flutter, hiss, hum?

4. *Operation of Equipment:* Remote controls for tape and cart machines, turntables?

5. *Special Console Functions:* Auxiliary mix ability, mix–minus ability, equalization, "solo" function, patch points, metering, cue positions, talkback?

6. *Outboard Equipment Available:* Reverberation, delay units, compressors and limiters, filters, equalizers? Clocks, tape timers and counters?

7. *Unity Gain Set–Up:* Board master pot(s) and recorder input/output calibration (system design–centering)?

8. *Fader Action:* Taper–type? Smooth, noise–free operation? Tracking uniformity?

9. *"Hotpot" Ability on Playback Sources?* (i.e.—can machines be started with the pot open without hearing "clicks" or "thumps"?)

10. *Quality of Monitoring Sources:* Secondary monitors available? Mono–stereo switching?

11. *Quality of Studio and Control Room Acoustics?*

Appendix C:

Sample Production Script/Plan

Sample Technical Script for Folk Festival U.S.A.

Technical Notes	Program Material	
Bring up music (guitar), hold for :35, then bring under for *Insert A* (Music peaks at +3 db).	*Doc & Merle Watson* Cannonball Rag	2:00
Add applause cart (:10 secs) at end of music. Crossfade to ambience cart and roll Cut #2, *MC Wallace.* . . .	*Insert A (Rathe)* in: "that's some pickin' . . . out: ". . . our MC onstage."	1:15
0 level—should be minus 6 db on MC.	*MC Wallace* in: "Welcome to the . . . out: ". . . Peg Leg Sam."	1:45
Backtime the applause for *Peg Leg Sam* :06 secs from end of MC Wallace, and mix into master tape "A"	*Peg Leg Sam* (set begins w/ applause)	:11
Level 0 db, then jumps to +3db at 1:00 into *Talk*. Level normal at start of song *"Greasy Greens."*	*Talk and jokes* *Greasy Greens*	1:24 3:24
Equalization needed on *"Greens"* . . . roll of bass, boost high end slightly	*Hard luck story*	4:00
Check ambience change at splice—occurs at 3:15 into *Hard luck story*	out: :16 secs applause and "thank-you's"	
Fade applause after second "thank-you" (occurs :10 secs into applause) and roll *Insert B*	*Insert B (Rathe)* in: "At this 3rd annual . . ." out: ". . . Malvina Reynolds"	1:24

Appendix D

Unity Gain Procedures for Tape Decks Without Calibrated Output Function

The following explains procedures necessary for performing the unity gain studio set–up described in Chapter 11, using machines of the "semi–pro" variety (Teac, Technics, Pioneer, Sony, Akai, Tandberg and Telex, some Ampex, and others). These procedures do not apply to machines of unusual or non–standard electronics/metering arrangement (Revox, Nagra, Stellavox). For this latter type, contact authorized station or service personnel for assistance in determining the unity gain structure.

To perform this procedure, you *must* have a standard tape recorder alignment tape. These are available from professional audio equipment dealers, and are manufactured by several firms (Magnetic Reference Laboratories, Standard Tape Laboratories, Taber, and others). Every professional facility should already own one or more alignment tapes and replace them occasionally, since they do wear out with use. They are used as part of the maintenance technician's routine tape machine alignment procedure.

First, make sure that the alignment tape is of the proper *reference level* for the type of tape you are using to record in that studio. Next, making sure the machine is in "SAFE" and set to the proper speed for this tape, place the tape on the tape machine. Play it with the machine's monitor selector in "PB" or "TAPE." After an introductory announcement or identification, the first tone on the tape should be a 1 kHz sine–wave recording at reference level. While playing this tone, adjust the output level control of each channel on the machine so that the machine's meters read "0 VU." If the tone runs out, and the announcement comes back on, rewind to the head of the first tone and play it again until you have completed your adjustment.

Once the output level controls are set, mark the machine in some permanent but non-defacing way so that this setting may be retained or re-established at any future time. (Ways of doing this include marking the front panel with tape cut out in the shape of an arrow or using magic marker on masking or other suitable adhesive tape.) Some people permanently fix the output level controls with adhesive tape or even epoxy glue.

Once this procedure is completed, you have effectively placed the machine in the calibrated output ("CAL") mode, assuming the machine is otherwise in good working order and has received proper maintenance. After you have performed this procedure on all tape decks without calibrated output function, you may proceed with the unity gain procedures outlined in Chapter 11, treating these machines as if they are all now in the CAL mode.

Appendix E

Peak Reading Meters

The standard "VU" meter used by broadcasters to measure audio levels is actually a holdover from the past. In the early days of broadcasting, audio signals didn't extend into the high frequencies (not much beyond 5 kHz), and all equipment in the audio path used *tubes*. Today, we have wide–bandwidth audio systems (20 Hz to 20 kHz) and mostly solid–state (or transitorized) audio chains.

The slow, "average–responding" VU meter was adequate in the past because of the small audio bandwidth, which ignored any of the very fast, high frequency "transient" sounds. Moreover, when the audio signal passed through the tubes, the tubes gradually increased distortion as the audio level increased, so the "averaging" VU meter display was accurate enough. Transistors, on the other hand, keep distortion very low and *constant* with increasing level, up to a certain fixed point; when that level is exceeded, *extreme* and sudden distortion ("clipping") results in most cases. One can see the need for a more accurate ("absolute" rather than "averaging") meter to display levels in today's wide–bandwidth, transistorized audio systems.

Perceived Loudness

An additional concern involves the confusion between audio levels as displayed by a meter (*any* meter), and the "perceived loudness" of that same audio, that is, how loud it sounds to the human ear. All an audio meter does is monitor *electrical* levels, regardless of how the audio sounds. Although the VU meter was designed to visually display audio levels in a way that would seem analogous to perceived loudness, that really isn't the case—the meter is telling when the parameters of operation of an electrical circuit or system are being exceeded, not how loud or soft something *sounds*. The problem with the VU meter is that it doesn't tell us very much *exact* information about the *electrical* levels, either!

The Peak Reading Meter

Instead of measuring a short–term average of audio levels as the VU meter does, the peak reading meter reads the absolute maximum, instantaneous, peak levels of audio.

The peak meter does not really do the job as far as perceived loudness is concerned either, but it does display with greater accuracy the *audio levels* it measures. Since high–frequency transients and wide–bandwidth signals are desirable and feasible elements of today's audio, and fairly exact distortion tolerances must be observed, a peak meter would seem to be the obvious choice over a VU meter.

Why, then, the proliferation and longevity of the VU meter? One answer is that the VU meter has been strictly standardized throughout the international audio world; the peak meter is not (at least not in the U.S.). The confusing variety of peak meter types can be disconcerting to anyone used to the good old VU.

The "PPM"

In Britain and parts of Europe, one particular type of peak meter has been established, and is the standard meter used by the BBC and others. It is called the peak programme meter or "PPM," and works very nicely as a peak reading meter, with some limitations. Visually, its pointer rises somewhat faster than the VU meter, and falls much more slowly, so it does take some getting used to for someone familiar with the response of VU meters to audio signals. The PPM is a much more accurate absolute audio measurement device, designed to relate maximum audio levels to the human *eye* so they can be viewed; it does not attempt to relate them to the ear at all.

The PPM is beginning to be accepted in the U.S., and is probably the only meter other than the VU to be found here to any great extent, but it still exists in far fewer numbers than the VU meter. However, the fact that the PPM is a *standard* meter is helping dissolve one of the preferences for

Fig. E-1. *The Peak Program Meter* (PPM), with EBU-A scale.

the VU—its consistent operation. As the PPM becomes more accepted in the U.S., perhaps it will push aside the currently ubiquitous VU and provide a more accurate standard meter.

One further note on the PPM standard: Although the meter's operation is standardized, its calibration and meter face notations are not. The meter shown in Figure E–1 is the EBU–"A" scale meter, which is perhaps the easiest to adjust to for those familiar with VU meters. It should be set up according to manufacturer's instructions, and levels can then be observed much like a VU meter, such that the pointer does not go above "0." Once the operator adjusts to the timing response of the meter, it's smooth sailing.

Appendix F

Tips on Recording from the Telephone

For news and information programming, audio recorded via the telephone is a staple. Even in these days of satellite transmission, fiber optics and digital technology, the telephone remains the most common conduit for on–location sound (actuality) to hit the air quickly. But, as audio technology improves, telephone audio becomes even more of an "earsore." Nevertheless, we must resign ourselves to the fact that in many cases, a phone-feed is the only way to air something newsworthy from a remote location in a timely manner, and will probably remain so for some time to come.

Programmatic Concerns

Your first approach should be to reduce the use of "phoners" to a bare minimum. Don't use a phone feed for anything other than a breaking story. Feature pieces or other non–dated productions should never use phone–quality audio. (There are ways to avoid the use of phoners entirely for distant interviews which are explained below.)

If a phone feed must be used, keep it as *short* as possible. Rewrite whatever is appropriate into announcer copy, leaving only the pure actuality or live sound from the location via phone. If a reporter is filing a story from the field, the report should be as concise as possible, leaving all superfluous or background information to the anchor or studio announcer. Highly–produced documentaries and the like should not use phoners at all.

Interfacing

When phone audio is recorded, it is imperative that the proper equipment be used. Recording *from* the phone in the studio is somewhat more difficult than feeding *into* the phone from the field.

One simple device for this purpose is the **voice coupler,** known in telephone company parlance as the "QKT." This small box is permanently wired into a phone instrument or line, and provides a quarter–inch phone jack output for feeding a line–level signal to a console or recorder input. When using a coupler, it is most convenient to have the telephone instrument on–line with it equipped with a push–to–talk switch on its receiver. This is because the instrument's receiver has to be "off the hook" while a feed is coming in, and the push–to–talk switch turns off the receiver's mouthpiece microphone when it is not depressed, thus insuring that noise and conversation from the studio side will not be included in the recording. (The coupler also allows feeding a line–level signal *into* the phone line as well, in lieu of "clipping on" to the receiver.)

For professional quality phone feeds or *two–way* phone recordings (the phone interview) or broadcasts, a much more complex arrangement is required, which usually involves a variation on the "speaker phone" or "telephone hybrid." This is beyond the scope of this book, but a detailed article on the subject can be found in the *NPR Engineering Update,* Vol. 2, No. 9 (April 1982).

Improving Phone Audio Quality

Once the phone has been properly interfaced with a line–level input on a console or similar device, some amount of audio processing is usually in order. This can be done as the phone feed is being recorded, or the feed can be recorded "flat" (without processing) and then processed during subsequent production or dubbing. The audio processing that is useful for phoners can be divided into three steps: **filtering, equalization** and **compression.**

Filtering: The first step, filtering, should employ a device with a very steep "shelving"–type high frequency roll–off (a "low–pass filter"). This should be set to roll off at three to four kHz (but adjusted by *ear* to each phone feed). There is little or no audio above this frequency on a standard phone line, but there is *noise*. The longer the distance of the call, the more noise there will be on the line, generally. The filter's roll–off point should be adjusted relative to the amount of noise on the line. The trade–off to removing much of the noise is loss of high–frequency audio (i.e., intelligibility), so not all the noise can be filtered out. Your ear will determine the exact adjustment for the filter on that particular line, balancing the amount of noise removed to the amount of intelligibility lost. It is better to err on the side of caution here, meaning that a little noise left in is preferable to a quiet but "dull" phone voice, which is more difficult to understand.

On some phone calls, or with some phone interfacing devices, low-frequency noise ("hum") is a problem. This can generally be removed without further audio quality degradation by the use of a "shelving"–type low–frequency roll–off ("high pass filter"), set to around 150 Hz. So–called "notch–filters" can also be used to remove this hum or any other discrete tones often found on phone lines. A good device of this kind is the UREI 565 Filter set.

Equalization: The next step is equalizing the phone line to increase intelligibility. Using an equalizer (see Appendix G) to reshape the frequency response of the phone line within its audio bandwidth can result in marked improvements in intelligibility. The equalizer should be patched in to the audio chain *following* the filter(s). (Many processing devices offer high–pass and low–pass filters *plus* equalization together in a single, multi–stage unit.)

Although the equalizer's settings will be different for every phone line, the following basic curve is usually helpful, with the sections of the curve listed in decreasing order of importance:

1. 6dB CUT at 400 Hz, wide bandwidth
2. 3dB BOOST at 2.5 kHz, narrow bandwidth
3. 3dB BOOST at 200 Hz, narrow bandwidth
4. 2dB CUT at 800 Hz, moderate bandwidth

Basically, what this equalization curve does is decrease the energy in the middle of the phone line's bandwidth and increase the energy on both ends, in an attempt to flatten out the response. The typical phone line's excess of energy in the 400 Hz region has a particularly negative effect on intelligibility. Reducing 400 Hz region energy alone will improve almost any phone line's sound.

Compression: Because of the reduction in energy caused by equalization, the phone line's intelligibility is improved, but its overall *volume* or "loudness" is reduced. For this reason, a moderate amount of *compression* after equalization is recommended. This will restore or even enhance the loudness of the phone line, which further improves its listenability, beyond the intelligibility increase afforded by equalization. Compression can also serve as a protection device by helping to catch any excessive audio peaks that the phone line signal may have, which may even have been further accentuated by the equalization. More importantly, when the phone audio is to be mixed with other full-fidelity audio (such as a phone interview, where the interviewer is in the studio and the guest is on the phone), compression of just the *phone* audio can help increase its loudness relative to the studio voice. Without such compression, proper loudness–matching of the elements to ear will result in widely divergent VU meter readings between the studio and phone audio. (Typically, an uncompressed phoner hitting 0 VU will sound loudness-matched to a close-miked studio voice reading around –10VU.) This can result in difficulties when matching *that* studio–voice recording to other studio–voice–only recordings in the same program, in which the studio voice is generally recorded at a much higher VU level. It is also an inefficient use of the dynamic range available on the tape, resulting in an overall noisier ("hissier") recording.

One drawback to compression is that while the phone audio's apparent loudness is increased, so too is any background noise on the phone line. In many cases, this noise level is rather high to begin with, and compression just makes it worse. Therefore, as with any audio processing tool, use it with moderation.

Dynamic Noise Filtering

Another effective processing device for phone audio improvement is the Dynamic Noise Filter or "DNF," manufactured by KLH/Burwen, Audio and Design Recording, and others. This device serves to filter out noise between the words of the voice on the phone, and can often clean up a noisy line without much negative effect on the desired audio. Some DNF units are very easy to operate, and other, more flexible designs are quite complex. Some are designed specifically for telephone audio. Beware of using a DNF on digitally–processed phoners (such as the ITT/ROLM system and others), or other extremely noisy, satellite–fed long-distance lines. In these cases, the "gating" (opening and closing around the words) effect of the DNF may make the noise more distracting by its "coming and going" with the words than if it were just there at a constant level all the time. In many standard phoner situations, however, a good, simple DNF can be a very useful and expedient tool for improving phone audio.

Additional Enhancement

Some people have experimented with phoners played back through so–called **aural exciters,** with some favorable results. These devices are patented processors intended to enhance the realism or richness of high–fidelity recordings, but seem to have some degree of improving intelligibility and listenability on phoners, without a trade–off in excessive noise increase. These devices are manufactured by Aphex, EXR and others, and are somewhat expensive, but are generally available on a rental basis. They must be used with moderation, and will not always help, but often can help to put the "edge" back in otherwise dull–sounding phone audio.

The Phone-Sync

A technique that can eliminate the phone entirely from an interview done over the phone is one called the **phone–sync** or **tape–sync.** It requires more production time, and is therefore generally inappropriate for breaking news stories, but can be quite helpful in feature–type stories or other highly produced pieces, where phone–quality audio is especially inappropriate.

The process requires a stereo console and two–track machine at the studio end, and any good recording equipment at the remote end. At the studio, a typical phone interview is done, but with a twist: the studio voice is assigned *only* to the LEFT channel console output, and is thereby recorded only on the left track of the tape. The phoner output is assigned *only* to the RIGHT channel console output, and is thereby recorded only on the right track of the tape. (It is helpful if the interviewer in the studio can hear a mono sum of both tracks in his/her headphones.)

Meanwhile, on the remote end, the guest merely conducts a normal phone conversation with the interviewer, speaking into and listening from the telephone receiver. However, someone at that location is simultaneously making a high–fidelity recording of the guest's end of the conversation, by merely placing a microphone in front of the guest's mouth, and rolling tape. No interface with the telephone is required at the remote end. In fact, it is important that no phone audio "leak" into the microphone from the receiver earpiece, so the mike should be placed on the opposite side of the talker's mouth from the telephone receiver, and the guest should be instructed to hold the phone tightly to his/her ear, and not move around a lot.

Once the interview is completed, the recording made at the remote location is sent to the studio via as fast a carrier as is necessary. Once it arrives, this recording is placed on one tape machine, and cued to the beginning of the interview. The studio (two–track) recording is cued to the same point, which is found by listening to the right (phoner) track. Then both machines are started at the same time, their outputs mixed, and a new, combined recording made on a third recorder. Only the *left* (studio–mike) track of the studio recording is used in this mix. The right track is used purely as a reference, since it is the only common element (or "sync–track") between the two tapes. This track should be occasionally listened to in "cue," to see how far apart the two tapes are drifting (which they will always do). Once the two tapes have drifted sufficiently far apart to affect the dynamics of the conversation, all recorders should be stopped, fader levels left untouched, the two playback machines rewound a few seconds back, re–synched, and the recording restarted. A pick-up edit in the new mix recording is made later. Any audible leakage on either end will make sync–drift instantly apparent, whereas without leakage, a full half–second or so of drift is often tolerable before re–synching is required. If you're careful, and there is not a lot of background noise on either tape, re–synching can be done "on-the-fly," by stopping the machine that is leading for the amount of time that the lead appears to have accrued, and then restarting it (while the person on the lagging machine is speaking, of course). Quick fades up and down around the stop usually help. By the way, varispeed [varying the tape speed] during the synching process is generally not recommended, since it generally creates more error than it fixes, except when a gross speed error exists on either the studio or (more likely) the remote-end recording. [The new digital audio processors which can change tempo without changing pitch could be useful in this situation—Ed.]

Once the synched recording has been made, only then can editing take place, on the new mixed recording. A generation is lost, and so is a lot of time, but if the latter can be tolerated, the former is certainly outweighed by the total elimination of the telephone from the new recording. The limiting factor is usually the quality of the recording equipment at the remote end.

Additionally, audio processing can be added to either side of the conversation independently, in an attempt to match acoustics, or whatever. Differences in microphones can be readily apparent to the listener in such a situation, so every effort should be made to put the remote guest in a quiet, "dead" environment, and use identical or similar sounding mikes on both ends. (The remote end of the phone call can be another radio station, if the guest is willing to travel to a nearby facility, and studio time is available. Or, a remote recordist can go to the guest.)

Should the remote tape be lost in transit, or not arrive in time, the studio two–track recording can be mixed-down or "summed" with optional audio processing on just the phone track, and a regular phone–interview recording is the result; nothing lost—nothing gained, except time.

Other General Tips

Remember that in most cases, you need not be satisfied with the quality of a phone line on the first attempt. Redial the call if the first connection is very noisy, distorted or low–level. If the call is long distance, call the operator and say, "This is station KXYZ, and we have been unable to get a broadcast quality line to (phone number). Can you please help us get one . . . ," etc. Occasionally the words "Press Urgent" can have some effect, especially when dealing with overseas operators. Of course, if IDDD (International Direct Distance Dialing) is not available to the desired location (such as many Eastern–bloc or Third World countries), and a call must be ordered for later delivery, you take what you get, unless you can wait another six hours or whatever for another (possibly worse) line.

When someone is speaking into a regular telephone receiver on a phone–feed or interview (especially from an outdoor pay phone), and the sound is muddy and/or distorted, ask the person to rap the receiver mouthpiece sharply against a hard surface a few times. This serves to break up any coagulations of carbon granules in the microphone that ambient humidity may have caused (much like a saltshaker in the summertime). Often the sound will be greatly improved after this technique has been applied.

Finally, consider the situation when a reporter is filing a *voicer* from the field, but has a portable recorder and microphone along. If time permits, the voicer should be filed through the portable recorder and mike rather than just using the telephone handset, even though no tape cuts are to be filed. The quality improvement will generally be well worth the extra time and effort.

Appendix G

An Introduction to Audio Processors

Audio processing is defined as the artificial manipulation of audio, and can basically be divided into three areas: manipulation of *frequency response, dynamic range,* and *time*. In the first case, the processors are called *equalizers* or *filters;* in the second, *compressors, expanders, limiters* and *gates;* and in the third, *reverberation* and *delay units* of various types. And there are occasional hybrids between categories.

Equalizers and Filters

These devices are designed to change the frequency response of an audio signal, such that the resulting sound has a different tonal balance after being filtered or equalized. A "dull"–sounding recording can be "brightened" by having its proportion of high frequencies increased or "boosted" by an equalizer. A "tinny"–sounding recording can be "mellowed" by having its high frequencies reduced or attenuated (or "cut") by a filter. An equalizer can usually boost or cut, and a filter can generally *only* cut frequencies.

The actual design and layout of an equalizer or filter varies from unit to unit, but equalizers are generally denoted as being of the **graphic** or **parametric** type, with the hybrid "paragraphic" showing up now and then (see Figures G–1, G–2). Filters are generally referred to as **low–pass** (filters out *highs*), **high–pass** (filters out *lows*), or **band–pass/band–reject** (*filters around/filters out* a certain middle band of frequencies.) An extreme version of the latter is the **notch filter,** which can severely attenuate a very narrow band of frequencies, and leave all other frequencies basically untouched (see Figure G–2).

Compressors, et al.

Compressors, limiters, expanders and gates are all devices which change the dynamic range of an audio signal. For example, if a voice recording has VU meter readings that varied from –10VU to 0 VU, a **compressor** could make that same voice read from –10VU to –5VU, or from –5VU to 0 VU, or whatever. In other words, it *reduces* the dynamic range of a sound, or makes the difference between its loudest and quietest extremes smaller. A **limiter** does the same thing, but in a somewhat more brutal fashion. It acts as a sort of brick wall, that does not allow any audio level to exceed a certain point, generally for protection purposes to avoid overmodulation, distortion, or tape saturation. Compressors can be used in a more creative fashion to increase the perceived loudness of a sound without increasing its maximum audio level. In other words, the meter never goes into the red, but stays at a higher level *more often* due to compression, which to our ears sounds *louder*. The *average* level over a period of time can be increased without the absolute maximum level being made any higher (Figure G–3).

Expanders and **gates** are much less useful devices that basically do the opposite of compressors and limiters, respectively. They *increase* rather than reduce dynamic range, and are rarely seen in broadcast productions.

Reverberation and Delay

These devices are used almost exclusively for special effects or in music and drama recordings. They can simulate a different (larger) acoustic space than the one the sound was really recorded in. They can also be used to create surreal or "spacey" kinds of sounds, and can be quite entertaining and convincing (albeit expensive!) (See Figure G–4).

A tape recorder can also be used to create a similar (though less versatile) effect by feeding its output back into its input. While the tape machine is recording something from a mixing console, put its monitor switch in the "PB" or "TAPE" mode, and carefully bring the recorder's output up into the mix on the console, so that now the recorder is recording the original sound *plus* a bit of its own recording of it, with the latter delayed in time by the amount of time it takes for a point on the tape to travel from the record head to the playback head (see Figure 11.4, "Tape Monitor Switch Positions.") You can experiment with tape speed as well; 15 ips produces a faster tape echo than does 7½ ips.

Fig. G-1. *A Parametric Equalizer* (Ward-Beck Systems). This model is built into a mixing console.

Fig. G-4. A spring reverberation device.

Fig. G-3. A pair of simple compressors.

Fig. G-2. *A Rack of Audio Processing Equipment.* From top to bottom: A "de-esser" or dynamic sibilance controller, a telephone interfacing device, a "paragraphic" equalizer, a "notch filter," another "paragraphic" and another "notch filter." This system could be used to process two separate phone lines simultaneously, or one stereo tape.

The Dynamic Sibilance Controller

This device, usually referred to as a "de–esser," combines some functions of an equalizer and a compressor/limiter, in an attempt to reduce some of the excessive "s" sounds that some close–miked voices exhibit. They cut high frequencies in this sibilant region (roughly 5 to 8 kHz), but *only* when sibilance is present. In this way, non–sibilant audio in this same frequency area is not lost, but when a quick burst of it comes along, the "de–esser" drops the level of this frequency band very quickly, and equally quickly restores things to normal once the sibilance has passed. Excessive use of this device can make a person seem to have a severe speech impediment, so care in its use should be exercised, in order to avoid causing a greater problem than the one you started with (see Figure G–2).

Summary

In summary, these devices can be handy tools to help solve problems, but they are *never* a primary solution. There is almost always a better way to fix the problem, but when worse comes to worse, audio processing *may* help. Moderation is the key here; overuse of any of these devices is a common trap, so beware. When using one, experiment with it to become intimately familiar with its operation and its effect on various sounds, before using it on serious production. This will both improve your eventual results as well as save you much time in the heat of the production battle.

Obviously, the above is just a brief overview and introduction to these devices. There are several other texts available which explain their design and operation in greater detail. See the *Bibliography* for suggested readings.

Appendix H

Tape Track Configurations

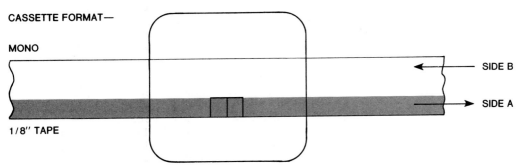

Fig. H-1. *Cassette format—Mono.* Almost all mono cassette recorders use this bidirectional format, operating at 1⅞ inches-per-second (ips). Cassette tape's width is 0.150 inches, or slightly more than one-eighth of an inch.

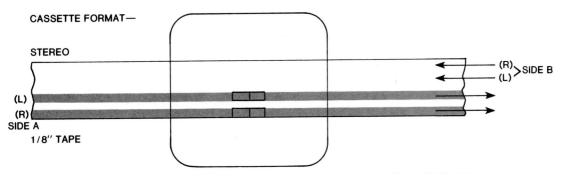

Fig. H-2. *Cassette format—Stereo.* Stereo cassette recorders use two adjacent tracks in this bidirectional format. Playback of a stereo cassette on a *mono* cassette machine provides a compatible mono sum of the two stereo tracks at the playback head.

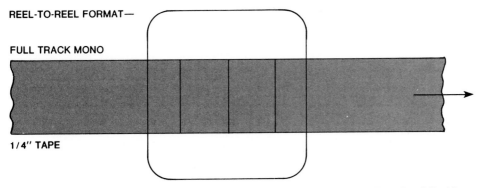

Fig. H-3. *Reel-to-Reel format (¼")—Full Track Mono.* This monaural format uses the entire width of the tape in *one direction* only. Standard tape speeds for all reel-to-reel formats can run anywhere from 15/16 ips to 30 ips, but professional broadcast (non-multitrack) recorders use ¼" tape at 7½ ips and 15 ips.

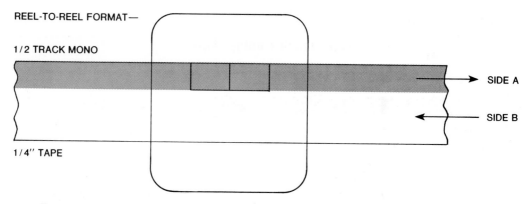

REEL-TO-REEL FORMAT—

1/2 TRACK MONO

SIDE A

SIDE B

1/4" TAPE

Fig. H-4. *Reel-to-Reel format—Half-Track Mono.* This monaural format uses half of the width of the tape in a bidirectional format (also known as "half-track mono.")

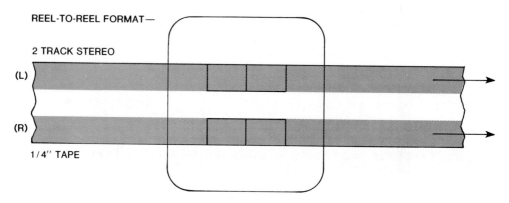

REEL-TO-REEL FORMAT—

2 TRACK STEREO

(L)

(R)

1/4" TAPE

Fig. H-5. *Reel-to-Reel format—Two-Track Stereo.* This format splits the tape into two tracks with a rather wide "guard band" in between, for stereo recording, only in one direction. (Format shown is the U.S. two-track; European formats use wider tracks and a narrower guard band.) Also known as "half-track stereo." When this format is used for monaural recording, it is occasionally referred to as "twin-track mono." The upper track corresponds to the left channel input/output and the lower track corresponds to the right channel. (Half-track mono plays back compatibly on this format, but provides a left-channel-only output.) This is currently the most commonly-found professional broadcasting format.

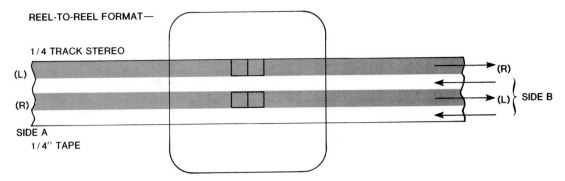

1/4 TRACK STEREO

(L)

(R)

(R)

(L) } SIDE B

SIDE A

1/4" TAPE

Fig. H-6. *Reel-to-Reel format—Quarter-Track Stereo.* This format splits the tape into four bands with guard bands in between, for use as two pairs of stereo tracks in a bidirectional format. Unlike the cassette format, the two tracks of each stereo pair are not adjacent but alternate, such that the top track is the left channel, and the *third* track (from the top) is the right channel, of the side playing forward. Tracks #2 and #4 are the right and left channel respectively of the "other side." Mono summing can only be done electrically after stereo playback.

CART FORMAT—

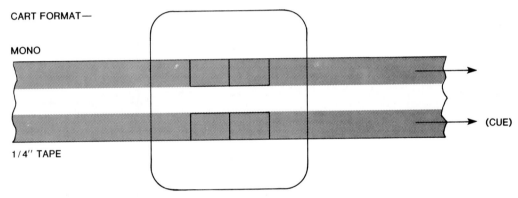

MONO

1/4" TAPE

(CUE)

Fig. H-7. *Cart format—Mono.* This two-track, one-direction format is used on all mono broadcast (continuous loop) cartridge machines at 7½ ips. The upper track is for audio, the lower track for cue tones.

CART FORMAT—

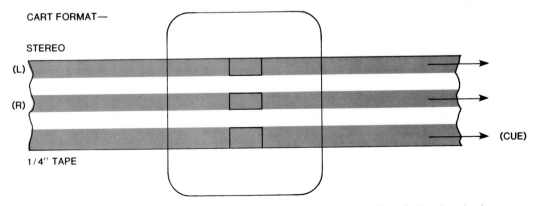

STEREO

(L)

(R)

(CUE)

1/4" TAPE

Fig. H-8. *Cart format—Stereo.* This three-track, one-direction format is used on all *stereo* broadcast cartridge machines, usually at 7½ ips. (Some new cartridge machines have a 15 ips option.) The upper track is usually for left channel audio, the middle track for right channel audio, the bottom track for cue tones.

Appendix I

Bibliography

I & II: News and Features

Bittner, Denise A., and Bittner, John R. *Radio Journalism.* Englewood Cliffs, New Jersey: Prentice–Hall, 1977.

Bliss, Edward Jr., and Patterson, John M. *Writing News for Broadcast.* 2d ed. New York: Columbia University Press, 1978.

Brady, John. *The Craft of Interviewing.* New York: Vintage Books, 1977.

Charnley, Mitchell V. *Reporting.* 3d ed. New York: Holt, Rinehart and Winston, 1975.

Gans, Herbert J. *Deciding What's News: A Study of CBS Evening News, NBC Nightly News, Newsweek, and Time.* New York: Vintage, 1980.

Metzler, Ken. *Creative Interviewing: The Writer's Guide to Gathering Information by Asking Questions.* Englewood Cliffs, New Jersey: Prentice-Hall, 1977.

Stamberg, Susan. *Every Night at Five: Susan Stamberg's All Things Considered Book.* New York: Pantheon, 1982.

Strunk, William, and White, E. B. *The Elements of Style.* 3d ed. New York: MacMillan, 1978.

Terkel, Studs. *Hard Times: An Oral History of the Great Depression.* New York: Pantheon, 1970.

Zinsser, William. *On Writing Well: An Informal Guide to Writing Nonfiction.* 2d rev. ed. New York: Harper and Row, 1980.

III: Recording, Editing and Production

Alten, Stanley R. *Audio in Media.* Belmont, California: Wadsworth Publishing Company, 1982.

Eargle, John. *The Microphone Handbook.* Plainview, New York: Elar Publishing Company, 1982.

Gifford, F. *Tape: A Radio News Handbook.* New York: Hastings House, 1976.

Goldberg, Mortimer. "The Art of Tape Editing." *db magazine:* December 1976, pp. 36–40.

Nisbett, Alec. *Techniques of the Sound Studio.* 2d ed. New York: Hastings House Publishers, 1974.

Runstein, Robert E. *Modern Recording Techniques.* Indianapolis, Indiana: Howard W. Sams Company, Inc., 1976.

Schwartz, Tony. *The Responsive Chord.* New York: Doubleday, 1974.

Tall, Joel. *Tape Editing.* New Hyde Park, New Jersey: EPLA Marketing Industries.

Thom, Randy et al. *Audiocraft: An Introduction to the Tools and Techniques of Audio Production.* Washington, D.C.: National Federation of Community Broadcasters, 1982.

Woram, John M. *The Recording Studio Handbook.* Plainview, New York: Sagamore Publishing Company, 1976.

IV: The Law and the Market

American Bar Association. *Law and the Courts: A Layman's Handbook of Court Procedure, With a Glossary of Legal Terminology.* Contact the Publications Department, American Bar Association, 1155 East 60th St., Chicago, IL 60637.

Bakan, Joseph D. and Chandler, David L. *The Independent Producer's Handbook of Satellite Communications.* Contact: The Association of Independent Video and Filmmakers, 625 Broadway, New York, NY 10012.

Bittner, John. *Broadcast Law and Regulation.* Englewood Cliffs, New Jersey: Prentice-Hall, 1982.

Circular R1: Copyright Basics. Address requests to: U.S. Government Printing Office, Washington, DC 20402.

Code of Federal Regulations: Title 47, Parts 70–79, "Broadcast Radio Services." Address requests to: U.S. Government Printing Office, Washington, DC 20402.

Communications Act of 1934. (Basic legal document upon which FCC operations are based.) Stock no. 004–000–00366–7. Addresss requests to: U.S. Government Printing Office, Washington, DC 20402.

Federal Communications Commission. *The Law of Political Broadcasting and Cablecasting: A Political Primer*. Free upon request from the Office of Public Affairs, Federal Communications Commission, 1919 M St. N.W., Washington, DC 20554.

Gadney, Alan. *How to Enter and Win Video/Broadcasting Contests*. New York: Facts on File, 1981.

Gillmor, Donald M., and Barron, Jerome A. *Mass Communications Law: Cases and Comment*. 3d ed. St. Paul, Minnesota: West Publishing Company, 1979.

Gora, Joel. *The Rights of Reporters*. New York: Avon, 1974.

The Grantsmanship Center. *The Grantsmanship Center News*. Published six times a year. Contact: The Grantsmanship Center, 1031 South Grand Avenue, Los Angeles, CA 90015.

National Association of Broadcasters. *NAB Legal Guide to FCC Rules, Regulations and Policies*. Contact NAB for current price information: NAB Publications Dept., 1771 N St. N.W., Washington, DC 20036.

National Federation of Community Broadcasters. *NFCB Legal Handbook*. Contact NFCB for current price information: 1314 14th St. N.W., Washington, DC 20005.

Sanford, Bruce. *Synopsis of the Law of Libel and the Right of Privacy*. Contact Jane Flett, Newspaper Enterprise Institute, 200 Park Avenue, New York, NY 10017.

INDEX

227